How to Build a Village Town

The Third Edition

A Settlement not a Development

Why do we build communities?

The timeless answer for all eras but our own, is that

We built on the foundation of a self-supporting local economy to enable people to pursue *a good life*, **meaning the social pursuits of:**

    Conviviality
    Citizenship
    Artistic & Intellectual Growth
    Spiritual Expression and Fulfillment

The VillageTown is

- a settlement, not a development. This distinction is paramount.
- a town made of villages based on a *walking home-range.*
- a 5,000 to 10,000 population, self-contained, medium-density community
- built on 100-500 acres around multiple plazas with cafes, shops, workplaces and artist guilds
- car free. everything is within a ten minute walk
- established on the foundation of its own local economy, with affordable housing and beautiful sustainable buildings.

The VillageTown provides a wonderful, thriving and fulfilling place for all ages and diverse peoples, carefully balancing public and private, based on a seven-generation wealth-creating settlement plan.

The book on a Post Card

Claude Lewenz
VillageTowns Stewards & Co.
www.villagetowns.com
RD 1 Waiheke Island,
New Zealand

People used to come to new lands as settlers, and they built settlements. They built their homes for their families; they built places to work to create wealth, and they did so without zoning rules; they made decisions that they would have to live with, so their places served their needs and values. In the 20th century we introduced a new model where developers built developments. They built for pecuniary interest (profits); We began to pass laws to curb their excesses. Life became bland, citizens became consumers.

The VillageTown is a settlement, not a development. It does not use a developer. Instead it organizes its villagers who, like settlers of old, plan their homes for their families, and their work places to create wealth. By aligning their interests, they are able to retain the net profits of their initiative, to be invested in the VillageTown's small-to-medium enterprises as well as social and cultural support and enrichment; a place of, by and for the people.

The difference may seem subtle, but it is profound. It addresses a host of challenges facing society today, and then aims higher: to create a wonderful place to live that is about conviviality, citizenship and artistic, intellectual and spiritual growth.

Join us in building VillageTowns.

— Claude

POST CARD
TO:

"THERE IS NOTHING MORE POWERFUL THAN AN IDEA WHOSE TIME HAS COME."
— Victor Hugo

How to build a VillageTown is the big book with color photographs that introduces the idea.

Life Liberty Happiness, by Claude Lewenz with cameos by Stewart Udall and others, is written as a story, following Ed Rice, retired town planner of Blandville — the town that could be anywhere, as unexpectedly he finds himself visiting a VillageTown. Having devoted his fifty year career to approving what his detractors labelled as suburban sprawl, he only began to understand the mess he and his peers created when a judge took away Ed's drivers license. He found his only option was to consign himself to a retirement home where he would keep himself busy until he died or lost his mind.

Follow Ed as he is introduced to a very different future, meeting the founders of a VillageTown who took control of their future, creating the town and life that serves their needs and aspirations.

VillageTowns - the next step is the third in the series. It sets out the details and provides the information that folks will need when they are serious about their future and want to learn more.

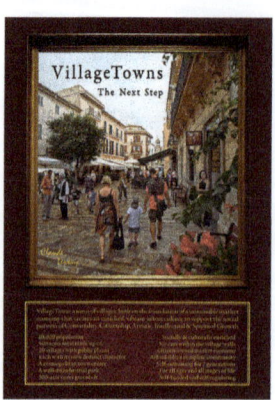

Ten Elements of a VillageTown Settlement

1. **A Settlement**: Established of, by and for the people, a VillageTown is not a development but rather is a settlement. In settlements, people build communities for themselves and for future generations, building for public & common interest not pecuniary interest. They build to provide what they need and to pursue aspirations and dreams for a better future. They live with the results so they invest well while protecting the environment.

   A VillageTown promotes local, wealth-creating private enterprise with a framework of a local economy that is diverse, self-creating, self-informing, self-regulating, balanced, transformational, reciprocal, empowering, responsive, resilient and protective. It protects its food sources, homes, community, money and employment. It cares for its young, weak and elders. It cooperates with national & global systems, but keeps them out of its life and bank. It de-monetizes daily life using design and capital investment to reduce or eliminate ongoing unnecessary personal and community costs.

2. **The VillageTown Purpose - *a Good Life:*** The VillageTown creates and sustains a self-supporting local economy that enables people to enjoy *a good life*, understood as the social pursuits of conviviality, citizenship, and artistic, intellectual & spiritual growth.

3. **Design – *A Walking Home-Range***: Construct a compact, affordable, comprehensible and wonderful human-scaled settlement made of multiple villages within the larger common locality of a town. A town whose urban core is car-free and all day-to-day destinations are within a 10-minute walk. A town that is socially, culturally and economically enriched. A town that is sufficiently diverse, complex and authentic to provide a continually motivating, inspiring and worthwhile place to live. Discourage outbound commuting. Move destinations not people; proximity creates community.

4. **Ecology: Sustainable Management of Resources**: Enable the community and people to provide for their economic, social, cultural and spiritual wellbeing while protecting and preserving the natural & physical environment for present and future generations. Use the budget to buy the best sustainable technology. Note that sustainable systems, architecture and design are the basis of good policy but not bragging points – building a wonderful community based on fear of catastrophe makes no sense. Plan for seven generations.

5. **Authenticity, Character and Beauty**: The most wonderful places in the world are shaped by the people who will live with the results, long after the hired experts move on to their next job. Beyond architecture's utilitarian purpose of protection from hazards and climate, well designed, built and cultivated spaces exist to provide connection, stimulation, production, contentment, hospitality and daily delight. Beauty, harmony, utility, efficiency, durability, authenticity, character and timelessness are all valuable attributes. These are best accomplished by enabling the people who will live there to shape the look, feel and function of their home and village to meet their needs and aspirations. Make reference to locality and history, but also create it.

6. **A Complete Community**: A community is complete only if it can be called home by all ages and stages of life, a wide range of incomes, education, occupations, skill levels, social and cultural backgrounds, outlooks and ways of life. In economies with a wide range of purchasing power, parallel markets for home-ownership prevent gentrification without bureaucracies. In human-scaled complete communities there is no poverty, only the weaker and stronger, where all participate and the stronger help the weaker. In complete communities, there is no unemployment, for there is always work that can be found. Build and maintain such a settlement.

7. **Diversity of Talent**: Seek out, identify, invite, foster, educate and train diverse talent that enriches the community in every way – business and economic, social, cultural and spiritual. Especially provide for the creative class that breathes life into a community; protect their ways of life, and preserve their platforms for creativity. In the education of the young, place classrooms in the center of each village, so children are exposed to the diversity of talent every day by witnessing adult role-models going about their business.

8. **Local food & drink**: Food and water are the basics of life. Know your farmers, know your food. Conviviality embraces food and drink; make it nourishing, healthy, flavorful and delightful. Control and protect your food and water sources. Grow for quality, not for yield. Put on festivals and celebrations around food and drink. In the public establishments on the plazas, go beyond the popular stimulants of sugar, alcohol, caffeine and other drugs; invent and serve drinks that are convivial and also good for you. Avoid food produced by organizations whose pecuniary interest is not aligned with your culinary interest.

9. **Liberty and governance**: Protect personal freedom and respect the values of dissimilar communities. Keep the peace, preserve civility, protect private property, care for the infirm, give a hand-up to the poor, support the family and protect the commonwealth. Govern locally using checks and balances. Regard and speak about your people as citizens not consumers. Liberty and freedom are important. Cultivate free communities. Use design, such as soundproof walls, to shape behavior before resorting to rules to enforce conduct. Balance public and private space so people can find solitude within proximity. Limit rule-making to enabling people to get along, rather than telling people how to live.

10. **Invest in your life**: VillageTowns are not for everyone, nor are they intended to be. They are intended to be the ultimate tangible investment – investing in that which affects you, your family and friends, on a day-to-basis, paying returns that can last for generations. VillageTowns are settlements, not developments; live the difference.

© 2007-2015 Claude Lewenz – All rights reserved
Third Edition – 31 August 2015
Jackson House Publishing Company
Auckland New Zealand

ISBN 978-0958286855

Favorite photo: taken in the plaza of a town in Italy. Between 4 and 7 pm the people come out and walk the plaza and car-free cobblestone streets. Some ride bicycles, others push baby prams. The same early evening pattern is repeated in many Italian towns because their plazas remain human scaled. On this perfect warm evening this group formed a rolling dialogue as people came up and joined in, one that went on for some considerable time.

No part of this publication may be reproduced or transmitted in any form or by any means, electronic, mechanical including photocopying, recording, or by any information storage or retrieval system, without written permission from the publishers. "VillageTown"™ is a registered trademark of the VillageTown Stewards and Company

post: VillageTown Stewards & Co - RD1 Church Bay
Waiheke Island, Auckland, New Zealand
web site: www.villagetowns.com
e-mail: contact@villagetowns.com

Author: Claude Lewenz
Photographs unless otherwise noted: Claude Lewenz

Table of Contents

Orientation (This upper section is designed to be read before you buy the book.)

If you are: Please turn to Page:

If you're a baby boomer worried about retirement... 8
If you run a small business or small field office... 12
If you are a creative or performing artist or musician 15
If you are a scientist, scholar, educator or engineer – the Creative Class........................ 17
If you are retired now or an elder in settled work... 19
If you are parents of a young family.. 22
If you are single and wish to enjoy it 25
If you are a young adult wanting to buy your first home 26
If you are an elected official or a government policy maker 28
If you are a government planner/regulator 33
If you are a master planner, architect or designer 35
If you are a wage-earner priced out of the market.. 38
If you are a nearby farmer 40
If you are an Investor or Developer... 42

~~~~~~~~~~

Ten Elements for a VillageTown...i
What is wealth? An essay to set the tone iv
The Home-Range – A way to understand how people get around vi
Settlement not Development... vii
Rooftop Rainwater Harvesting and Rooftop Farming.. viii
Note from the author... x
Executive Summary: Can We Design and Build for Quality of Life?........................... 1
A Personal Journey.. 2
What is a VillageTown?... 4
If You Are a... (See top section of this index – above) 8-45
Chapter 1 – Challenge and Solution 47
Chapter 2 – The Big Picture – Imagine.. 53
Chapter 3 – VillageTown Layout 58
Chapter 4 – Landscape Architecture – Plantings 70
Chapter 5 – The Local Economy.. 73
Chapter 6 – Food and Slow Food... 92
Chapter 7 – Local Transport Area: A Walking Home-Range 96
Chapter 8 – Utilities and Convergent Technology.. 102
Chapter 9 – Education and Culture.. 116
Chapter 10 – Governance.. 128
Chapter 11 – The Design Brief.. 137
Chapter 12 – The Design Code... 158
Chapter 13 – Building Design... 178
Chapter 14 – Building Materials and Process.. 206
Chapter 15 – Building the VillageTown 213
Chapter 16 – Getting There... Funding and Organizing... 216
Chapter 17 – Recap 218
Index 220

If you see yourself in one or some of the groups of people in this top part of the Table of Contents, or even if you don't, but are in search of an authentic, supportive, wonderful place to live, read this book – borrow it, buy it, stand here and read it, at least the first parts.

When you have read it, make it known that you want to be a part, that you want to build your village or see a VillageTown built. When you and 200 other individuals and families come together with one intent, a village will begin to form itself. That is all it takes to create the momentum for a VillageTown.

It's about people.

To connect:
www.villagetowns.com

An essay to set the tone

What is Wealth?

What is Wealth Creation and what is Wealth Conversion?

What is the relationship between Wealth and Technology?

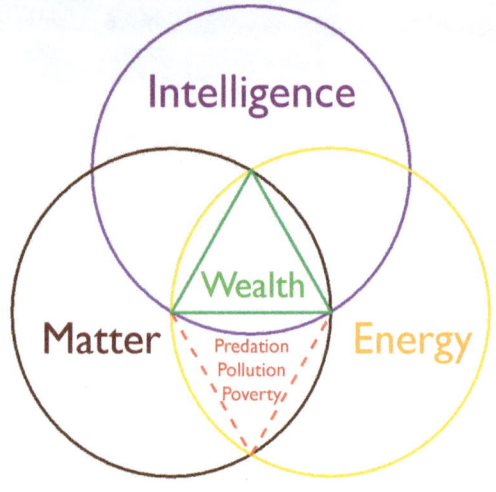

Let us agree that on earth reality consists of three spheres: matter, energy and intelligence.

On earth, matter is a closed system – all the matter which exists has always been here, all we can do is convert it from one form to another. Earth holds 6 sextillion tons of matter, about one trillion tons per person alive today.

On earth, energy is an open system; every day new energy flows in from the sun. In just twenty days, the energy value of sunlight striking the earth is equal to all the energy stored in all the petroleum, natural gas and coal that exists in the earth's crust... give or take a day or two. On average each square meter of earth collects 4.2 KW/hr of energy per day.

Wealth is created when we transform matter from one form to another using energy and intelligence. The sun causes grass to grow using earth, water and air. Human intelligence figured out that if we domesticate sheep and cattle that eat the grass, nomads become wealthy because in a society where starvation is possible, a year-round supply of livestock to feed and clothe them improves their ability to meet their needs.

Tunnel Vision is the down side – it does not look at negative side effects. If to increase the pasture yield we spray all sorts of toxic chemicals that pollute the land and the rivers, and then years later cause cancer for the farm workers (and others) we are less wealthy. We have not created wealth but converted it. To grow more grass we took wealth from future generations by fouling their environment and forcing them to pay more for medical services to treat the sick.

Wealth creation occurs when Matter and Energy and Intelligence are combined to enable humans to live better. Wealth is a human value and humanity's values change, based on circumstances. For nomads, wealth was livestock. The more sheep and cattle the tribe owned the richer they were. For the Haida Indians of the Pacific Northwest, where the food supply of fish and game was naturally abundant year round, wealth was the opposite. The richest person was the one who could give away the most in the potlatch ceremony.

Wealth conversion occurs when no value is added, but one party takes wealth created by another. It also occurs when wealth is created but someone else gets saddled with negative side effects such as predation, pollution or impoverishment. Strip mining where no land restoration occurs afterwards comes to mind. When a warrior says to a farmer he will protect him from another warrior who wants to steal the farmer's food, both warriors are converting wealth. When a lawyer writes a contract to assure two parties will mutually create more wealth, that clarity is wealth creating. When a lawyer writes a complex contract to generate non-essential billings for more lawyering, that is wealth converting. Indeed as we look at the world, we begin to realize far too many accepted human practices in society are wealth converting. Investment banker Catherine A. Fitts named this the Tapeworm Economy.

When technology shifts, the definition of wealth also shifts, as does the hierarchy of governance, the basis of the economy and social status.

Nomadic society was tribal, governed by elders holding parental authority (which is why in one nomadic society "honor thy father and mother" ranked as one of the top ten fundamental laws). In nomadic society law was simple – to enable tribal members to get along with each other and avoid fights. Severe punishment included banishment.

Nomadic life worked until man discovered if he domesticated the horse and mounted it with a sword in hand, he could convert the nomad's wealth to his own by taking their livestock. When this became the norm, nomadic life gave way to a new definition of wealth based on land ownership.

With the shift in technology, owning land protected by fortified towns became the new definition of wealth. A class system emerged with strong armed families dominating

$(E+M) \times I = W$ or in real life $(E+M) \times I - Tv = W - P^3$

(Energy + Matter) × Intelligence − Tunnel Vision = Wealth − Pollution, Predation and/or Poverty

weaker ones. Over time a hierarchy emerged based on who was the top warrior. Governance became feudal. Warriors ruled by fear – fear because the top warrior, a king or emperor, had the power to execute, imprison or fine transgressors (later this became protected as the right to life, liberty and property).

Then in the middle of the 2nd Millennium, around 1,500 AD, another major shift in technology occurred – machining. Men applied their intelligence to machine glass and metal for navigational aids, to forge bolts to build ocean going ships, and guns and canon to enforce (or prevent) wealth conversion. Wealth became that which could be transported in a ship. Large quantities of gold were brought back from the Americas. Silks, spices and drugs were shipped from the Orient. The rise of the merchant class with their royal navies as enforcers eclipsed the descendents of the warrior landlords, and wealth conversion became a major industry. Treaties, laws and contracts became the weapons of wealth conversion. As a friend asked recently "How's it been going now that businessmen have been running the world for 400 years?"

In this era from 1,600 to 2,000 AD, wealth became defined as money, first gold and now pieces of paper or numbers contained in computers. Swipe a plastic card at the butcher and you get a package of slaughtered lamb. The nomad would be awestruck... so easy, so clean, so little work to get food for the family.

Now, early in this new millennium we are experiencing another shift in technology, one in which intelligent energy becomes dominant. In this new era, matter matters less.

The information age gives us tools of brain power. In writing this essay on my computer, I clicked to the Internet to look up the weight of the earth, the statistics on solar energy hitting the earth and the date when Queen Elizabeth 1st chartered the East India Company (December 31, 1600) marking the transition from the warrior era to the era of the businessman. At my desk on an offshore island in the South Pacific I am able not only to write a book and access scholarship around the world, but typeset it thanks to the intelligence applied by thousands of cooperating software engineers. When done, at the press of a button 100,000 words and 400 photographs become electronic signals pulsing off to an overseas printer to become a physical book. New technology vanquishes what is called the tyranny of distance.

This human intelligence is cumulative. Once a new tool is invented, like Computer Assisted Design, it becomes part of the global asset base. The reason Bill Gates became so rich is that he was able to charge an old technology price (price per box) for new technology product (packaged intelligence).

When we make the transition to this new era, what will be the new definition of wealth? Will it still be having more possessions? Will it be having more power over others? Will it be having more money than others?

Perhaps not. If there is an emerging theme among those who are benefiting most from this new technology it appears to be that what they value most is Quality of Life, or what Aristotle called *a good life*, the social pursuits of conviviality, citizenship, artistic, intellectual and spiritual growth. Richard Florida described their pioneers as *the Creative Class,* an emerging class of people that drives the wellbeing of a city or town. They move in because the place is interesting. Their presence then raises the social and cultural life of the place, making it more interesting. For them, wealth is more than income and accumulated investments. It is how they use both their working and leisure time. It's their Quality of Life.

Quality of Life is based on biological principles that simply say that for any part to be healthy, all parts must be healthy. In other words, I cannot be rich if my neighbor is poor and, with global communication and movement, the poorest person in the world is my neighbor. Case in point – comedian Bill Cosby became fabulously successful in his profession, by all American standards of education, fortune and fame he was rich. Yet in 1997, his son Ennis was murdered. Ennis was changing a flat tire on his Mercedes on the side of a California freeway when a Russian immigrant, in an attempted robbery, murdered Bill Cosby's son. Wealth is not money when one must fear for ones children's lives. Wealth is not land when one must be protected by patrolling guards, security systems and locks on everything one owns.

Quality of Life comes primarily not from matter but from intelligence, a higher level of consciousness. The role of organized matter is to enable Quality of Life.

Having spent 400 or 4,000 years subduing Nature, human beings no longer fear Nature. We now are beginning to realize that we are a part of a living system called Planet Earth, and we are powerful enough to devastate that system.

We now realize if we do so our quality of life will suffer greatly, and we are beginning to find that we value Quality of Life most highly. This is a fundamental shift; one brought about by our collective intelligence, the third sphere.

When wealth becomes quality of life, humanity can no longer accept predation, pollution or poverty. It may take several generations to make the transition, but it looks like the right direction. It's a good place to put our energy.

Definitions essential to understanding the context of VillageTown

The Home-Range

Many of the problems facing humanity today can be traced back to the expansion of the human home-range by the introduction of rail and then more recently the automobile as the means to transverse the home-range. The *Driving Home-Range* causes the problems. The *Walking Home-Range* is the solution.

Home-Range was coined in 1943 by Zoologist William Henry Burt to refer to the territory that an animal travels day-to-day. While it has become a central principle in understanding animal behavior from bees to bears, unfortunately it was not adopted by city planners in understanding human behavior. As a result, planners analyze all human travel, rather than differentiating between home-range travel and *extended-range* travel. This hobbles the planning profession, resulting in flawed plans that never solve the problems.

When one commutes to work, that is home-range. When one then walks, drives, flies or takes a train or bus to meet a client, go to a customer to deliver or repair something or conduct any other sort of business activity, that is not home-range because it is not day-to-day. It is their extended-range. Going to church on Sunday is home-range; going for a Sunday drive afterwards is not. One may debate if a school bus driver who drives the same route every day is driving home-range, since that activity is how the driver earns a living to feed the family, but certainly for the children riding on that bus, it is home-range. Why do we bus children anyway?

What makes this distinction useful is the choice it gives to urban planners. Make a distinction between the size of ones home-range travel - in effect going in same-circles, in contrast to extended-range travel that benefits most from driving. Plan differently for home-range than for extended-range. By plan, do not just look at roads or rail, look at destinations and purpose.

The problem is not the roads and the cars. The problem is how we use roads and cars.

The US Department of Transportation reports the average American drives 35 miles a day in a car. This means that in a normal community of 10,000 people, where about 7,500 drive cars (allowing that the remainder are children or infirm or old people who do not drive), the home-range for that community is over a quarter million miles a day, every day, all year long. Most of this daily driving is not commuting. It is shopping, driving the kids, running errands and social/recreational activities.

The VillageTown proposes to create a walking home-range by moving destinations, not people; . It is not anti-car, and cars (and other forms of transport) will be used when one needs to go somewhere beyond the home range. But for local transport, it eliminates the need to drive. It improves quality of life, returning more quality time, while lowering the costs and the adverse impact of driving.

Settlement not Development

A VillageTown is a settlement, not a development. The difference is significant; it completely changes the way that place-making is thought about, built and done. As a 21st century settlement so many of the environmental, social and economic problems caused by modern development vanish – they cease to be issues.

Development is driven by developers and backed by investors. It is essentially speculative, which inherently encourages a herd mentality: same, bland and boring and usually not at all sustainable. After reading the first edition of this book, a developer asked *why are you making it so difficult for yourself? Just do what they want, get in, get out and bank your profits*. The "they" he was speaking about included the financial backers that fund it, insurance and engineering companies that frame it, regulatory agencies that grant permission and the real estate sales industry that sells it; in other words, the whole money-spinning system that has grown out of the fundamental human need for shelter. While developers have been around for centuries, the suburban-sprawl industry is the dominant force today.

Settlements have a much older pedigree. From the time humans shifted from migratory patterns to settle down, the driving force behind settling was not pecuniary interest (return on investment for investors) but personal, family and social interest... settlers came to a new land and built a home for themselves and their families, and they built or took a job in a work place, be it a farm, factory, shop or office, to create wealth and wellbeing for themselves and their fellows. This model worked well. The settlers were stakeholders; they did not need regulation because people do not soil their own nest. As Christopher Alexander put it: *"...most of the wonderful places of the world were not made by architects but by the people."*

We now live in a highly-regulated environment where the players, such as officials, will have a great deal of difficulty getting their heads around a settlement initiative. They will keep saying "*you*" and then be confused when the reply is *"there is no 'you', only the people and their communities; there is no developer. A VillageTown is not a development.*" Yes, there will be a civitas corporation (the ViTo) that will be incorporated to organize the process, and subsequently to operate it. But the ViTo serves the people and communities who will live there. Its citizens are shareholders; its stakeholders are the citizens of the host community. Everyone is on the same side; no *you*, only *us*.

The proper purpose of regulatory agencies is to protect the public interest from the inherently exploitive practices of pecuniary interest. Settlers don't exploit themselves. Developers makes more money if they externalize costs; they do what they have to do, collect their profits and leave. In contrast, settlers and their hosts will live with the results, thus externalizing makes no sense.

The 21st century settlement process begins when the host community, both the jurisdiction such as a county, and the people and communities who live there decide to allocate open space, greenfield or brownfield, of sufficient size to become a VillageTown. Their motivation can range from wanting to strengthen their economy, attract jobs or make their region more sustainable, to more personal motivations: attracting the businesses that will enable their adult children to come home, or a kinder place for elderly parents.

The locals take on a leadership role, drawing upon the volunteer resources inherent in every community, to reach out to the VillageTown stewards who bring in the framework for settlement. The framework represents decades of research, but it then is up to the local hosts to transform that framework into a specific plan that fits local conditions. Once that plan is in place, the ViTo is set up, and the hard work of attracting businesses begins. Rather than focus on selling houses, the ViTo focuses on attracting head-of-household jobs. This not only sells homes, but it ensures that the buyers will not commute by car to a job outside the VillageTown.

A VillageTown is a settlement, not a development. It is possible because technology is vanquishing the tyranny of distance. It is an ancient form of habitation whose time once again has come.

Reston Virginia Townhouses 1973 - a thoughtful development but no personality…In contrast, Waterford Virginia 1733, a settlement has similar scale but each home oozes character. The Reston homes are not welcoming; the garage door is what greets one; they give no sense of a neighborhood, they feel like places where one is just passing through.

Rooftop Rainwater Harvesting

WITHOUT WATER THERE IS NO LIFE

In 2013 stewards travelled to a California county whose leadership had expressed interest in a VillageTown. As the stewards examined the potential, several major issues leapt to the forefront: fully-allocated water rights and prime-agricultural land as the only suitable place to build.

California water law is a zero-sum game. In order to take water from the surface, one must secure water rights; someone else must lose their rights, a politicized process that effectively bars a VillageTown settlement from happening. However, in 2012, the state legislature passed the Rainwater Capture Act that says: *"Use of rainwater collected from rooftops does not require a water right permit..."* The VillageTown water plan is based on rainwater harvesting, thus this Act opens up the way for a VillageTown to happen.

Rooftop collection can come from any ordinary roof except that the VillageTown works best if instead of a backyard each house comes with a rooftop garden. It is not safe for the rainwater to be collected from a platform that also supports human activity, thus the need for an elevated collector. In climates with rainfall year-round, it is imagined that a shade panel that does double duty as a solar collector and rainwater harvester would be sufficient to harvest the required rainwater. Not so in California, especially since 2013, when California suffered the worst drought in recorded history. Consider this chart:

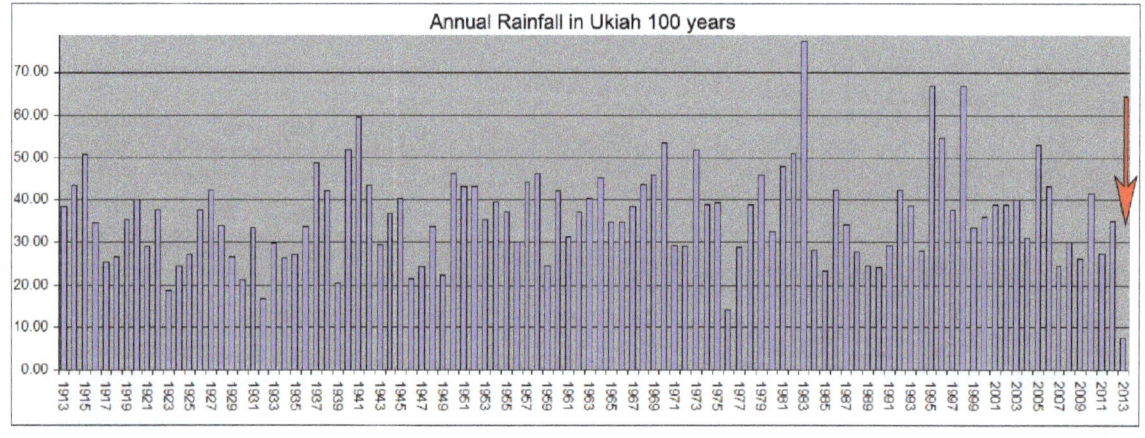

The 2013 year could be an anomaly, or it could signal a change of climate where the extremes become more frequent. In any case, it would be unwise to plan a settlement based on the hundred-year average. Better to plan for the worse case.

Accordingly, the plan for this initiative includes rooftop greenhouses; glass enclosures that collect all the rainwater that falls on the footprint of the building (estimated at an average of 1,000 square feet). With 100 acres of residential rooftop and an additional 50 acres of walk-to industrial park rooftop, this should provide sufficient fresh water for human consumption for 10,000 people (requires storage of 60 acre/feet - rounded up to 100 acre/feet to provide a margin of error). As explained earlier in this book, the water system is based on extensive re-use of water for all other water uses. Washing, toilets and plants are supplied with clean water that is re-processed in closed-loop systems.

Kew Gardens Temperate House from the Pagoda, 1859 designed by Decimus Burton. It was the largest glasshouse in the world, and is still the largest Victorian one. © Copyright David Hawgood, licensed for reuse under Creative Commons Licence.

Rooftop Greenhouse Farming

ELEVATING AGRICULTURE LAND

The secret is charcoal, a.k.a. biochar - © DryPot GNU Free Documentation License.

For the California initiative, greenhouse water harvesting becomes a mandatory requirement for each building. Also thousands of rooftop greenhouses capitalized as part of the house opens up a whole new set of possibilities for farming. This became especially apparent when we had a visit from a doctoral candidate whose area of expertise is soil science.

As he explained it, in 1542 the Spanish explorer Francisco de Orellana traveled the Amazon River and reported "*There was one town that stretched for 15 miles without any space from house to house, which was a marvelous thing to behold. There were many roads here that entered into the interior of the land, very fine highways. Inland from the river to a distance of six miles more or less, there could be seen some very large cities that glistened in white and besides this, the land is as fertile and as normal in appearance as our Spain.*" Yet, the rainforest soil is known to be very poor; how could it support large towns?

When the Spanish returned to the Amazon, a century later, these towns were gone, and it was presumed that de Orellana had exaggerated. Scientists now believe that the European diseases wiped out the natives. Of significance was the scientific analysis of *Terra preta de índio*, a dark, highly-fertile soil that science has now shown was able to feed these dense populations. In fact, it was far more fertile than the lands of Spain. Soil scientists are rediscovering the secrets known to these native peoples. Terra preta is a natural way to increase soil fertility and much greater yield of healthy, flavorful foods.

The excitement of our visiting scientist was palatable. Securing grants to do studies of soil science in controlled environments is the usual slog of academics. There is never enough money, unless a corporation seeks a particular study to serve their pecuniary interest. Yet, here was the prospect of 4,000 enclosed environments, elevated farms raised three stories above the ground and covered with a glass roof and controlled heat, light and moisture. While some owners will choose to do their own gardening, many can be expected to be very happy contracting with the ViTo to grow whatever food is needed. The rooftop gardens are expected to have outside staircases and elevators, thus they serve as a modest income stream for owners.

The yield from Terra Preta soils, or as scientists are now calling it, *synthetic terra preta*, are considerably higher than conventional farming. Indeed, if the VillageTown is built on flat prime agricultural land, the topsoil will be first set to one side, the subsoil covered with a three-story building, and then the topsoil will be elevated to the rooftop garden. It will be mixed with the biochar and other ingredients that generate an exceptionally fertile soil with the trace elements humans need for health, and the VillageTown will become a farm at 50 feet above ground level. The ag land is not paved over, it is elevated.

The economic case for these greenhouses is based on displacement funding. Farmers may find it difficult to compete on the open market if they had to capitalize an investment in a greenhouse. However, when the greenhouse becomes a mandatory part of the building construction, and amortized as part of the mortgage, the capital cost is displaced and not factored into the cost of food. If you want to live in a VillageTown, you must pay for your part of the water collection system; relative to the cost of housing, it is an affordable addition that is a warm, semi-outdoor space during winter.

In addition to the rooftops of the urban core, the walk-to industrial park is expected to have flat-roof farming on top. This is expected to add about 50 acres. The design discussions include making openings in the roof, so that the industrial workers can look up and not only see the sky (something sadly lacking in most modern industrial buildings) but also have stairs, so that during breaks and lunch, they can walk up stairs and enjoy sitting in the warm sunlight surrounded by plants. This also means better air to breath as the greenhouse needs CO_2 and emits oxygen.

The other potential for these greenhouses is to not use all glass panels but just enough for the plants. In addition, use a new type of solar panel that not only converts sunlight into electricity but also collects the thermal energy that is then fed to a water-to-water heat pump to provide climate control and hot water to higher temperatures than passive solar water heaters.

The implications of this rooftop gardening system will need further exploration, including examining the capital and operating costs. However, if it works as the scientists hope, it could end the contest between human habit and agriculture for prime land. Indeed, it could become a way for human habitat to turn poor agricultural land into a rich source of healthy, flavorful foods with a extended growing season.

Note from the author on the Third Edition

When the first edition of this book was released, we, the Village Stewards, proceeded with considerable caution. We had no book launch, no public relations campaign. It's one thing to talk about an idea; it is quite another to go public with it. How would it be received? Is the idea potent, or would it wither under the bright light of public review. Would it be muddled or clear? Would it be on target or miss the mark? I quietly stepped on stage with no fanfare.

Within a few weeks, the word got out, and reviews began to appear on web sites. Invitations to give keynote speeches began to come in. The first speech was in front of over a thousand people at the Woodford Festival in Australia. What a challenge! I had sixty minutes to explain an idea that came from a very different place, to reduce years worth of research and study into a coherent presentation. The concept of a VillageTown is what people in Silicon Valley call "market disruptive". When you start by sweeping all preconceptions off the table, where do you begin? Speech-making demands distillation.

Two months later I found myself giving a keynote before the Thought Leaders Conference in Sydney, Australia, only this time I had to distil the message down to 30 minutes. Then in May 2009 I was asked to speak at the TEDx event in Sydney where the ground rules were 18 minutes maximum and toss away your speech. That was tough.

Book sales came in from all over the world. It was clear the idea hit home with many people. Projects began to come together... Sydney, Melbourne, Auckland, Austria, Ecuador and Northern California. Circles began to form; volunteers coming together to do their part to move VillageTowns from a good idea to a place cast in concrete. Volunteers emerged to set up the web site, to get a forum going on www.villagetowns.com, to promote book sales and to put together week long site visits including radio, television, evening town meetings and daily meetings with politicians, planners and others in the business. They did so not out of pecuniary interest, but of passion.

Consider this heartfelt book review found at Australia's www.nourishedmagazine.com.au:

Many of us have these secret dreams. Dreams that don't fit into our current experience but we can't get them out of our hearts. Dreams of a life without alienation. Where we live close to our relatives but not in their laps. Where the daily drudgery of traffic is replaced with a jaunty walk to work along a promenade where the only wheels are those of bicycles, buggies and prams. We dream of living in a village where we know almost everyone. Where artists color our streets and children are safe to play. Where our waste water is used to fertilise the village farms and create biodesiel to run our small, quiet, community buggies. Dreams of living close to the land and close to each other. Dreams, dare I say it, of community.

For many years I've been praying for village life. With three children under 6, stuck in a tiny box in suburbia, I was so lonely I thought my heart would break. I was lost in the needs of my children and there was no outlet, much less any one to share the joys and burdens of mothering with. I dreamed of planting a garden with sisters while other sisters took turns at holding babies. I dreamed of sending boys off with my brothers to become men...

On the other side of the world, a staunch Republican wrote a book review at www.baconsrebellion.com:

Claude Lewenz is an American living in New Zealand. He has absorbed the keen environmental conscience of his Kiwi compatriots, but he retains an Yankee conviction that he can change the world if he's just bold enough to try. He has published a book, "How to Build a Village," which amounts to an audacious thought experiment. If you could design a community from scratch with the goal of maximizing the quality of life, what would it look like? How would it function?... Lewenz offers a powerful vision for market-driven transformation of society. It would be marvelous if his dreams took root here in Virginia.

The breadth of positive response surprised me. Libertarians loved it as much as liberals – albeit for different reasons. Conservatives embraced the idea as strongly as conservationists. The idea of VillageTowns addresses a universal need; it's not for everyone, but it offers an alternative that many seek and cannot find.

In the first edition, I named Libby Rouse as the person I thanked for her early support. In the next edition, I name another elder, Stewart Udall, former US Secretary of the Interior and one of the most important advocates for Nature and Earth, who agreed to serve as Chairman Emeritus of our VillageTown stewards. I last visited Stewart about two months before he died at age 90, and he said to me "You are young enough to see this through. It is very important that you succeed, that the VillageTowns get built. It is of the utmost importance; you must do it." Words from elders like this are what keeps us going.

If you like the idea, and agree with Stewart that it is important, I invite you to join with me and the other Village Stewards to help make it happen – We invite you to go to www.villagetowns.com, and become involved.

Claude

Claude Lewenz
Author and Photographer

Executive Summary
BUILDING COMMUNITIES FOR A GOOD LIFE

A VillageTown™ is a self-created, self-funded, self-governing archetypal settlement; a town made of villages, that is settled, not developed, that is car-free within its urban core, where people work within walking distance of home, and where the net profits derived from the settlement are retained and invested in "a good life", meaning the social pursuits of conviviality, citizenship and artistic, intellectual and spiritual growth. Based on common sense, not utopian ideals, it is what happens when timeless "patterns" proven to work are integrated with the best potential of new technology. Environmentally, socially and culturally, it focuses on balancing life to be sustainable, so present generations leave the earth and its people in better condition than what they inherited from those who came before.

Settlement not development: Until something shifted in the mid-20th century, the new world was settled by settlers. Then settlements gave way to developments; places developed by developers. Developers make decisions driven by pecuniary not common interest: too often decisions good for the investors but bad for the people, communities, civilizations and the planet that must live with the results.

Challenges: We all know the problems. Alienation, depletion, degradation, pollution, unhealthy food, new diseases, social insecurity, fractured families, youth and elder segregation, drug, alcohol and electronic addictions, economic insecurity, voracious consumption, unsustainable debt, schools that can't educate, occupations detached from wealth creation, communities living with fear, crime as normal, essential systems increasingly vulnerable to calamitous collapse. In an era of the broadest-based wealth ever, humanity faces challenges that seem overwhelming.

Answer: As soon as we shift to settling settlements, instead of developing developments, we avoid the root causes of these problems. People don't soil their own nests. They make place-making decisions not on how they will profit, but how they will live. They think about long-term wealth creation, rather than hit-and-run development.

Aim Higher: When people focus on place-making their attention is not solely or even primarily on mitigating the negatives. People would prefer to live in wonderful places, although what wonderful means is different for each of us.

In *A Pattern Language*,* Christopher Alexander wrote *"...people should design for themselves their own houses, streets and communities. This idea... comes simply from the observation that most of the wonderful places of the world were not made by architects but by the people."*

A *Good Life:* In looking for an all-embracing concept for the positive, we found it had been written 2,300 years ago by Aristotle who observed that when several villages come together to become self-supporting or nearly so, the purpose of the continuance of *the polis* (city-state, or in our case VillageTown) is to enable its citizens to enjoy *a good life* understood as the social pursuits of conviviality, citizenship and artistic, intellectual & spiritual growth.

These are positive aspirations, because while fear is effective in motivating people for short bursts of energy, *you cannot build communities based on negatives.*

Conviviality: A good life begins with conviviality – having fun, laughter, playing sports, singing, enjoying others company, often around slow food and good drink. While people can have fun anywhere, investing in infrastructure that supports it makes a difference. A public plaza in each village provides the platform for connection without an appointment. Cafes, taverns and restaurants, especially outdoors in good weather gives people a place to connect and linger. Sports fields, especially home-made sports, add to a convivial atmosphere.

Citizenship is about taking care. It can be formal (politics) or natural, what happens when people look after each other. In support of citizenship, classrooms are on the plazas, not in segregated campuses. Eldercare is integrated into the community, made easier because the urban core is car-free. Governance uses a citizen-owned private corporation that is used first to build the settlement and then to operate it – retaining an estimated $100-200 million in net profits that is used to build a strong economy. *Re-read this last part; it's unprecedented.*

Artistic, intellectual and spiritual growth is supported by purpose-built buildings, including artist guild halls to foster cultural enrichment, libraries, university extensions and research facilities to add to the intellectual rigor, and sacred halls on each plaza that may be consecrated if the villagers so wish (if not, they serve for rites of passage, sanctuary and places of peace).

The Economic Foundation: All of this is built on a solid economic foundation based on a private, market economy that invests in local wealth creation. With an estimated capital investment of $1-2 billion to build the VillageTown, the initial focus is not on selling homes, but attracting head of household jobs. The critical mass of the VillageTown is large enough that everything an employer would want for its employees is self-contained, meaning the target audience to recruit is national in scope, not based on regional growth.

The distinguishing features of the VillageTown include:
- To attain economic critical mass, it requires 5-10,000 population
- The town is made up of 10-20 villages, about 500 people each
- 100-200 acre urban-core, 50-acre industrial park, 300-acre greenbelt
- A walking home-range, no cars. 10-minute walk to all destinations
- Target zero outbound commuters, minimal impact on host region
- About $1-2 billion capital value, net profits retained by the citizens
- Non-combustible buildings to permit human-scaled streets
- Parallel real estate markets provide affordable housing for target groups
- A Civitas corporation owns the land, the citizens own the civitas corporation
- Environmental sustainability is a given, but not a bragging point.

Construction uses economies of scale.
- 200 homes per village all built at the same time, but each home distinctive
- 20 villages all constructed in parallel, each using a separate, on-site factory
- CarveCast™ rapid construction system enables significant time/cost savings.
- Each home is funded through individual construction loans/mortgages
- Minimal investment risk; all units are presold.
- It's a settlement, not a development

To learn more, see: ***www.villagetowns.com.***

---
* Available at www.patternlanguage.com ISBN 0-19-501919-9

A Personal Journey

My father spoke about the importance of preparing for life. He worked hard, left for the office in his Plymouth at 7:30 in the morning, back home at 6:30 and worked half a day on Saturday. He did it for a family he only saw for a few hours in the evening and on weekends. We lived in a place where we had to drive a car to get anywhere – for me the rite of passage came at 16, the day I earned my drivers license and my wings. Sadly my father became ill while he was still preparing for life – in some ways a life not fulfilled.

When I traveled to countries built before the automobile and visited towns and villages where people work, live and shop within walking distance of the central plazas, I saw a different way of life. People were living, interacting, working and taking care, all at the same time. The children traveled in packs, actively playing for hours. People working in the shops and workshops could keep an eye on them; old people sitting on benches in the sun became friends and mentors. In these villages, no one hired babysitters – the pressure on parenting was far less than what we know in the suburbs. I saw teenagers in first flush, posing, posturing, but also genuinely interacting and modeling real adults – not the electronic substitute role models of rock stars, punks and professionally angry young men and sex-kitten women. They were friendly and helpful. Some hung around the shops and workshops and became apprentices, continuing the circle of village life. I saw no graffiti or litter – everyone held a stake in the village.

In those places, people actually made things – they created wealth. Most products were outstanding, designed for quality not solely for profit because their customers were also their neighbors – who expected good products. Things made were distinct, made in no other place, yet they were functional things used by people of the region for daily life. No one got absurdly rich, but all seemed to have everything they needed, including much laughter.

In these villages, I found the food to be consistently outstanding – flavorful, fresh from the local fields and gardens, often from old local recipes, and inexpensive – good food was expected, not a luxury. The house wine, also local, never gave me a headache, smooth and simple. No matter how long I lingered over a meal, I observed the locals stayed longer – engaged in spirited dialogue, arms waving, voices raising, loving every minute of their own stage and their own theater. When I spoke with them, I found them remarkably well informed and engaging; ready to challenge my views of the world, yet they laced discourse with kindness. They were confident in their home.

The villages provided a safe and high-stature place for their old people. They were elders, not senior citizens, and no matter how bent and frail, they knew they were secure. Because the villages were not dependent on driving, and everything was within walking distance, they kept going – on canes or in wheelchairs – and when they became bedridden they stayed in the village.

Decades ago, sitting in a café in Trefdraeth, Wales, while eating the best summer pudding in the world, I noticed that people would walk by and call in, "And a good day to you, Mrs. Owen", or, "Lovely weather we're having, Mrs. Owen"... even the children would greet her. After lunch I glanced in next door to see a home where the front window had been converted to very large glass door, open on that summer day. Within was a clearly infirm, paralysed elderly woman who had suffered a debilitating stroke and could hardly move, yet her eyes held bright fire, and her friends and neighbors spoke not to the withered body, but the clear soul within. What a contrast from my father, who lay for seven years in a Veteran's hospital as his brain slowly turned to spaghetti – where the only ones who saw him, except for the faithful visits of my mother, were well meaning, overworked nurse aides who had no idea who this man was or how many people had loved him in his time. We call this progress.

I grew up in a place where local citizens wrought great change for the good. A family friend, Marty Millspaugh would visit friends homes, including ours, and set out his dream to restore the heart of Baltimore – then a downtown waterfront of rotting, rat-infested warehouses serving a slowly dying banana boat trade. Sitting at our kitchen table, he put into words a vision – enrolling my parents and many others in a restored harbor, a place of people, shops, food, music, homes and offices. His vision is now the Baltimore Inner Harbor, world famous and the archetype of a restored heart of a city. While Baltimore still faces many challenges, his vision sparked hope. Marty was a reporter for the Baltimore Sun, who covered the problem of urban slums. In 1958, he wrote

> Experts and laymen can agree that slums breed a hopelessness in people's hearts. Amid the piles of rotting garbage, tumbledown porches and junk-filled back yards, the human spirit seems to wither away.

Rich or poor, it's about the human spirit.

Other partners in Baltimore's urban renewal efforts included Jim Rouse who later conceived of Columbia – a new 90,000 population town built to prove blacks and whites, rich and poor could live together in harmony in the American south. Another powerhouse was William Donald Schaefer a city councilman who became mayor and a terror to his employees until they understood his passion was about making his town a

Mayor William Donald Schaefer and Jim Rouse
Reprinted with permission of The Baltimore Sun.
All Rights Reserved.

better place to live. While he was mayor, Pulitzer Prize-winning journalist Richard Ben Cramer wrote about Mayor Schaefer and captured the spirit of Baltimore's unique leadership:

One time he popped them an Action Memo: "There is an abandoned car... but I'm not telling you where it is." City crews ran around like hungry gerbils for a week. Must have towed five hundred cars.

That was NOT... GOOD... ENOUGH: Schaefer called in his cabinet, the best municipal government in America. The mayor held two fingers up, and he poked them at his own glittery eyes.

"Do you know what these are? Do you? These are eyes" The mayor was jabbing at his face now. They thought he might hurt himself.

"I GOT TWO. AND YOU GOT TWO. "

Then he grabbed a cabinet member and started menacing him with his fingers in the eyes. The cabinet guy's head was burrowing between his shoulders.

"So how come my eyes can see and a smart young fellow like you can't see a damn thing, huh? HOW COME?"

But today it's worse. He won't look at them. He's staring down at the table. His head, in his hands, rocks back and forth in sorrow. At his shoulder is the easel with the single word he'd written:

ERR-JEN-C.

"You think we been in this job twelve years and we've done this and we've done that. Well you're wrong. This is a new administration

(Schaefer was reelected last year, with 94% of the vote).

"What has this government done for the city? Nothing. Not a thing. Where's the new ideas? WHERE? What's NEW? NEW! There isn't a damn thing new. I don't see it. I don't see it...

...At city hall he railed at the experts, the bright young men, planners, urbanologists. His pencil made a mess of their careful plans for new suburban-style housing.

"People here want to live in a row house," he said.

"But there'll be grass, here, as you see, Mayor, provision is made for a lawn for each, ranging from 26.5 square..."

"I want a row house."

"... and each with a tree, with varying placement in..."

"Dammit, I wanna live in a row house. I don't want a tree. I don't want a lawn. I live in Baltimore. I like a row house, I'm gonna have my row house. I AM BALTIMORE, I LIVE IN A ROW HOUSE – GET IT?" They got it.

As a child at the kitchen table, I learned the power of building with heart, building with spirit. Marty was a journalist, Jim a mortgage banker, William Donald the oddest politician you can imagine. They made a difference because they wanted something better – not for themselves, but for all. They put their heart into it and they did it.

Years later, I looked at those wonderful overseas villages where life flowed like spring, and then contrasted these with the reality of our present day choices: live in a suburban sprawl; downtown apartment; or a small town dying when the big box mall opens up. They call this progress?

Look at the mess we have made. We have created problems and then spawned massive governmental, NGO (non government organization) and private sector industries to address problems that did not exist a century ago. These great job machines for service providers devour resources yet things seem to get worse not better.

The people who find solutions do not go to school to major in solution finding. They don't hold degrees in it. Instead they bring both passion and willingness to cooperate to make change. It worked in Baltimore when journalists put it into words, bankers found the money and politicians told their public servants their job was to find a way to do good now, not frustrate good people until the project got so watered down they went away.

Today we face new challenges. We witness the unravelling of the great experiment in suburban living. We segregate our lives by age, create untenable pressures and don't understand when our systems – both external and within – begin to break down.

So early on I began to ask questions. I asked them of many people, both experts and people driven by passion. From those questions a dialogue began, first as an interest, and then as a passion, and now as a mission. Why can't we live in places that offer a good life for all, for all ages and incomes; places that remain interesting and beautiful?

Nothing in this book is a new idea. Parts of it have been done before – somewhere. Architect Christopher Alexander calls them *Patterns* – A Pattern Language.

The purpose of this book is to put all these patterns and ideas together to enable people to create a brilliant place to live. Do not think utopia, this is a real framework based on many years of collecting, generated from many people in focus groups, dialogue and travel – looking at what actually exists, understanding what works, and carefully listening to the indicators pointing to a likely future.

Some people want to live in suburbs, some are very happy living in city apartments, but many seek something more fulfilling. This book proposes that if you can't find it already built, join with others to build it yourself.

What is a VillageTown?

We all know the problems:

Alienation
Depletion
Degradation
Pollution
Unhealthy food
New diseases
Social insecurity
Fractured families
Youth and elder segregation
Drug, alcohol and electronic addictions
Economic insecurity
Voracious consumption
Unsustainable debt
Bland architecture hardly noticed
Canned, packaged music and arts
Schools that can't educate
Occupations detached from wealth creation
Communities living with fear, crime as normal
Essential systems vulnerable to calamitous collapse

A VillageTown offers answers:

Proximity, interdependence and social connection
Restoration, sustainable management of resources
Reclamation and regeneration, drive less (a lot less)
Maintain clean air, water, land and healthy ecosystems
Slow food, local food, seasonal food, heritage food
Good diet and exercise, spend more time walking outdoors
Self-supporting societies that care for their weak and frail
Elders, friends and relatives who spend time with children
Car-free streets, safe for children, elders who don't drive
A proximate socially and culturally enriched life
A strong, diverse, self-funded, self-sufficient local economy
Durable goods, use less, need less, enjoy more
A wealth-creating local economy where money recirculates
Beautiful, wonderful buildings reflect their owners' character
Arts guild halls, festivals, home-made music, funded creativity
Storefront schools on daytime-active village and town plazas
Self-supporting local economy that invests in its businesses
People live and work locally with a low tolerance for crime
Local power, local food, rain water, walking home-range
… and a whole lot more

In an era of the broadest-based wealth ever, humanity faces challenges that seem overwhelming. National and global systems consume vast resources, but too often seem to be the problem not the solution. Every day it becomes more obvious that the solutions for ordinary folk will be local, human-scaled solutions.

Human scaled street — as long as the buildings are non-combustible, it works. It's beautiful. It feels delightful

It also is less noted that we currently live in the most democratically-wealthy era in human history. Ordinary people have access to resources that kings lacked 500 years ago. The change is now so rapid, that three editions of this book had to be written since it was first launched in 2008. In 2008 we wrote about $100,000 Telepresence; six years later Skype offers it for free on a laptop.

A Framework for Settlement

A framework is not a plan. This book provides a framework. The framework is then shaped to fit the local conditions, geography and the needs and aspirations of the people and communities of the host region where the VillageTown is to be built.

What it is, what it is not

Let's start with the negatives; what it is **not**:
- It is not an intentional community
- It is not an eco-village
- It is not co-housing
- It is not a utopia; it is not based on utopian ideals
- It is not a real estate development

It **is** a **settlement**.

The first 3 categories (intentional, eco and co-housing) are often presumed by people who don't listen very carefully, and want to put the concept into a familiar box. When they hear the numbers, 5-10,000 people, $1-2 billion, 400-600 acres, they get confused. While the VillageTown is environmentally sustainable (eco) and socially supportive (co), these are not its definition or core purpose, but merely common sense.

Folks who say "oh, it's a utopia" are confusing idealistic projects with something that is quite the opposite. A VillageTown is pragmatic. Utopias are places where everyone and everything works in harmony. VillageTowns presume and plan for human corruption and therefore base their governance system on Jeffersonian principles of checks and balances.

The one that causes the most difficulty, especially among professional planners is explaining that it is not a real estate development, but instead a settlement.

Everything within a ten minute walk means people connect with each other on the plazas – no appointment necessary

Developments are developed by developers. Developers are motivated by and make decisions based on pecuniary interest, meaning the profits they will make for themselves or their investors. Real estate development is a purely monetized industry in which the public or common interest is only served if it happens to align with the profit motive, or if the government has mandated certain things that the developer must do. Unfortunately, in the big picture, big business manages to sufficiently influence government that laws and regulations are made that are good for big business, but not necessarily good for people, communities, societies, civilizations or the planet. For example, suburbs were invented to sell cars and related products.

Modern real estate development exploded on the scene after World War Two. Farmland was converted to suburban housing; roads began to stripe the land and more millionaires were made subdividing land than any other way. But this was a new phenomenon. The older, indeed timeless model was settlement, especially in the New World. The first wave of settlers come to a new land, and with apologies to the indigenous peoples who were there first, they seek to carve out a new life, build a home for their families and work-places to create wealth (be it farm, shop or factory). Then when those settlers have settled in, and want to see their economy or society grow, they designate some greenfield for a new settlement, and they invite new settlers to come in. Sometimes they invite family members who are working in the cities; other times they attract new folks. What is important though is that the people who will live with the results, both the hosts and the new comers, participate in the settlement process, and they make decisions based on reasons very different than those made by developers. As Christopher Alexander wrote in *A Pattern Language* "...*people should design for themselves their own houses, streets and communities. This idea... comes simply from the observation that most of the wonderful places of the world were not made by architects but by the people.*"

Why not a town? In a village you are known and you know others.
Why many villages? Diversity, variety, stimulation, social & economic critical mass

Why are such places wonderful? Because they are human-scaled and they reflect the character and aspirations of the people who will live there. In building a new home that the founding family expects to house their descendants may decide, for example, to commission a beautiful front door that a developer would never buy, because the return on investment does not pencil out. The founding family does not care about ROI; they will open the door every day for decades, and they want it to reflect what is important to them. This is what it means to say it is a settlement.

The Numbers:

- 5,000 to 10,000 population, depending on what the land will support and the host community wants
- 400-600 acres total. Figure 10± acres for a 200-house village, plus 20 for the town center. Total urban core, 100 to 220 acres
- 50 acre walk-to Industrial Park with an agricultural and/or rainwater harvesting roof
- 100-300 acre Greenbelt that surrounds the urban core and industrial park
- $1 to 2 billion capital investment, one quarter to one half billion dollars per year in income
- Takes at least 6,000 cars off the road permanently and eliminates about a quarter million miles of driving per day

Pitigliano Italy

Los Angeles, California on a rare clear day

A recently built suburb in the Auckland region of New Zealand

Villages and towns almost died when the Industrial Revolution put cities on steroids

In the 1950's many cities fell into ruin when the automobile gave us the suburbs.

Now, we assert, the suburb is obsolete. We suggest

with the introduction of advanced, affordable telecommunications, we have come full circle. Economically, villages and small towns are viable once again, and can be a most satisfying and fulfilling form of human community. The time of the settlement has returned– but only if it is done right.

Attention to detail is essential. This book is about those details. It contains recipes, "how to" sections, intended to show the way to get started, and to finish.

Before we get to the details, realize that VillageTowns emerge from individual needs – needs as different as the cycles of life and the path of life each of us choose. Each home reflects the dreams and aspirations of a unique individual, and if empowered to mark their home with their personality, the VillageTown as a whole emerges with a distinct and authentic character.

Consider the difference between this distinctive building found in Italy in the photo to the right, and this suburban home in a subdivision, below. One reflects the character of the owner in a glorious riot of color, artistry and potted vines. The other reflects a developer who picked designs from a stock design and fit them on a road plan, intended to maximize profits within the local zoning rules. One contributes to a sense of place, a sense of community. The other provides a place to sleep, to watch TV but no sense of identity or place – it is functional and distinctly temporary, devoid of character – as if life is something to get through.

In this book, we seek to empower the individual in hopes of engendering the

Yes, the letters of the sign really are backwards

individual character found in the example of the Italian building. To do this we offer a framework to enable people to provide for their wellbeing. We provide the framework, the people and communities write the plan.

In this first part of the book, we invite you to identify the stage and focus of life that matches your life and aspirations. The remaining two parts of the book guides you though the steps on how to build a VillageTown.

The front face of a home makes a statement. The garage door dominates the streetscape. Cars define the suburb. Interesting how the front lawn was converted to blacktop. Practical in the dry climate of California, but so lacking in beauty.

If you're a baby boomer worried about retirement

On 12 July 2006, I opened the New Zealand Herald to read syndicated columnist Rupert Cornwell's commentary with the headline that read:

Baby boom to bust in a bankrupt nation
Comment: US finances face meltdown as post-war children reach retirement.

On 17 January 2008, David M. Walker, Comptroller General of the United States showed the unfunded liability of the US Government was $52 trillion and the net worth of all Americans was $58 trillion (before the crash). $42 trillion of that liability is for the Baby Boom's retirement and medical care. In 2014, some quote the unfunded liability at $127 trillion, roughly $1.1 million per taxpayer. Projections say that today there are four payees to every beneficiary, but by 2030, this will drop to 2:1. While these many reports address America's challenge, the same problem faces many western nations. Simply put it is very unlikely there will be sufficient money to pay for the promised elder care for the next generation of retirees.

It will get worse. The 2008 crash was due to greed. What's coming is an immutable wall of demographics. When baby boomers go to sell their suburban homes and their stock portfolios to pay for retirement, who is going to buy? In the US with 79 million boomer sellers and 69 million next generation buyers, real prices may drop and a lot more net worth may disappear.

Sounds grim, and I wish I could say "Don't worry; they'll take care of it."

Regrettably, I'm simply not confident that *they* have a solution in the wings. Most likely, we will see quality of life decline, personal wealth shrink and less transparency to mask decisions that would be politically unpopular. As much as well-meaning people would want the governments of the world to solve the problem, unless we find a new way to create wealth and then use some of it to support our aging population, the laws of economics will be working against us. We can't solve the problem by manipulating tax systems or printing more money backed by nothing. The laws of economics are against us. With more elders and fewer young, the balance falls over – Baby Boomers need to find another way, to reinvent aging... and to do so very soon.

The way to understand this challenge is to begin thinking about the difference between wealth creation and wealth conversion. This book will focus repeatedly on the difference. Let us take as an example the Baby Boomer's suburban home.

Once a suburban home is built, most of the wealth created is completed. Land, timber, cement and petroleum have been combined to make a place of shelter. After that, the market demand that increases the home's price is wealth conversion, because nothing new on earth is added to shelter people. If market demand declines, as we can expect it will when millions of Baby Boomers go to sell their suburban homes, the seller is the loser.

- Wealth conversion is about winners and losers
- With wealth creation, there are only winners.

If Baby Boomers want to provide for their elder years, they need to begin now – and think direct action, wealth creation in very concrete terms, both figuratively and literally. They need to reinvent the very concept of aging and retirement. They need tangible investments that provide them security, care, protection and beyond that a good elder life.

How did we get into this mess? It all began with WW-II. Dad and nine million of his fellow soldiers came home from the war, determined to resume a normal life with a wife, children and a new home in the suburbs. They all had babies at the same time, thus producing a demographic bubble and a competition for resources that defined their generation from birth onward.

When we were babies, Dr. Spock wrote the book on parenting; we became a focus of attention as if parenting had just been invented. When we got to school, the classrooms overflowed. I remember one high school English class where my desk was in the doorway — simply too many of us to fit in the classroom. When we became teenagers, society suddenly became youth obsessed, something many of us still haven't grown out of.

When we went to university, competition for admissions became intense, and the same thing happened when we got out and were looking for jobs. When we went to buy houses, prices boomed, too many of us in the market.

Every stage of our lives has been marked by competition for resources, and now baby boomers are starting to look ahead to their graying years and beginning to worry. Many, having put a parent or grandparent in a retirement home and that living

From ages fifty to one hundred – the remaining stages of our lives

purgatory we call a nursing home, swear they won't go there. Where will we go? What happens when our children or that nice young judge takes away our drivers license and our driving home-range suddenly becomes inaccessible? What do we do when walking a hundred yards knocks the stuffing out of us? Where do we want to be when mobility is a wheel chair, and we need help getting out of bed? Where do we want to be buried?

Some will be happy to go to Golden Sands Retirement Village in the desert or a tropical paradise to watch our skin slowly turn to leather and our consciousness devolve to nattering about Judge Judy. However, many have no interest in hanging around a bunch of old folk.

One curious effect of aging is that the person inside does not feel old, they feel just like they always have, albeit a bit wiser perhaps, with a longer perspective on history, and feeling a bit betrayed by a body that creaks and brain that sometimes suffers memory lapses. We'd rather be among people of all ages, watching the folly of youth, enjoying the company of peers, happy to assist the stressed-out parents next door, knowing that when we get tired of their children, we can send them home.

For most of history, elders held a special and honored place in society – elders were not banished to some sort of an apartheid township or when ill, a kind of leper colony; they remained in the community. In many European countries, even the lord of the manor would take a ground floor apartment in the village, for villages can be kind to the elderly.

The VillageTown is important to baby boomers because it gives them a better alternative for making the transition from employment and parenting years to retirement and eldership. It provides them with a social structure designed to have a place for them, so they don't feel like redundant, inconvenient baggage. It provides an economic plan not dependent, (or at least less dependent) on government funding, for we fear such funding may dry up when so many of us switch from taxpayers to benefit recipients. The VillageTown becomes the ultimate tangible investment.

If you are a baby boomer interested in building your village in the VillageTown, you become important for two reasons:

• You are the most motivated of all the target groups. You need to see the VillageTown begin now, so it is ready when you need it. While boomers should not be a majority of the residents (we don't want to build another retirement village), it is likely you will be the primary drivers, the most motivated Founders who make certain it gets built now.

• You are the decision makers. People born between 1945 and 1965 hold the positions of authority, the bankers, the politicians, the company directors, the local government officials. You are at the peak of your earnings power. Consistently, when we present these ideas to decision makers, government officials or experts whose assistance we need, they then comment, "I'd be interested in living there myself."

This is now beginning to change. As more boomers shift from contributors to beneficiaries, those looking to the promise of government pensions and health care may be disappointed. Even for those boomers who cash in successfully we can expect exactly the same competition for retirement dwellings that they had for desks back in high school: High demand for elder housing coupled with limited supply.

It seems reasonable to suggest that the best plan boomers can latch on to is one that creates a system and infrastructure neither dependent on central government nor on fragile global economic systems, and to create a highly diverse community, not just one for old people.

After moving into a VillageTown, the baby boomers may move two or three times. First, they move into the big house, lots of room for visiting children, grandchildren and all the furniture and possessions they tend to collect over a lifetime. Then as they get older, these things become clutter, difficult. They find it best to simplify, to move into an elder cottage where life-focus shifts to the plaza, walking to it becomes a daily ritual. Some will die in their cottage, but others may become infirm, and for this the VillageTown provides the third stage of housing – nursing facilities on the plaza, allowing them to remain part of their community even to death.

Life for elders worked for centuries before we invented pensions, retirement villages, nursing homes and a society where one is dependent on ones drivers license. Now that we are witnessing the failure of these 20th century systems, due to overload and insufficient funding, it's time to implement models that proved to work before such systems came along.

For now, boomers want a beautiful, stimulating place that supports an active life – these are people who are still jumping out of airplanes and running marathons in their 60's and winning at Henley at age 70. As they look ahead, they also want to know a place for their eldership is prepared and waiting. The VillageTown we envision has several special features for them:

Elder Housing: Smaller, ground floor residences especially designed for old people. Located within 50 yards/meters from the plaza, elder housing would be level, have kitchens with smoke sensors that shut off the stove, be wired to call for help, and overall be designed for people when their bodies are weaker. Each should have good light, and however small, a garden – the sunlit garden is important.

Pedestrian and bicycle priority, no cars in the VillageTown, only in a motorpool for outbound trips. Local streets will permit golf-cart-sized, slow-speed local vehicles and mobility scooters, but not cars. Losing ones drivers license becomes irrelevant; everything one needs should be within walking distance, or using a local vehicle.

On-plaza nursing care facilities. For incapacitated elders, on each plaza the VillageTown pays for building a small facility to provide nursing care. The initial capital cost to build the facility should come from the VillageTown capital fund, the same fund used for streets, parks, underground wiring and pipes and other public amenities. The operations cost, mostly for 24=hour supervisory staff, utilities and operations costs, should come from an annual levy, fee or tax paid by everyone in the VillageTown.

In this way, the levy becomes a form of local collective insurance. Everyone would hope they never need to collect, hoping instead to die at a merry old age in bed, at home. For those not so lucky, if afflicted by ill-health or systemic weakness, they would know that they would get to remain in their community. They would never face the ignoble end of being wheelchair or bed-bound in an alien, overheated institution smelling of rank urine, with crying or shrieking strangers in the next room and patronizing underpaid, overworked staff treating them like senseless children.

When the VillageTown keeps its elders (and its infirm of any age) in the community, the cost of their care is less. Who needs weekly art therapy or classes in basket weaving to occupy empty time, when instead they wheel out to the plaza café or the plaza's tropical arboretum where old friends and good neighbors join them for a cup of tea?

Providing for these three stages of eldership within ones community offers a far more human and dignified way to get old. The time for the baby boom generation to begin making these provisions is now – or to add urgency, we really should have begun back in 1995.

The time is now.

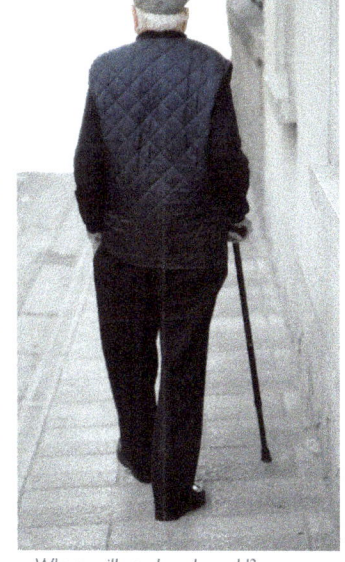

Where will you be when old?

If you run a small to medium enterprise (SME) or field office

A VillageTown settlement is advised to not focus on selling houses, but instead attract head-of-household (HOH) jobs. In this way it builds the local economy while avoiding outbound commuters. Initially, the ViTo (the civitas corporation) should look for 3-5 "anchor businesses", medium-size enterprises that sell local to global (L2G). At about 200 employees each, such businesses create the critical mass that attracts local-to-local (L2L) businesses as well as ancillary smaller L2G companies.

Why will businesses move to a VillageTown?

Talent: Talent attracts talent. Businesses will move to the VillageTown to be a part of a creative, exciting new life. In California, this is what is happening in Silicon Valley, for example. Reach a critical mass and it becomes a *cluster*.

Quality of Life: The most important draw for businesses will be personal. Business owners and decision-makers are human. They have families and they have personal concerns like the rest of us. Families with school-age children will move to get into a good school zone. They will select locations that work their way up Maslow's hierarchy of needs, starting with safety for themselves and their families.

Economic Security: Creation of a local economy enables a community to protect itself from the suffering that economic downturns bring. Basic needs are provided locally; the capital fund derived from the initial home sales enables the VillageTown to look after its own.

Child raising and eldercare: In car-free villages where adults work, rather than commute out, it's safe for children to play outdoors; to learn independence & autonomy in an environment that is safe. This is important both for the business owners bringing their own families to the VillageTown, but also because it is attractive for their employees. The same applies to the concern for their elderly parents. The present options of retirement homes followed by nursing homes do not appeal to many. For some decision-makers, the alternative of purpose-built elder housing followed by nursing care within the village will tip the balance, either for their parents or their own old age.

Conviviality and fun:

Each village will have its own cafes, restaurants and taverns. All will focus on *slow food* meaning an emphasis on flavorful, locally-grown, locally-made food and drink.

Cultural Enrichment: The VillageTown invests in social and cultural enrichment with artist guild halls on each village plaza, festival fields, sports fields and performance halls. It ensures that no less than 5% of the community are active members of what Richard Florida calls the *Creative Class*; a demographic that stimulates the host community's local economy.

Investment Capital and Lower Costs: The Legacy Fund will have hundreds of millions of dollars in capital to loan or invest in inbound businesses. The ViTo may offer subsidized leases in the industrial park. The absence of commuting, more efficient buildings and other savings will lower the cost of living.

In the last decade or two, new technology reduced the need for physical proximity. It also cut the cost of the tools of the trade to a level affordable by an individual. Today, the home office desk might cost more than the home office's computer, with software obtainable for a few hundred dollars that reflects millions of dollars in research and development. As a result, for many people the priorities change for selecting business location. If we can locate our business anywhere we are linked into the global networks, quality of life becomes a prime decision factor. Note the caveat "anywhere we are linked into the global networks". The VillageTown must meet this condition if it is to secure a stable and diverse local economy. Home offices became popular in the 1990's, until people discovered commuting to the converted spare bedroom in a bathrobe did not feel right. We need to be in a work environment, and to have contact with colleagues, even if we are running a one-person business. We need to have breaks during the day where we can have intelligent conversation with more than the dog or the courier delivering overnight mail. This is not possible with suburban zoning rules. It works well in traditional settlements.

The VillageTown is micro-zoned. It includes plazas ringed with workplaces – the zone for offices, shops, low-impact workshops (example: the village toymaker) and cafes, taverns and restaurants. Set on the ground floor, these workplaces face the plaza, with careful attention paid to the design of the windows to create a balance between public engagement and privacy. In this way, the workers in the workplaces go about their own business, yet by their presence, bring the plaza and village alive. Because the plaza has no cars, children can play knowing that the village workers are keeping a watchful eye. Each plaza has open sitting with tables, cafes and restaurants, providing a better alternative for coffee break than the institutional work-place kitchens.

In establishing the zoning rules for the VillageTown, provision should be made to permit owners of the workplace to have a studio apartment attached, either a proper apartment overhead, or in the back, a bedroom with shower and kitchenette, where the owner can live if they can't afford both to start the business and buy a home. The rules should require an attached studio be small, just big enough to be functional, but small enough to encourage the entrepreneur to move into a proper home when the business turns a sustainable profit.

Industrial Park – Outside the urban core, near the motorpool and freight depot, a VillageTown should have a 50 acre (20 ha.) walk-to Industrial Park. It is important that the economy make things. It is important that the VillageTown provide jobs for a wide range of people, not just white collar or new-tech. During construction, the VillageTown will need a place to make the components related to new homes and businesses. This provides a market opportunity for new businesses who can capitalize their equipment on the first burst of local sales.

By building an Industrial Park, the VillageTown can attract a wider range of entrepreneurs and small businesses.

Funding – By using a civitas corporation (ViTo) instead of a developer, the people who will live in the VillageTown pre-identify. The reward they get is that the ViTo's net profits remain in the community. These profits are vested in the ViTo's *Legacy Fund* that could be in the hundreds of millions of dollars. This fund is to be invested in the local economy (both the VillageTown and the host region), to level the playing field for its small and medium private enterprises, in loans, direct investment and in professional assistance.

Broadband – The VillageTown should have fiber-optic-speed broadband, installed in a way that can be easily upgraded when technology advances.

A word of warning – wireless is cheaper to install, but do we really want to create a fog of microwaves? We don't know the long-term health effects of filling the air with radiation. Play it safe, spend the extra money, install wired broadband, be it fiber-optic cables or plugged-in telephone wires. If wireless is essential, select limited distance signals, such as a wireless table with a range of a few inches - it only works with a tablet or smart phone sitting on it.

Technology – We recommend the VillageTown provide community accessible technology so small offices need not invest in expensive good equipment. Commercial grade printers, binding machines, video equipment are a few examples where including the capital cost as part of the initial infrastructure makes the VillageTown more attractive to this essential part of the village demographic – the money importers.

Proximity – Our research conducted in the 1990's found that the VillageTown works best within a two-hour drive of an urban center (overnight mail and parcel delivery by noon).

Critical Mass – The VillageTown needs about 5,000 - 10,000 people, to support:

- a reasonable range of local shops and services
- an industrial park
- rapid freight delivery
- a feeder airline service (even if just morning and evening)
- a stimulating quality of life sufficiently diverse to provide perspective and on-going interest for a lifetime
- sufficiently accessible and interesting to have a refreshing flow of interesting visitors (but not tourists paying to be entertained). Visitors keep a place from becoming boring.

> History 101: Prior to global communications, most professions and businesses needed to locate in a city. Business is about cooperation as much as competition and previous generations needed to be able to meet with other businesses and professionals. Offices needed to be in close proximity so couriers could hand deliver papers. The post office made several deliveries each day. To keep communications flowing and profits monitored, businesses needed to be big enough to support whole departments of typists and bookkeepers. When computer systems cost millions and photocopiers cost tens of thousands of dollars, companies needed to have hundreds of workers in an office to afford the support tools. All of this was swept away by telecommunications.

A population of 1,200 supports one general store; my watchmaker says 5,000 people are needed to support one watchmaker. 4,000 to 10,000 people support a whole street of shops, services, restaurants and cafes. Over 10,000 people, bureaucracy creeps in and sense of place declines. Beyond business, this critical mass also ensures the non-work hours are interesting. VillageTown life works when a broad range of people are represented and actively engaged in day-to day life of the community.

Provided proximity and critical mass are met, selecting a VillageTown site becomes a joy... by the sea, in the mountains, or in a bucolic rural setting. If you can, select a place near a national, state or regional park, a place with ample outdoor activities, so a healthy and active life is just outside the village gate.

When one is freed from the tyranny of distance, one no longer needs to pick a place to live that is far from the better things in life but near the rat race.

So what will it be? Close to the snow-filled mountains or down by the sea? Perhaps in the bucolic countryside?

What a wonderful problem to have.

Welcome to VillageTown planning.

If you are a creative or performing artist or musician

The VillageTown needs artists. Artists need the VillageTown. To keep its artists, the VillageTown must prevent gentrification. It must have a plan where artists never get priced out of the market. Why?

Creative and performing artists hold an important place in any community, they hold the mirror up to society, showing not the image we want to see, but the masks we wear, and what lies behind the mask. The artists transform a community into a vibrant, interesting place. Communities need more than television, CD's, videos and Internet performances, more than posters of great art; they need living, creating artists, making live music, creating original works of art, street theater, making the films and dancing. To achieve this, the community must understand the needs of such artists, and provide for them – long term.

Artists need support of a community – traditionally they had it

In indigenous societies, the artist was not only valued, but supported. They were fed, clothed and sheltered by the tribe, so they could focus on pursuit of their art. When we monetized society, many artists struggled because they are not masters of the art of moneymaking.

The VillageTown cannot change the economic reality of the art market, but it can reduce the cost of living for artists (it's easier to save a dollar than earn one), and provide a collective creative space to allow them both a supportive arts community and more time to create their form of art.

If the VillageTown pays for buildings for the artists to work plus provides affordable housing reserved for them, the artists have more time to create. What's important for them in this is permanence. That they are permanently protected from gentrification. The best model the VillageTown research found has its roots in history, when artists clustered in guilds. The medieval guilds had a weakness in that they became a monopoly and began to calcify, but the VillageTown can prevent this through a system of checks and balances.

Thus, we propose that the VillageTown build an Artist Guildhall on each village plaza with 25 members each. This works out to 5% of the population being permanently supported members of the Guildhall. The Guildhall is paid for out of the general construction budget, so the artists get their workspace rent/mortgage free. Owned by the VillageTown, it is a

non-monetized exchange following the ancient model of indigenous societies. The artists add to the cultural enrichment.

The clustered artists form a guild based on their medium of expression: painters in one, musicians in another – and if, for example, there are many musicians, perhaps one becomes a classical music guild, another jazz or contemporary. Decisions about how to form a particular Guild is made by the artists in collaboration with their host village.

After reviewing several options for permanent housing, designers suggested oblique-angled, free-base housing. To explain:

A desirable feature of the VillageTown is avoidance of the grid – allow the streets to curve. However, with attached housing this means either wasted wedge space or some homes must have a trapezoidal floor plan. Build the latter, with two or three floors of apartments reserved for artists and other people the community deems important to support.

Angled artist housing in a converted warehouse

Provide the apartments rent-free to the Guildhall members. They can live in them (only paying the ongoing costs and maintenance), or, if they prefer to live in a bigger home (perhaps because they have a family), they may rent it and keep the proceeds as the community's acknowledgement of their contribution to culture. This subsidy is deed restricted by the civitas corporation (called the ViTo) to the VillageTown at the onset to make it permanent. It is paid for out of the profits from sales of unsubsidized homes and workplaces.

Collaborationz 2007 – artists come from around the world to create together

The guild should be given substantial authority over the design and construction of the Guildhall; the collective artists know best what they need. We imagine a Guildhall for writers – a place to write – might resemble an Oxford library or club, with book-lined walls, comfortable chairs and modern technology with book printing and binding equipment. In contrast, a music guild might have rehearsal rooms, perhaps a recording studio, near one of the VillageTown's performing arts halls. Sculptors may be located near the industrial zone, so noise and dust would not interfere with more tranquil parts of the VillageTown.

Note that the definition of artist, when qualifying for Guild status goes beyond the traditional painter, musician or actor. See the next page that discusses what sociologist Richard Florida calls the Creative Class, noting that a village formed around the theme of entrepreneurship, for example, may elect to sponsor a Guild of inventors and engineers who invent great new stuff.

Waiheke Jazz Festival

Finally, while the ViTo would set aside funds to support construction of the Guildhall and free-base housing, efforts should be made to secure outside sponsorship, offering naming rights to build and equip better, more enriched buildings for the Guilds and their members. Make the VillageTown one of the great cultural centers of the world.

If you are a scientist, scholar, educator or engineer – the Creative Class

The Creative Class – For the VillageTown to thrive, it needs what Richard Florida named as the Creative Class. This includes, but is more than the artists and performers. The Creative Class encompasses a wider range of front line creators: scientists, engineers, architects, designers, filmmakers, scholars, authors, inventors, innovators, as well as secondary professionals who provide essential support to the creators. Peter Jackson is one of New Zealand's front-line creators who funded a whole film industry of creativity in Wellington. The investors and the various professions including lawyers and accountants who believed in him, formed part of the secondary creators. Both are important to the wellbeing of the VillageTown. The Creative Class plays a major part in securing VillageTown prosperity and it should be at the core of any VillageTown settlement plan.

To attract the Creative Class, the VillageTown must offer certain amenities... what they need to live there, and a quality of life that provides the things they love. Location and infrastructure become important. Critical mass becomes important – the VillageTown needs enough interesting, creative people to make life interesting for the Creative Class.

Location no longer demands proximity. In the 19th century, being in the city was essential. Now creators like Peter Jackson can develop one of the most sophisticated film production industries in a remote country at the bottom of the globe. Technology enabled him to continue production in New Zealand while he was at Abbey Road studio in London, with live video conferencing literally spanning the globe. Infrastructure for the VillageTown demands a first class, upgradable telecommunications network. First class today means a fat broadband cable capable of supporting high bandwidth multi-media video conferences, so people can meet and share work without travelling.

The Creative Class of centuries past invented the tools that opened up world trade and changed the fundamentals of the economy.

> If we look to history, we find certain places at certain times have been hotbeds of creativity... Babylonia, Egypt, Classical Athens, ancient India, timeless China, the Indian tribes of the Pacific Northwest, the Huron, the Inca and the Mayan, Oxford and Cambridge, Paris, Greenwich Village in NY in the 1950's, London in the Age of Enlightenment, the Arabic lands during Europe's Dark Ages, Venice in the Renaissance and Florence still today.
>
> The list is large and spans all continents. Places once thriving later became backwaters of deprivation. What does it take to make such a place emerge?
>
> It seems the binding character of each of these places in their time was
>
> (a) affluence in relative peacetime
>
> By affluence, we mean sufficient wealth that people have leisure time and discretionary resources, in an environment of freedom, peace and stability.
>
> (b) valuing learnedness and the creative and performing arts.

Upgradable includes low-tech elements such as easily-accessible underground channels to enable replacement of today's cables with the unknown product of the future. The Creative Class needs an infrastructure with good transportation for when local-to-global businesses whose staff must fly to other places and for rapid delivery of goods. Location demands a country with stable national governance, but not too interfering in day-to-day life.

Beyond the infrastructure the creative class needs to work, location also addresses elements they need for quality of life. Borrowing from the work of Abraham Maslow, the Creative Class (and others) also seek a VillageTown that is:

- Healthy and nourishing, safe and secure
- Well-ordered, with clear boundary conditions but a strong sense of personal freedom
- Welcoming, supportive of family and friendships
- Offering a sense of community and of belonging and of tolerance
- Environmentally well balanced, with places both of activity and silence
- Designed with clear delineations between public and private
- An honest and good place, not unnecessarily complex or bureaucratic;
- A place that values justice, not tolerating injustice or lawlessness
- Interesting, not boring, with sufficient diversity to keep one active and alert
- Culturally enriched, with a thriving arts scene, intellectually stimulating
- Playful, valuing excellence and humor
- Tolerant of, indeed delighting in, eccentricity and non-conforming behavior
- Part of global society, yet be substantially self-sufficient
- Beautiful, a wonderful place to live without ever feeling the need to move on.

At the village walls a clear delineation where urban stops and the rural begins
- open land within walking distance, and set in a countryside of interest:
- by the sea, in the mountains or a bucolic rural setting
- easy to engage in outdoor activities... walking, cycling, climbing or more active sports

Giacomo Puccini

The Creative Class seeks these qualities because they have selected careers that enable them to look beyond survival, and recent shifts in technology enable them to do their work away from the cities. Thus, they look for quality of life. By their presence, they will add to the quality of the VillageTown, and the more Creative Class people attracted to the VillageTown, the more dynamic it becomes.

If one group should be over represented in the VillageTown, it would be the Creative Class. Create a milieu that attracts such people and one can expect more of this group to move to the VillageTown. This group then increases quality of life for all in the VillageTown.

This gentleman was busy writing on his laptop while sitting outside an Oxford concert hall listening to an orchestra playing with the windows open. Multitasking artistic and intellectual growth.

If you are retired now or an elder in settled work

I went to Cornwall in the UK to visit two friends, a Kiwi and a Scot, who had just launched a book on the Scot's 79th birthday. He used to be a successful CEO of a furniture manufacturer, but a near-death experience in the peak of his career caused a change in his life-view. As a child, he always wanted to be a blacksmith, so he closed his company, moved to Cornwall and started a new life at an age when his peers began thinking about gated-golfing communities. In addition to becoming a blacksmith, Hamish Miller took up dowsing and that took him to writing books on his experiences. His new life has taken him around the world; I first met him in New Zealand when he gave a talk at our place. He was an elder, not a senior citizen.

Aging isn't what it used to be, thanks to advances in medical science and the way people live. We no longer expose ourselves to hazardous conditions and environments, we eat better foods and when we do break, doctors fix our bodies the way mechanics replace parts in our car. We slow down, our faces change shape, but in many ways while the retirement age has remained around age 65, in body terms our 70 year olds look younger than our grandparents did at 60.

This change creates a need for a different form of retirement, one with three stages – active retirement, settled retirement and infirmity. To provide for these stages, the VillageTown concept envisions age diversity, not age segregation. It is not a retirement village (a monoculture of old people), but its intent includes providing for elders from the time they retire to the time they die. To achieve this, specific design elements, or *patterns*, become an essential part of the framework of the VillageTown.

Three Stages of Elder Housing

In our post WW-II society, we failed to develop an infrastructure for old people, in part because most died within a few years of retirement. Now the first stage of retirement can be extended for decades, and the VillageTown needs to provide for all these stages.

Large – When first they move into the VillageTown, retired people may have a houseful of furniture and a need for guest bedrooms to house visiting children and grandchildren. Standard VillageTown homes would be available for them, needing no special architecture, placement or price protection.

Settled – The next stage of elder housing provides smaller, simple, ground-floor homes designed for one person or a couple. Specifically designed for elders, these homes should have level access, no steps or stoops, special smoke detectors

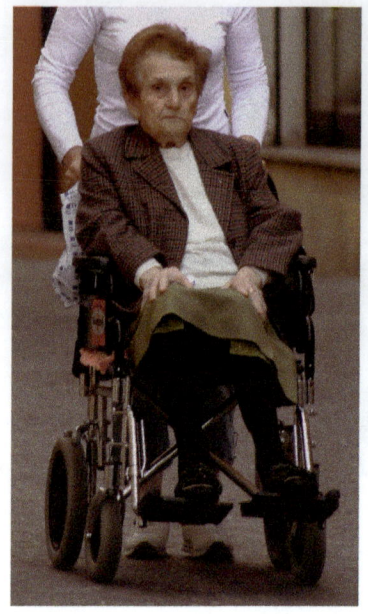

that shut off the kitchen stove, wiring for a wristband panic button to call for help in the case of emergency. Kitchens and bathrooms should include handicap access, and each home should have a sun-facing garden, no matter how small it might be. In order to assure this housing remains available for elders, at least some should have deed restricted pricing, with subsidized original price and a restriction on the deed limiting resale to people living on a modest pension or to physically handicapped people.

Care – In the final stage of eldership, some need to move to nursing homes. In the western world nursing homes all too often are sad, depressing places only visited by dutiful grown children accompanied by grandchildren who make embarrassing comments about the stench of urine and ammonia. Nursing homes often are institutions inhabited solely by old people in sad states of decline. This need not be life's endgame, and in the VillageTown, we propose a better alternative.

As part of the capital investment in the infrastructure of the VillageTown, build small – say 6 to 10 bed – nursing care facilities on, or by, the plazas. Pay for the staffing and operations costs out of the levy, fee or tax paid by all VillageTown residents, just as street maintenance and the village halls are supported. In essence, VillageTown citizens pay a form of local insurance, hoping they never have to claim it. Such a system is far more civilized and caring, as infirm elders are not forced to leave their home and friends. During the day, they may be wheeled out to the plaza café, to catch up with friends and neighbors, or simply to watch the public life of the community. Bedridden elders not wanting the curtains drawn should be placed by windows looking on to the plaza, as elders lived for many centuries in traditional villages. Such an approach costs less because the service need not hire people to help combat the isolation and boredom that comes when one is removed to a nursing home.

Critical Mass

As part of the element of *critical mass*, the population of the VillageTown needs to be of a sufficient scale to provide for a local medical center to provide emergency services, and recovery beds. This tends to work with a population of not less than 5,000 in the VillageTown. If the center is also available to people in the surrounding countryside, the center can offer more services.

In a society based on the car, to lose ones license is to lose ones freedom. The solutions for elders in this state brochure are adaptations to a hostile car-spread-out infrastructure.

The VillageTown infrastructure places all within a 10 minute walk. VillageTown streets are for walking, bicycles, ebikes, wheel chairs, mobility scooters and golf-cart-sized electric vehicles.

Solutions you can use

Lifts from family and friends

This works well for many people, but it can be helpful to use other forms of transport as well. Using a mix of solutions is good, especially if you don't like asking for a lift too often. Neighbourhood Support groups can be a good source of help.

Taxis and public transport

Taxis and public transport can be excellent ways to get about easily. How useful these solutions are to you will depend on how regular and reliable services are, and whether access into and out of buses is good. Sharing rides with your friends will help keep taxi costs down. The Total Mobility Scheme administered by Regional Councils may provide Total Mobility Vouchers for discounted taxi fares.

Community transport

Many community organisations provide free transport for people to attend their activities. Hospitals and medical centres sometimes provide transport for patients, and some shopping malls provide shoppers' buses and mobility scooters.

Walking

If your health and mobility are good, walking more often can be a very good solution. Walking costs nothing, and promotes health and independence.

Settled Work

> "Give each person, especially as they grow old, the chance to set up a workplace of their own, within or very near their home. Make it a place that can grow slowly, perhaps in the beginning sustaining a weekend hobby and gradually becoming a complete, productive, and comfortable workshop"
>
> *Pattern 156 "Settled Work" A Pattern Language - Christopher Alexander ISBN 0-19-501919-9 1977*

Zoning around the plazas embraces offices, shops, cafes and services. It also allows a form of settled work, provided the noise, smells and dust are mitigated or not present. This provision specifically envisions workshops run by elders: the village toymaker, the baker of glorious cakes, the quality businesses that probably can't be run profitably to support a growing family, but work well for someone who does it mostly for love, appreciating the top-up it gives to ones pension.

Plaza Design

The plazas are designed for elders, as well as all other stages of life. Benches and steps facing the warming sun or shaded from the hot burning sun are carefully placed so they are out of the firing range of children kicking balls. Borrowing from the Italian model, the cafes spill out into the plaza, but the VillageTown goes one better: it owns the additional seats that allow people to sit and to visit without having to buy a drink or meal.

Old People Everywhere

Future generations may look back on how we treated old people the way we look back at slavery. How similar are retirement homes to Apartheid? How similar are nursing homes to leper colonies? Old people belong in the community, not locked away –out of sight and out of mind. Certainly, people should have the option of such homes but not as the only option. Communities, especially children, need their elders.

Rely on government to provide a safety net, but not quality of life. To secure quality of life, design villages that have a place for old people until they die... and a cemetery so we remember them.

There was something exceptionally sad about this invitation hanging on the side of the wall of this seniors' home.

'Try our 90 day test drive' shows the extent to which the automobile has taken over our culture. Ironic since the reason to move to such a place is loss of mobility – the state takes away the senior citizen's license to drive.

The building was in a commercial zone with busy, noisy streets. There was no sense of community and one can imagine what life is like inside: The occasional visit from dutiful family members, but a life essentially out of synch - politely, sadly waiting to die.

If you are parents of a young family

Parenting can be exhausting. You don't think about that when you're getting married.

Yes, it's become a cliché "It takes the village to raise the child" – but behind the cliché we find wisdom – children need more adults around than their parents and school teachers. The VillageTown provides proximity: children living next door; safe nearby places to play; a thousand neighbors looking out, adults as role models; and elders with time and interest.

For as long as humans have been human, sharing the burden was part of community – until we invented the city and then the suburb where we then had to pay people to supervise children. We also shifted to the nuclear family, with the unintended negative side effect that the children began to drive the parents crazy. We added a new twist by shifting to a two-earner family, thus requiring day-care, and we separated home from school, play, work and entertainment to the point where a whole new type of car was invented – the people mover, and a new bumper sticker "Mom's taxi". Then we wonder why families break up.

A key element in VillageTown design becomes that of inherent safety. Inherent safety is not the nanny state, but attention to design details that protect children. The most obvious safety measure is banning cars from streets, then designing plazas to be a place children play – a place where adults, friends and neighbors, are present in natural proximity – whether, having a meal or cup of tea – natural proximity. For older children, especially teens, the VillageTown design includes places where they can express their independence from parents (and dependence on each other in packs) without it becoming self-destructive.

Children: Boredom is a major issue for many children, especially those of the comfortable classes of Western civilization. Television and shopping malls don't cure boredom; they aggravate it. VillageTown design engages children to include patterns that stave off boredom. In the design process, input is solicited from children who set out the patterns they want to see. In one workshop, the children lobbied for children's caves, small places to play. Give children play areas and real life will win out over television and computer games every time.

Parenting can be exhausting

Teens: Architectural design for teenagers is an art form different from that of design for adults. It combines activity places, social contact places and shielded places – shielded enough to explore, but not enough to get into trouble. Build climbing walls, soundproofed skateboard parks, solid concrete walls to bounce balls where the noise and stains don't bother adults.

Students: Parents will move home to place their children in a good school. In creating a new VillageTown of say ten thousand population, the needed new primary and secondary schools becomes an opportunity. In New Zealand, education law provides for state funded schools to have a special character and it draws upon local citizens to form the establishment board of trustees. Similar opportunities exist in other countries, although sometimes by persuasion and negotiation rather than specific clauses in law. For example, in the 1960's educator John Bremer started the Parkway Program in the Philadelphia School District – a public high school, but a "School Without Walls" that transformed the student's educational experience.

Bird shot fell like sleet around me as the armed escort cleared way for the musicians and then the bride and her family.

In creating a new VillageTown, the opportunity opens for the Founders to create an outstanding school, potentially very different from the factory models we still build – place the classrooms on the plazas, make each village a campus, integrate learning with the rest of VillageTown life so students have many role models and see the value of education.

Apprentices & Internships: Plaza-based workplaces create opportunity for youth apprenticeship and internships: At a young age children observe role models, then as they become teens, they may take after-school jobs with a future track.

Tom Sawyer childhood: Children who grow up with fields, trees, swimming, fishing, surfing, climbing or riding ponies experience a level of fulfillment no video parlor or play center can offer. The outdoors teaches the young to act, to be active, whereas the suburban life of malls and organized entertainment teaches them to buy, to passively consume. We call it the Tom Sawyer childhood, one in which children learn independence and autonomy through active living.

Money: Of all the stages of life, parenthood is generally the most stressful economically. One supports not just oneself or spouse, but demanding little people who need and want. Thus, a major focus of VillageTown planning is to use design to reduce the cost of living. Eliminating the expense of cars is one mentioned; another is reducing the cost of food and purchased goods. Cutting energy costs, reducing home maintenance expenses and replacing paid entertainment with more interesting free entertainment all work together to reduce the pressure on parents. Child care is replaced by a caring community.

When we moved from Greenwich, Connecticut in the USA to New Zealand's Waiheke Island, we found you don't hire baby-sitters, you buy an extra bed. Your child's bedroom is either full of children, or empty. Parents trade children – sleepovers – and noticed it's much easier when your child has a friend over; they're off in the bush down by the stream discovering the joys of mud.

It's safe to let even young ones go over to Artworks, our closest equivalent to the plaza, playing with friends while parents buy a coffee. The shopkeepers and other parents kept an eye on the children, and if a child needed help, they offered it gladly. Everyone looks after everyone.

If you are single and wish to enjoy it

> Email from VillageTown web site:
>
> *"I love the idea that you're working towards and to be honest, my experience living in that kind of community, which happened to be at my college where you could indeed walk everywhere, was one of the happiest times of my life. I know college is like that for most people, but perhaps it is that way because you have such a strong sense of community. Living in the city now, the community and ongoing casual interaction with people is what I miss most."*

Single, unattached, unencumbered. For some, being married, partnered or living with someone is not viewed as their first choice. For others becoming single is less than voluntary – death, divorce or separation finds them living alone. At one time, living solo was considered out of the ordinary… men were widowers or confirmed bachelors, women were widows or spinsters. Today it is normal. For some it is a passing phase as they date until they find the right person. But for others, it is a life choice.

Single living for some is living alone. For others it opens the possibility for sharing space without entering into an intimate relationship. University housing, fraternities and sororities, religious orders are all examples of single, cooperative living.

The most obvious form of single housing is the apartment, the one bedroom, sometimes elegant, home. Another is the roommate or flatting form where someone buys or leases a conventional apartment or home and then sublets to single people who come and go. The older university model offers some interesting alternatives. One can envision a large building that has a formal dining hall with professional chefs, a club room or library with many comfortable reading chairs, round tables with board games, full gymnasium and indoor pool, perhaps even an arboretum and cafe. Such a building would be collectively owned and on the upper floors it would have individually-owned bedrooms or small apartments; the ultimate in conviviality.

Other single people may prefer something more akin to the monastic model with a focus more on the holy than the convivial. Or it may be academic, sharing a passion for learning or creativity. In addition to these voluntary life styles, the VillageTown should provide caring and supportive designs for those who find themselves involuntarily single. In times past, death of a loved one was the most frequent cause, now it is the breakup of a relationship. Provide for it.

Trend Setters: Make sure that at least one village is founded by what might be called trend setters. Often single or childless, these are the people who make things happen.

If you are a young adult wanting to buy your first home

Suburbs are not designed for people after they graduate from high school. Those who hang around home seem lost. For those who leave, many find the next five years is a struggle: flatting with mates or strangers who drive you nuts; struggling to get more than a menial job; or if you got a good job, trying to learn the rules, since they are so different from school... no tests, if you fail, the boss fires you. Why don't we provide better for young people starting out?

Design for the VillageTown's young adults – under the age of 26 – begins with creating the opportunity to buy your own home. That first home allows part of your salary to go into ownership, not rent, so when you sell it to move into something bigger (perhaps starting a family), you have cash for the down payment and good credit.

Youth housing is different from mainstream housing. For a start, noise becomes a design consideration, best solved by setting youth housing in its own zone, away from more settled folk. Young adults also want that separation, as their social life is focused on people their own age, partying in the street. Thus,

> I still recall the shock of leaving school. All my life, I had lived in society with my peers, making friends was easy, you sat next to them in class, sharing a common experience. Suddenly, at 18, I was tossed out. They put me in a cap and gown, shook my hand, gave me a roll of parchment and boom, I was on the outside. I had to learn to make my own way. Staying at home with my parents was not an option. Very few of my childhood friends remained in that community, there simply was no place for them.

Single workers lived in very small homes built in Nelson NZ in the 1860's

VillageTown design sets aside areas for youth housing and youth hang-outs.

The many village plazas with their workplaces offer employment opportunities for graduates and apprenticeship opportunities while still in school. Provided the local economy is sufficiently diverse, this would present a wide range of career and experience building opportunities.

In this book, we examine what we call parallel market housing. One target group for this would be youth housing. Such homes should be low cost to buy – made possible initially by VillageTown subsidies (which generally does not mean selling for below cost but setting the sale price lower than what the open market can command). Once bought, the young adult can live in the house until they are 106 if they want, but when they go to sell, the buyer has to be a young adult, under the age of 26. This assures the market price will remain affordable, as the purchasing power of young adults is generally lower than that of mainstream buyers.

In addition to this deed restriction to keep prices affordable, the housing design should be smaller and simpler, and hard-wearing. It should incorporate special sound-proofing, with an inner room designed for music – soundproofed so stereo, electric guitars, or a full drum set would sound great indoors but not be heard on the street or by the next door neighbor. It should have a well-designed kitchen, with trash and recycling bins in a drop in design… lift a cover in the bench or counter top, drop the recycling in. It falls into a wheeled bin below located behind an outside door where the collector retrieves it. Make it easy to keep clean.

For another reason, youth housing should be small and not able to be expanded in size. It should suit one or two people, but be too small when young people decide to start a family. At that point, architecture, not rules, should encourage them to trade up to something bigger, and in a nearby neighborhood with larger homes, more appropriate for raising children. Because they were paying a mortgage, not rent, they should have some equity for the next stage of housing, thus freeing up their initial home for the next generation of youth buyers.

Of course, not all young adults will choose to remain in the VillageTown. The VillageTown gives them choice: the choice to stay or leave. If they wish to stay, they will find a home to buy, challenging work and a strong network of peers and mentors.

If you are an elected official or a government policy maker

What are some of the challenges we face in Western countries?

Aging population – As discussed above in the part for Baby Boomers, a large block of voters will soon be looking to government to take care of them, and a smaller block of younger taxpayers may not be able to foot the bill. The time to begin addressing the issue is now, before it gets bad. A core part of the VillageTown concept builds a support system that can operate independent of government pensions and high levels of expensive medical care.

The VillageTown reinvents aging; redefining retirement as "settled living": slowing down but not stopping.

The VillageTown provides purpose-built elder housing; ground-floor, 50 yards from the village plaza, designed for independent living; affordable-priced and restricted by age. With no cars in the urban core, elders need not move when they stop driving.

The VillageTown self insures for infirmity. Using its initial capital budget, it builds 6-10 bed nursing care facilities on each plaza, thus capitalizing the building cost. 24-hour staffing is paid by a town-wide self-insurance plan (either out of VillageTown profits, or the annual fee voted by the citizens). The elder pays a nominal room rent and the actual cost of food.

The key to this working is critical mass: the earning population of the VillageTown needs to be large enough to make this a form of local old-age insurance. By capitalizing investment cost (the VillageTown pays for construction of the nursing facilities), perhaps in lieu of a developers contribution to the local government, the costs are lowered. By keeping the nursing bed facilities relatively small and located on several of the plazas, the cost of day care activities is lowered. When one isolates old people in concentrated masses, people must be paid to keep the elders from prematurely going mad in such a disagreeable environment. When they are wheelchair bound but still in their community, and able to be wheeled onto the plaza or into the cafés during the day, their friends and neighbors attend to them, just as was done for the many centuries of human existence before the 20th century invented nursing homes – an invention future generations may regard in the same way that today we regard apartheid.

Kicking the petroleum habit – It's a bit crazy when one thinks about it. We design cars to drive far in excess of the national speed limit, and then brand drivers as law breakers when they drive accordingly. We develop housing isolated from work, close the local walk-to schools, destroy main street shopping in favor of massive malls where people drive, then park, and then walk down a pedestrian mall... and then we buy and sell carbon credits to reduce air pollution from fossil fuels.

The suburb is obsolete. It served its primary purpose: enabling the victorious USA to transform its booming 1945 wartime economy into a booming 1950's peacetime one by reinventing how people lived. Its side effects are now biting back.

Old speed sign from the early days of the automobile

History 101: Toward the end of WW-II America's leaders feared the US would slide back into another Great Depression when wartime contracts dried up and millions of soldiers became unemployed civilians. Since the war was won with jeeps, trucks and shiploads of petroleum, America's industrial leaders naturally proposed their own products as the economic solution. They built roads, tore up the cities' trolley tracks, built low-cost housing and promised a car in every garage. Trouble is the unanticipated negative side effects are proving toxic, costly and if petroleum keeps going up in price, we foresee suburbs being consigned to history. While this way of life passes for normal, in fact it was a radical experiment in which people's lives were structured to serve policy instead of policy designed to serve people. Payback time is coming.

Suburbs failed to deliver on their promise. Not everyone wants to live in cities.

The answer is not to invent a new form of experimental living, but to look to the oldest, most proven model of common locality – the village and small town. Well-designed, the transport problems vanish. Everything is within walking distance. Rush hour is a promenade to the plaza. It may still take half an hour to get home, but 28 minutes of it was stopping to talk.

In this high resolution aerial photograph, we drew in markers to show the space taken up for cars and trucks. Much of this road coverage stems from zoning rules that mandate the driving home range – rules that separate destinations, requiring people drive from home to work to school to shops as part of their daily routine. Covering good land with pavement is wasteful, it costs a lot to maintain and it pollutes earth and water.

Reducing Crime – If crime is a social illness, it seems that modern society has resigned itself to being chronically ill, keeping crime below the threshold of epidemic, but never rid of it. Perhaps the answer is to think locally, one community at a time, to secure a healthy, crime-free way of life.

Traditionally, in many villages, crime was nonexistent because everyone in the village had a role, and its citizens had a low tolerance for crime. Crime often

Crime thrives in fractured communities

stems from boredom and a lack of rites of passage for the young. No, it's unlikely a contemporary village would bring back lion hunting to induct the young into the company of adults, but careful design of the VillageTown can create experiences that address the same human need... the rite of passage. When a child becomes a teen, acknowledge it with some meaningful and relevant ceremony – one that truly marks their passage.

Preventing crime begins at birth, when children are born into a supportive community that shapes their character. If we require both mother and father commute away to full-time jobs, it becomes harder for them to hold their lives together; it creates levels of stress that breaks the family and damages the children.

Re-create settlements where children play together, outside, within eyesight of working adults. Keep your elders in the community to provide connection for the young, and a rich source of child-minders when the parents need a break. Place work near home, within walking distance, and build the plazas with places children play, so parents can earn a gainful living and not have to park their children in front a TV to keep them occupied or find they run wild because no one is around.

Invest in child activities: places to kick balls, climb walls or run fast. Creating opportunities youth rites of passage, reduces the opportunity for crime to flourish. Development of innovative local schools works hand-in-glove with the VillageTown settlement, so what the children learn at school is reinforced by how they live in their community.

Stakeholding is an important element in preventing crime. This is why the VillageTown concept seeks to enable more of its residents to own their home and not be passing through. When people have a stake in their community, law enforcement becomes social pressure, not the job of police. In short, we can pay now, or pay later. Better to pay now, and get good children.

Graffiti is one of the first signs of a community in breakdown. It is about boredom, alienation, anger, revenge, defiance and eventually gang alliance.

Zoning for Settlements: *Byzantine* is a word that refers to a historic government to describe a system of government that is excessively complicated, typically involving a great deal of administrative detail. If we look at the regulations governing the development of land, it is Byzantine. Half the cost of real estate development is securing permission; too often enriching lawyers and consultants. It stems from a reasonable demand by citizens that the excesses of developers be reined in.

Before developers, it was not this way. Before developers, when greenfield land was to be converted to a built environment the local citizens agreed on growth. The difference is settlement versus development. Settlers come to land with the intent to build a home for their family, work places to create wealth (be it farm, factory or shop) and social centers to enjoy a good life. They valued education so they met, voted to tax themselves to build a school and hire a teacher. They did the same with governance and religion. In contrast, developers view land as a pecuniary opportunity. They have no stake in the future and they make decisions that too often are good for them, but bad for people, communities, societies, civilization and the planet.

Zoning for settlements is absent from too many local and state regulatory systems. The VillageTown is a settlement. It is a greenfield (or brownfield) initiative that is of, by and for the people. Do not try to force it into the developer model. It does not have the money to waste on lawyers, and its inherent checks and balances means it does not need the same red tape.

A village spring in Greece

Water – Who would have thought the world would be running out of good water? The problem is worse than we think, as traces of antibiotics, recreational drugs, and birth control chemicals are now showing up in the water many cities drink.

The cost of purifying water to drinking standard is high and cities find the average household consumes about 125 gallons (500 liters) per day. Of this, perhaps 1% is actually used for drinking. 99% of the purification is wasted as most water management still relies on 19th century technology – one clean pipe in, one dirty pipe out.

A new VillageTown offers the opportunity of a clean slate – the opportunity to adopt proven new technology instead of relying on older, more expensive and less sustainable systems. Instead of installing another 19th century water system, we need to look to better science, better engineering and more pipes going into and out of each home.

The technologies we need are already in operation – somewhere else. Rather than invent (and debug) a new technology, the best investment is in hunting and gathering. Travel to the sites where some local enterprise or government has already installed and proven a component. In 2006, after an internet search, I traveled to a quaint New England village, to see 7,000 daily gallons of sewage being treated in a specially engineered greenhouse with plants, pipes and lots of microbes. In operation now for almost a decade, the greenhouse is a few paces from the local dentist, in the back of the Main Street business district. No smell. No pollution. Very low operational cost. It's not the only such system, but I chose it because the state of Massachusetts is known for its very tough wetlands and water protection laws and old Yankee towns are governed with a high level of local watchdog democracy. The company's president said if he did it again today, he would use the nutrient rich water to make biofuel – where sewage becomes a profit center.

The VillageTown proposes in sites where water is scare, that rainwater is harvested and purified, and used for drinking. Water for washing clothes can be reused in a closed loop system, so make laundry services "free" so villagers do not do their own wash, but have laundry collected by a ViTo-run laundry service to save water, energy and provide low-skill jobs.

Greenhouse Rain Water Harvesting: In a VillageTown of 4,000 houses, approximately 100 acres is rooftop, plus an addition 50 acres of rooftop Industrial Park. The roof tops will be flat, and designed as rooftop gardens. In regions with water shortages or long winters, it makes sense to cap the rooftop gardens with greenhouses (glasshouses) that harvest pure rainwater that is then piped to a central storage and filtering system for drinking. In a climate that only has 8 inches of rain a year, with proper storage, this will provide all the drinking and cooking water 10,000 people will need. Such a greenhouse will extend the growing season and in winter, provide an outdoor living space that is warmer.

The Greenhouse Sewage Treatment facility in Weston, Massachusetts is next to the local dentist on Main Street. No smells.

From a Policy Perspective then, what's a VillageTown?

In defining what we mean by the VillageTown, consider the following parameters:
- It is a settlement, not a development. It needs a democratic, not bureaucratic process for providing permission
- It is a regional economic engine, pays taxes, asks little of government other than permission, solves problems
- It creates new markets for regional farmers to supply full range of good food for the VillageTown residents/visitors
- It not gated. Local people and visitors are welcome and will benefit by the amenities and enriched opportunities
- The foundation of the VillageTown is its own self-supporting, market-driven local economy (see page 73)
- The design principle of the VillageTown is to engender a high quality of life for all its citizens – to enjoy a good life.
- Population is best between 5,000 and 10,000, no larger. If less, critical mass is lost. If more it becomes bureaucratic,
- "Parallel markets" for real estate ownership to keep affordable housing for target groups (see page 39).
- Micro-zoning with a workplace and commercial zone including educational and nursing residential set around plazas and high activity pedestrian streets and residences above and behind. Walk-to light industrial park.
- Village buildings are three-floor, attached townhouses. Town Center has four-story office and public buildings.
- Walking home-range: Day-to-day destinations within 10 minutes walking distance, no more 15 minutes at the most.
- Cars banned within the VillageTown. Motorpool and freight depot outside the village gate. No garages, no shop parking lots, no on street parking (except for small golf-cart sized vehicles) no gas/petrol stations.
- With no cars, density is higher, streets are smaller, indeed, the proven pattern of pedestrian streets in Greece and Italy finds they work as narrow as 2.4 meters (8') wide, some even narrower (see the book cover for an example)
- No *design by fire truck*, all buildings are non-combustible & sprinkled. This is to permit narrow, human-scaled streets
- Advanced local utilities to manage power, water, waste water, solid waste. Goal = zero waste.
- High-tech telecommunications and sophisticated delivery and transport systems essential for local economy.
- Significant developer investment in civic amenities, most notably a multiple village design connected by pedestrian streets, subsidized artist guild halls, surrounding greenbelt (if land is available)
- Clear boundaries, possibly village walls, to mark where the VillageTown ends, countryside begins. If land is available, VillageTown to own a greenbelt around the urban core. Designate as historic district: once the VillageTown is built, no further changes to shape and scale of building exteriors, no additions or demolitions.

If you are a government planner/regulator

> **The Challenge:** You hold a degree in planning. Historically, your degree program evolved in the 20th century in response to a then new way of creating habitat called real estate development. Much of your work is anticipating the negative side effects of development and writing or enforcing rules to keep them in check. This is because development is driven by pecuniary interest whereas your job is to protect public interest.
>
> But what happens when instead of a development, someone proposes to build a settlement that is driven by public interest? There is no developer. It is fascinating to observe how professional planners struggle with this. They keep saying "you" to the stewards who provide the framework for the settlement, and get frustrated when they are told there is no "you", only "us". "We're all on the same side." It's a major head-shift.

The question: How do you fit a VillageTown settlement into your existing regulations written for suburban or urban developments? How do you work with a proposal with no cars allowed, narrower streets, with residential and commercial mixed use, with retail shops including with owner apartments and light-industrial with noisy-residential mixed in. These patterns of village life came first – long before suburbs, for thousands of years; yet today's zoning rules often prohibit such a mix.

We expect this means amending the rules. While these amendments often require political approval, the policy preparation begins with the staff or expert consultants – you. To put this in context, please reread *The Home-Range* (page vi).

In adopting rule changes, we first ask if a general set of rules need to be drafted or if the initiative is of sufficient complexity and scope that it is better treated as a "one-off". We recommend the latter, as you will be entering new territory and will need closer engagement with the process. The term we use to describe this is ***dynamic engagement***.

Dynamic engagement is intended to avoid unexpected rule interpretations resulting in undesirable outcomes or expensive and tedious battles in court – all of which consumes valuable time, resources and often producing lose-lose compromises.

The VillageTown process begins with a particular site, and a core of Founders – the host community plus the future villagers. Having the site means we can produce a 100:1 aerial photograph of the land, contour it, and make 100:1 scale models of proposed buildings, open space, walls and streets. This makes the process user-friendly, both in enabling everybody to get the picture and in allowing "what if" movement of buildings and infrastructure to model land use. This 100:1 modeling tool is supported with what we call Pattern Cards, which take key design elements (originally based on Christopher Alexander's book, *A Pattern Language*), reduced to fridge magnets and set out on a white board to support the planning process. What makes this scale method different from the usual modeling is its intent. It is not intended as a fixed representation to show a proposed plan, but as a way of testing, negotiating and evolving the plan. Once done, it is locked and the plan becomes a historic district.

In this process, the government planners or plan approvers can play an essential part. They are not there to tell us what to build (a conflict of interest), but rather to offer real-time interpretation of the rules and expectations of the approving department or local government. Plan details can be flagged as Green (yes), Yellow (maybe) or Red (no). In many cases, such a process will result in an immediate rethink to get a red or yellow to a green, and if something looks like it is stuck being a yellow, to seek an immediate executive or legislative ruling, thus converting it to a provisional green. We say *provisional* acknowledging that, in good faith, a decision-making body must reserve its final decision on the whole

In tests, we found that a smaller scale such as 200:1 does not provide for adequate visualization. 100:1 works well.

Throughout this book, you will find references to Christopher Alexander's A Pattern Language. Published in 1977, it remains in the top 2,500 of best selling books on Amazon for a reason. It gives language to the art of architecture, planning and design. If you do not have a copy on your bookshelf, buy one. While it can be ordered from bookstores or Amazon, we recommend you buy it directly from Alexander's web site www.patternlanguage.com as this way the full purchase price goes to supporting the author's work

package as finally presented. In some cases, the on-going yellow to green decisions may still, when all combined, result in a few red flags that must be altered to secure rapid approval without a judicial review.

In proposing such an approach, it also becomes important that management provide time for professional development training, as the mindset of this approach is different from the normal day-to-day work of local government planning. The typical work environment is often adversarial, a contest between pecuniary interest and public interest, with the government official seeking to strike a balance amid political pressures. In this Dynamic Engagement process, no such contest exists, because the expected contestant (the adversarial developer) is not in the game. Pecuniary interest is diffused into that of the future residents who are not driven by profit but by the desire to live in a wonderful place. Because these future residents represent the normal diversity of society, they become a representation of the public interest. Your job and their interests align.

Thus, in such a climate, your adversarial role is no longer necessary. For some planning staff, the best way to adjust is for management to provide professional development to (a) understand the new working relationships and (b) to model a different, more supportive role in such a working environment. To be more specific, when working in such a group, you must make clear you are dynamically engaged, but not a founder; you stand in the process not to plan the VillageTown, but to immediately give an opinion on the plan the Founders and their professional advisors are formulating in real-time.

In addition to this formal role distinction, the interpersonal behavior shifts, and for this professional development training also provides role-play. An abrupt "no", often the approach of adversarial zoning approval, may need to be replaced by helpful questions – asking what the Founders and their planners are trying to accomplish, and then explaining how their proposed solution might create challenges they may not have considered.

Admittedly, this approach may seem to take more time than the traditional where one receives a plan, approves parts and rejects other parts. However, the public interest being served by the establishment of such a VillageTown easily justifies the additional staff time. If funds are not budgeted for such time, or the process does not fit within established practices, we suggest it's appropriate for an executive or legislative decision to provide for it. In some cases, the financial matter may require the VillageTown initiative reimburse the local government for the additional staff time. If one considers that the capital value may be upwards of a billion dollars (land, infrastructure and all buildings), such an investment up front is minuscule yet invaluable.

Finally an opinion: **Time is of the Essence.** The need for such VillageTowns begins to hit when the first Baby Boomers begin to retire. While there are many other fear-based drivers for the VillageTown – peak oil, global warming, disenfranchisement of the young, hollow-house syndrome, and more – the immutable fact of the Baby Boom retirement creates the urgency. The Urban Village Forum in the UK says it takes 10 years to build a village. We believe the approval and construction process must be cut to three. This is doable, but it requires the full support of the political will at a policy level and senior management at implementation.

100:1 scale model in the foreground, magnetic pattern card process in use on the whiteboard.

If you are a master planner, architect or designer

> Perspective: VillageTowns are settlements, not developments. As you read this part, do not regard it as threatening your career, but rather opening up new fields of opportunity, perhaps the reason you originally were attracted to your profession.

We face a dilemma: Every human being is different, but the output of a mechanized world seeks uniformity, not as an end, but as a means of increasing profits for its maker. While humans appreciate the efficiency of uniformity, many find it not fulfilling. They seek authenticity, especially in their surroundings – their home and community. However, authenticity cannot be found in mechanized output.

Authenticity is a complex concept – you know it when you see it, but that's because visually, humans instinctively comprehend complexity, but verbally find it much more difficult to explain. To understand its elements, it's most helpful to go to places built before the industrial revolution, before uniformity became the medium of architects, designers, consultants and consent-approving government officials. The best place to go? Try old Europe and look for the signs for the historic city center.

Authenticity is not Disneyland®, which does a marvelous job of copying authenticity but never achieving it. Authenticity comes from individuals implanting their personality and character on their home or place of work. If we wish to secure

authenticity in building a VillageTown, then we must establish a system in which the end-result – each home, office, shop or café – reflects the individual character of its first owner.

If we look at the villages and market towns of old Europe, we find small-scale construction, rarely over three-story, often with a commercial use on the ground floor and residences above. The overall character is influenced by several key factors:

- Local artisans – If a village has a skilled blacksmith, it will have beautiful ironwork including gates, fences, window covering and exposed metalwork on doors. If it has skilled stone carvers, columns, outside seating, door lintels will add to the character of the village.
- Use of local materials – The Cotswolds in England are a famous example, where the color of the housing changes as the quarried native stone is different in color as one moves from part of the Cotswolds to an other.
- The skill of the local builders – Unlike large public buildings that are based on classical architecture, ordinary homes and workplaces derive from vernacular architecture, which in real life means an architect does not design the house – rather a skilled builder follows a basic sketch set out by the customer and then builds following conservative, proven principals.
- The permanence of the community and its residents – People who plan to live in a place for a long time tend to build for beauty and character because they and their descendents will live with the results. They do not always commission house-detail with an eye to profit; instead they buy what suits them, what gives them pleasure or makes the statement they wish to make.
- The village evolves over decades and centuries as buildings are modified to meet changing needs of its individuals. As long as the community remains stable, the pressure to make these changes blend in, to fit the neighborhood, remains strong.

In our research, pundits would comment that it was the last factor (time) that was pivotal, but when we examined it with a historian's eye, we found this to be incorrect. They key was owner-decision-making and local skill on offer.

How can we create authenticity rapidly?

One attempt at this can be found in Prince Charles' village, Poundbury in which master planner Leon Krier looked at many local and regional archetypal English homes, and replicated their design, scale and placement in the construction of a new village or small town. In many regards, Poundbury is a success, but in terms of authenticity, the buildings tend to have the precision that comes from a replica. This is because the decisions were made by professionals trained in attaining precision, thus lack the slight imperfections that characterize involvement by homeowners and by local artisans. Authenticity comes from this "human stamp" and the only way we know to secure it is to involve diverse human character and hand-shaping in the process.

Consider these two (or four) attached buildings, each of which has a double door, one painted blue and the other red. If three were blue, and one red, it might indicate an individual making a statement – political, non-conformist, just loves the color, whatever. Not so in this building – one recognizes the mark of a not-quite-right replica. The same lack of authenticity shows up in the trees – placed in exactly the right place and looking uncannily like the architects drawing or computer rendition—nature imitating art. The authenticity fails to come through.

Such a proposed solution may be challenging, especially to the professional's comfort zone, – or dare it be said – the professional's ego. The challenge comes from the prospect of doing something differently than in the past; or to be more precise, to go back to an earlier time when societies built settlements rather than developments. In settlement-building, the first owner would commission their home. The architect's role, if there at all, was to help the family articulate their vision; to provide the experience and knowledge to make sure all is considered.

Many of today's professionals in master planning and architecture are accustomed to being the person in charge; they ask the developer what they want, but then they, the professionals come back with their solution. Their solutions often tend to reflect the commercially available materials (those products that typically come pre-manufactured) and the way contractors assemble, no longer create, buildings. The developer accepts the professionals' plan based on sales projections. This tends to result in blandness, mediocrity and sameness – no character.

Instead, we propose an approach where there is no developer in the usual sense. The customers become the *Founders*, both in setting out the master plan for their village, and then having a substantially greater involvement in the design brief for their home, workplace and village. This changes the professionals' roles to that of mentor, and the skill set includes fostering collaboration. The professionals enable people & community to provide for their own wellbeing.

In addition, we propose that very early in the process of the VillageTown initiative, some of the first industries to be brought on-site are master makers – blacksmiths, carvers, joiners (doors and windows) and master builders prepared to work in vernacular building.

Your role, should you chose to accept it, becomes that of teacher, mentor, advisor in the early stages, when the people who will live there develop the design brief to a far more detailed level than the norm. It becomes their building, as they implant their personality on its size, shape, function and ornament. Then you take their dream, their vision, and transform it into working drawings, costings and contracts.

> A WORK OF ART OR A PLACE TO INHABIT?
>
> As I wrote this book, a young architect offered helpful critiques. But one area where we disagreed was the job of the architect.
>
> In his view, architects are artists, the building their work of art. They would not be interested in serving as mentor to the Founders.
>
> If true, perhaps the VillageTown needs a different kind of architect. It needs professionals to design plans that become buildings. Those plans need to incorporate beauty, harmony, functionality, affordability, flexibility, durability, and to embrace and enhance the spirit of the place where they stand – for a long time.
>
> They also need to reflect the character of the owner who built it. This is different than art, where the work is supposed to reflect the character of the artist, not the owner.

Prior to writing this book, I spent five years mastering the art of vernacular building – constructing five separate earth-brick buildings to form a compound that includes a large residence, a detached guest house, art gallery and Bard Hall, workshop, executive office and conference room and a 100 ft² (10 m²) writer's hut to test low cost artist housing.

Each stage was not only to construct required buildings, but to conduct research and development, testing out vernacular theory against the real world condition of limited funds, engineers and inspectors being asked to think outside the square, good ideas that don't work in practice, subcontractors failing to meet deadlines, unreliable workers, foul weather and variable quality in materials.

Construction was subject to building inspections by the largest territorial authority in the country, and all processes were driven to be affordable, wonderful efficient and beautiful. The result is said to be the largest earth-brick compound built in New Zealand, with a very high build quality, expected to last for hundreds of years. The cost was less than conventional stick-built housing and the ongoing utility and maintenance costs are substantially lower. Though only begun in late 1997, it now looks like it has been there forever.

Image reproduced with permission of the New Zealand Herald

If you are a wage-earner priced out of the market.

The other day over morning coffee, I noticed the property section of our newspaper – Affordable homes under $500,000. In this city, the average household wage is $50,000 per year, which means the average affordable home must be $200,000, not $500,000. To buy a half million-dollar house requires a six-figure income. The problem is that unless you bought a home back when they were affordable, and are now trading up using the capital gain for the down payment, you can't afford to buy an "affordable" house any longer.

People who are wage earners, especially in service industries in desirable communities find they cannot afford housing where they work. While there are many such wage earning *target groups*, the VillageTown will need to select ones it deems as essential. For the purpose of example, let us focus on public servants (but see youth housing p. 26 and elder housing p. 19 for two alternative lower wage-earning target groups). The local public school cannot pay a salary to teachers sufficient for the teacher to buy a home. The same goes for police and government employees as well as people in private service jobs with a moderate prevailing wage.

If central or state government wishes to help, pass useful legislation in lieu of relying on existing contract law:
- a simple clause for deeds/titles to be restricted to target markets defined by age or occupation.
- a simple clause for VillageTown governance using a form of corporate law that also operates like small local government:
  - *the right to place a covenant on all deeds/titles to auction a property whose owner is found to have breached VillageTown rules and deed restrictions.*
  - *the right to establish VillageTown prosecutor & court*
  - *the right to hold elections for VillageTown legislators*
  - *the right to employ a VillageTown administration*
  - *the right to assess taxes/fees for VillageTown services*
  - *the right to own non-profit and for profit enterprises related to VillageTown services*
  - *the right to set up public schools run as special character schools with latitude in structure*
- allow the VillageTown development to be substantially self-regulating, and not swamped with central government bureaucratic reporting, regulation or interference.

Providing subsidized rental accommodation is an undesirable answer, because it makes such workers into tenants, not stakeholders in the community. Having them commute long distances undermines the principle of walking distance from home to work and it removes important people from the local community.

The VillageTown proposes a simple solution devoid of regulatory overhead, based on existing law regulated by the market: "parallel market" housing.

> **What is Parallel Market Home Ownership?**
>
> In creating the overall business plan to finance the VillageTown, some funds are set aside to subsidise the price of some of the homes – perhaps 25% of them. The original sale price is set at an "affordability price" for specific target buyers such as youth, artists, elders, and workers in service where income would not compete with the open market demand for VillageTown housing (see the chart below where income determines affordability). The targeted buyer gets to purchase the home at a substantial discount, but when they go to sell, they must sell only in the "parallel market", meaning to another buyer in their target market. For example, if a target market includes public servants and teachers, a police officer moving on could sell to a teacher, but not to a stock broker who would be prepared to pay more. In this way, the average wage in the target market determines the average home price in that parallel housing market, and gentrification is minimized. Cheating is discouraged by a simple mechanism. If a buyer is found to have fraudulently claimed to be in the target market, the VillageTown retains the right of public auction – it notifies the buyer their home will be sold at auction if not sold privately to a qualified buyer in the target market within a reasonable period of time.

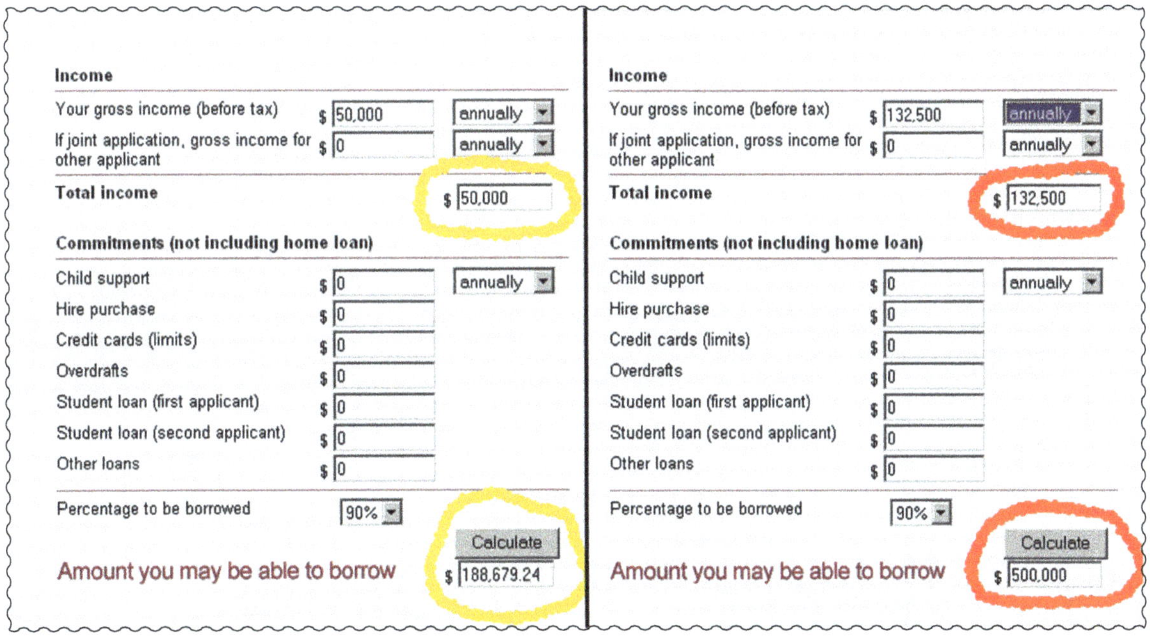

Let us take an example: A teacher or other public servant has a salary band of say $50,000 a year, upon which a bank will provide a mortgage to purchase a $200,000 home. Due to the desirable amenities of the VillageTown, the market price for unrestricted homes is $450,000, even if the actual construction cost was closer to $200,000. In the initial construction phase, the VillageTown sets aside say 25% of the housing stock as Deed Restricted. For teachers and other public servants in the $50,000 earnings band, they get to purchase their $450,000 home for $200,000. The $250,000 combination of actual and opportunity cost is subsidized by the overall VillageTown initiative. For that subsidy, the VillageTown places a perpetual deed restriction on the title, which says the owner can only sell it to a qualified buyer – one who also is another teacher or public servant in the designated (initially $50,000) band. That restriction becomes the property of the VillageTown.

The appeal of this approach is in its self-regulation. If due to inflation, the earnings band jumps from $50,000 a year to $100,000, then the market price of the house will also double. The collective VillageTown will benefit by being assured its teachers and public servants will always be able to buy a home in the VillageTown. To assure the needed housing stock remains available, the ViTo may build extra buildings, that the VillageTown leases until demand rises.

If you are a nearby farmer

Opportunity – If a 5 to 10,000 population VillageTown is built in your region, it opens the opportunity to create a new, more stable market for your farm produce. By removing the middlemen from the transaction, it offers you a higher return in a fixed market, while giving customers lower prices.

Villagers need to eat. This book stresses that eating well is an important part of the VillageTown's quality of life. This means securing a steady supply of fresh, healthy, flavorful foods of considerable variety. This creates a constant, predictable, profitable local demand for vegetables, fruits, nuts, grains, herbs, spices, fine meat, fish and dairy products. Research shows that the human body reacts adversely to certain chemicals even in parts per million or parts per billion. Thus, consumer demand increases for such foods to be grown with the minimum of chemical farming. Chemical-free farming is healthier for the farmer. The risk warnings accompanying farm chemicals make it clear to farmers they handle hazardous and toxic compounds. By increasing prices paid per unit, the farmer need not farm for yield, as demanded by the industry, but for quality as desired by the customer.

To make any local food buying effective we recommend two VillageTown design requirements:
- Cold-store, locking food box next to the mail-box at each home enabling home delivery of foods on a daily schedule without requiring the occupant be at home.
- An intranet software system designed to enable residents to place food orders from their kitchen that can be combined to produce wholesale orders for local farmers.

With these two systems in place, thousands of households will place daily (and future) orders for the full variety of foods. The software handles the consolidation, delivery routing and automatic bank debiting when the produce is delivered. The farmer is paid; the customer gets good, local, fresh food and the relationship is permanent.

VillageTown Farmer's Bank – We recommend the VillageTown and the local farmers enter into a dialogue on funding the planting season. Instead of going to large banks for seasonal loans, the farmers deal direct with their customers. Several financial models exist. The right one is dependent on the particular needs and interests of the local farmer. The benefit to the VillageTown is in keeping money turning locally, the funds remain in the community to continue circulating and increasing local wealth and wellbeing of both farmers and Villagers. The benefit to the farmers is less complicated and more stable credit.

Development Rights – To protect the farmland from the pressure to convert it to suburban sprawl, we suggest the VillageTown use some of its profits to offer to purchase development rights from willing farmers. For farmers who like the idea, this enables them to retire debt or invest in new equipment or realize a capital gain they can enjoy now. This offer should be part of a long-term food-purchase agreement. In this way, farmers who love farming get themselves out of the vicious debt cycle that is part of commercial farming today, and the VillageTown is assured they will have a permanent source of good food that is protected from the predations of suburban sprawl.

There are several models that work. Each VillageTown will work with the local farmers to find which each prefers.

Slow Food – About 30 years ago, an international movement emerged from Italy called Slow Food (see slowfood.com) in which a community designates itself as a slow food community, and then seeks to introduce an alternative to the fast food life. At one time, all food was local, offering great diversity. The best tasted wonderful and was good for health. Conviviality often occurs around food, it is part of what makes up a good life. Slow food seeks to restore the close link between the farmer and the table, thus nearby farmers becomes important to the VillageTown planning process.

A place for the children – In farming regions, one of the saddest things to see is when the children can't return to their community because they don't want to farm, but find no other employment opportunity in the area. Farming regions are coming under great pressure from the global economy. Farming families who held a presence for generations find in this generation, the children scatter. The VillageTown is inward focused, which means it won't upset the surrounding region, but it does provide opportunity for the children of the local people. We recommend the VillageTown initiative offer special concessions for the grown children of local families who might not otherwise be able to afford to come home.

Retirement – The other area of interest for farmers is having the VillageTown as a place to retire – not so far from the family farm, but easier to get around and less of a burden on the young ones who will take over when your work is done.

If you are an Developer or Investor

This book intends to redefine mainstream real estate development – the business you are in. It does not intend to put you out of business – to the contrary, it may prove more profitable, faster and more enjoyable. <u>But it will redefine your profession should you choose to participate.</u> It will require for many, a mind-shift.

It is a presumption of business that pecuniary interest is primary; that maximum return on investment is the purpose of doing a *development.* However, the presumption of the establishment of a *settlement* is not aligned with your ROI. Instead it is to serve the public interest, the common good and the needs and aspirations of the people who will live with the results.

Consider: real estate developers today find that half the job is securing permission because their pecuniary interest has clashed so often with the public interest that the people demanded zoning rules, environmental rules and eventually a Byzantine web of bureaucracy that adds to the cost; ultimately leaving less to spend on better buildings and landscape. What would happen if that web of bureaucracy were to go away, the red tape cut, the objectors became supporters, and most of your risk eliminated? The obvious answer is that it would be great, but we expect you would then ask *"How would that be possible?"* The answer is *"A VillageTown is a settlement, not a development."* A settlement is done of, by and for the people, where democracy trumps bureaucracy. This is not a slogan, and in some locations, it is a procedure embedded in law, although rarely used.

How investors and developers can fit in to a settlement plan

Limit your target scope for profit:

The VillageTown will have three primary building groups:

1. Mixed-use village buildings – the profits from these buildings (and land subdivision) are reserved for the people
2. Industrial park – it is expected that this will not be a profit center; instead leased at subsidy rates to support blue collar jobs
3. Town center office buildings – the commercial offices can be a profit center for the developer/investor

It's a trade off. When a developer builds a gated-golfing community, the golf course and club house is not a profit center, but a marketing cost; it is necessary to make a profit on the homes and land subdivision. In the VillageTown, view rezoning, the villages and the industrial park as your marketing cost. With the stewards help, they attract the critical mass required to make a profit on the town center office buildings. Those four-story office buildings will be a significant business opportunity, and commercial real estate is both profitable and stable when built in the context of a complete community. The key is the level of support you will get by doing something different than more suburban sprawl.

Most objection to real estate development objects to suburban subdivisions because they make very poor use of land, and bring in two or three cars for every new home. Invariably the local community must suffer traffic jams because the roads were not designed for the new subdivision.

> Some of the more attractive differences an investor or developer may find in building a VillageTown:
> - Global pool of potential buyers bringing their own jobs.
> - Expect extensive presales.
> - Higher density – Smaller development site.
> - Lower road building costs
> - Negotiate for faster and easier government approvals.
> - Expect public support not the usual opposition.

Lead with the settlement: The settlement process is about empowering the people and communities who often are the very ones who oppose development. The settlement process shifts their role from "No" to "Yes". They become the local people who work with the ViTo to take the VillageTown framework and transform it into a specific/precise plan for the designated greenfield or brownfield. In this process, you will be in perhaps unfamiliar territory, that may require a few human relations or communications workshops to enable both sides to see that they are working on the same side. No one should begrudge your profiting from the office buildings if that means you enable the people to get their settlement built, especially since your office building tenants or buyers will be the most significant source of high-paying, high-skilled jobs.

Doing Well by Doing Good

Perhaps the most important mind-shift is the reason to do a VillageTown and not another conventional subdivision. Doing well by doing good is not a new idea; it is how Philadelphia was settled. First and foremost, you are not your job, you are an individual and a participant in society and civilization. At present there are many aspects of society and civilization that are doing well, but also parts that urgently need correction. As an individual, you may be doing well now, but your eldership may be another matter entirely. At present even the most wealthy elders find life socially isolating when they become frail or infirm.

The Business Case

The town center will be a ten-acre business opportunity. It needs no subsidies, and the amenities of the villages will make it far easier to sell or lease white-collar office space. The process of settlement is intended to streamline the approval process, eliminate objections and enable greenfield development. It solves the *"which comes first, jobs or worker's homes?"* by doing both at the same time. Unlike a normal development, in a settlement everything is presold. The land is paid for out of presold mortgage-backed securities as are all the residential and village work-place buildings.

What is needed is a fiscal kick-start, and that can be you. The deal would be simple. Excluding the owner-occupied office buildings, apartment houses and public buildings in the town center, in exchange for providing the Stage 1 start up funds (estimated at $5 million with a high ROI), you would get the first right on all the commercial office buildings in the town center. You would work with the VillageTown stewards who would ensure the concept (aka, the brand) was not corrupted.

The Social Case

It promises to be a lot of fun.

The pedestrian plazas of Italy offer a quality of life that no suburban development can match. Pedestrian plazas and streets require far less land than suburban roads.

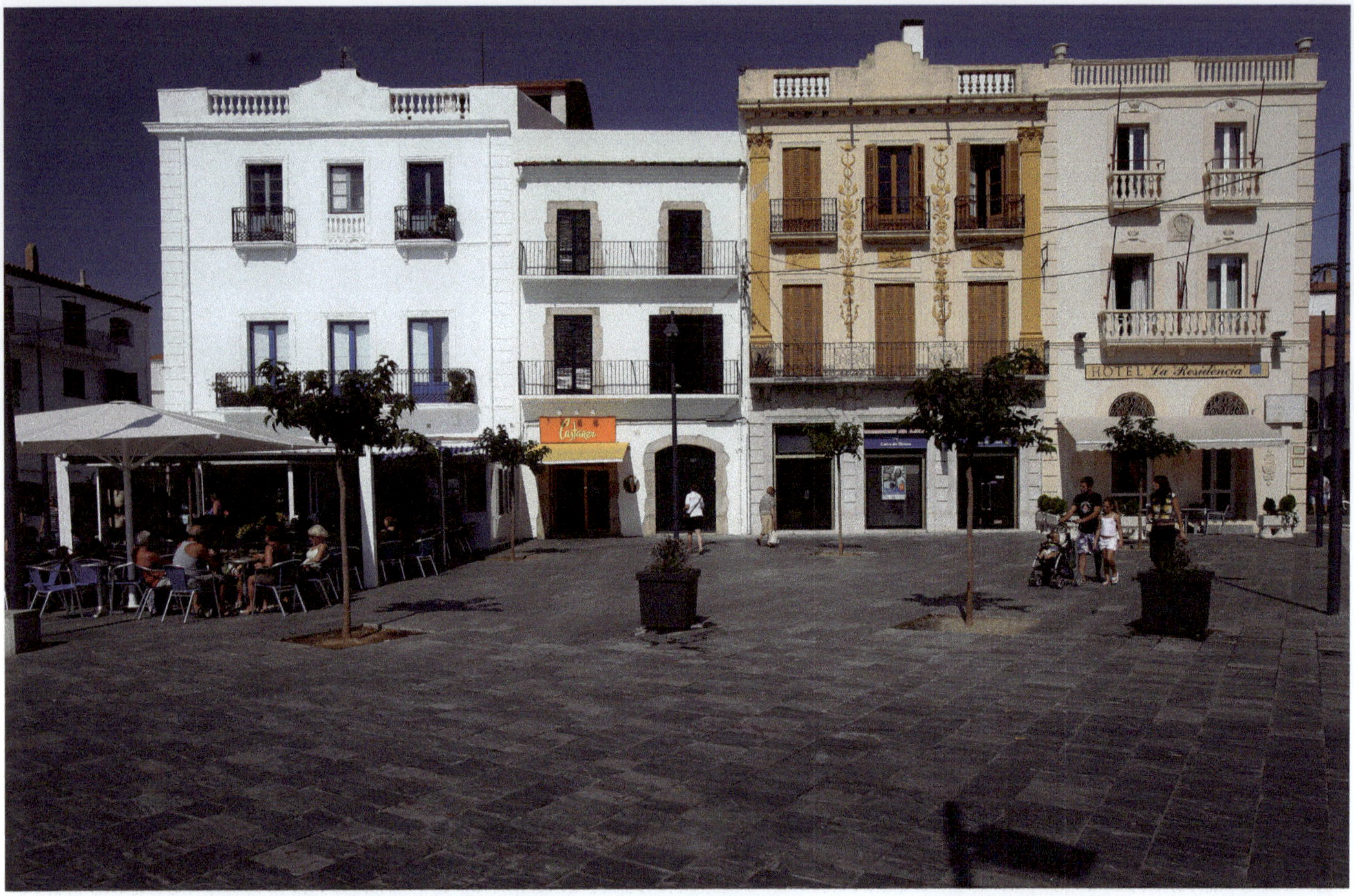
HOTEL La Residencia

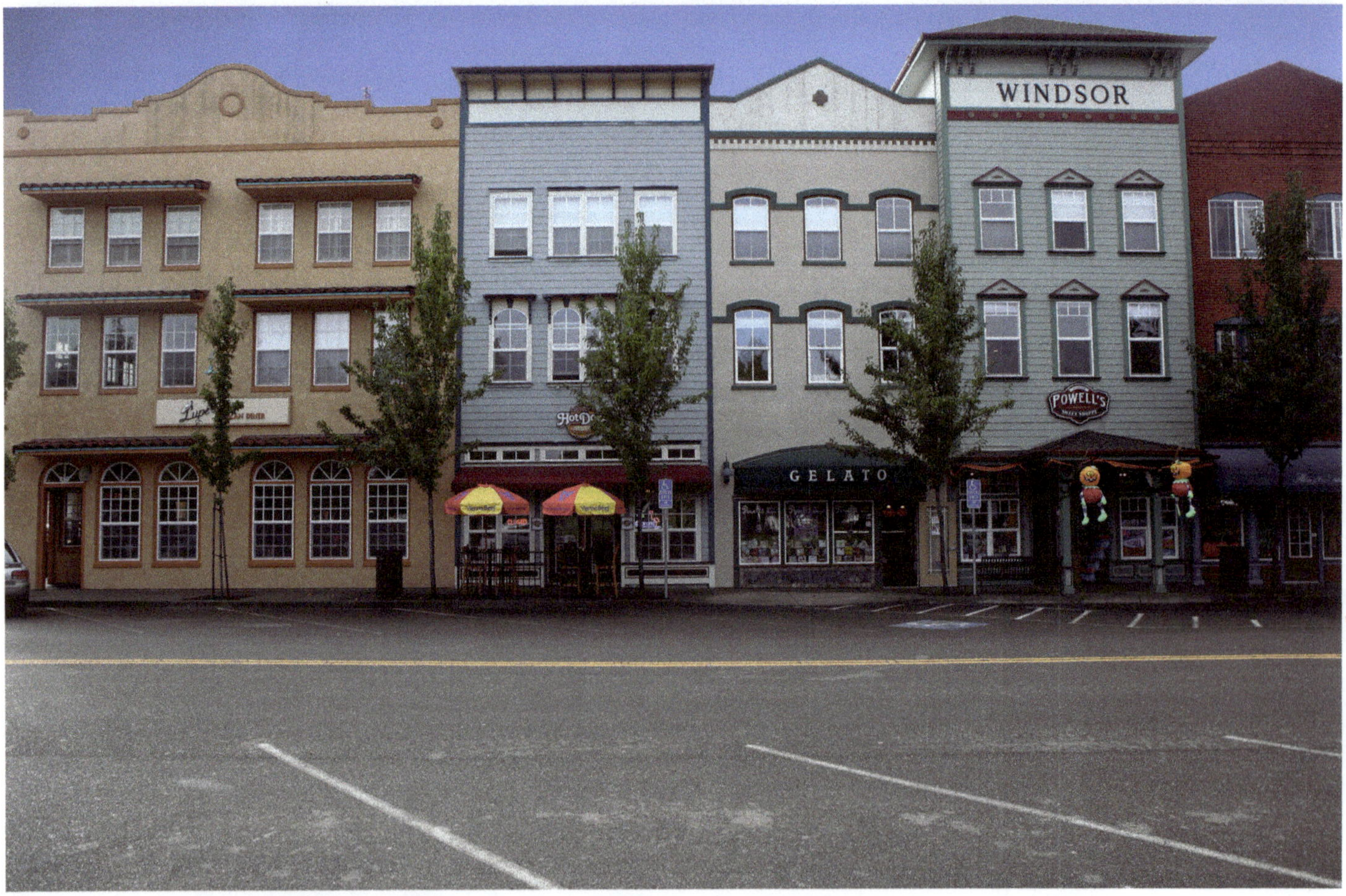
WINDSOR
POWELL'S
GELATO

Case Study: The difference between Settlement and Development

In the photographs on page 44 you see two sets of urban attached buildings. The top is Cadaquez in Spain, a settlement, built as a fishing village with buildings dating from the 19th century. At bottom is Windsor, California a retro, new-urbanism, smart-growth development, built by developer Orrin Thiessen in 2001. In Windsor, Thiessen built over 270 residential dwellings and 100 commercial units for shops, restaurants and offices. A decade later, in 2012 he went bankrupt because he had condominiums he could not sell, development debt he could not repay and projects he couldn't complete. The two sets of buildings look remarkably similar, yet their details tell how different they are – and why Windsor failed as a development.

As a developer, Thiessen made the decision to use the same windows for each building, thus stripping them of the character and authenticity that would come if those decisions were made by the person who would live with the results. In the Cadaquez buildings each building's openings are different; the windows are in fact doors with balconies, so people can step out into the fresh air. The wall surface in Windsor alternates between vinyl-imitating-timber and plaster-over-timber-frame imitating solid wall construction. In Cadaquez, the walls are authentic: brick, block and mortar with real plaster ornament.

Equally different is what happens in front of the buildings. Windsor is a busy street where cars dominate. Pedestrians must hug the edge, with two lonely umbrellas where people eat, squashed between parked cars and shopfronts. Sitting outside is not particularly enjoyable – it is noisy and the view is limited as cars and trucks drive by. In contrast, in Cadaquez the pedestrian is paramount. The cafe generously spills out onto the car-free plaza; it is peaceful, it is not a street, it is a human-scaled plaza.

Ultimately Thiessen failed because his development did not sell before the 2008 Global Financial Crisis killed his credit. He had seven years to sell, but the buyers were not there. There was insufficient attraction for businesses to move to or start up in Windsor. His main point of difference was the old-style new urbanism, the developer replicating a 19th century California town. However, building neo-frontier storefronts was not enough to attract the businesses needed to buy or lease his units.

The Cadaquez economy was local, a fishing village that reinvented itself as an arts community (hosting Picasso and Dali, among others) and then reinventing itself as a resort town for Barcelona. The businesses that came and thrived did so individually, not based on a developer's master development plan supported by spreadsheet projections of presumed unit sales.

Thiessen, as a developer – albeit one trying to do something better than the usual – made decisions based on pecuniary interest. Buying all the windows from one supplier saved money, although in the end, it did not save Thiessen. Cadaquez was a settlement in which decisions were made by the people who would live with the results – the locals and the folks they attracted.

Settlements are different than developments. For a start, risk is spread because the person or family who pays for the building will live and/or work in it. The risk of dozens of buildings stand unsold and unoccupied is alien to settlements because there is no speculative construction; no single owner holding a lot of bank-financed unsold units. In addition to diffusing risk, settlers make decisions for different reasons. One will decide to commission a beautiful front door that costs more, but will be used by their family for decades. Heights, widths and depths of buildings will vary due to different needs and budgets.

Today we have become so used to developments that we forget that for most of human history, places were built as settlements. When a new land was settled, be it America starting in the 17th century, New Zealand and Australia in the 19th, or Europe for several millennia, the settlers who laid out the greenfield to be settled knew precisely what should happen because the people who would make the decisions would be the people who would live with the results. They did not need, and did not have, zoning laws, yet the results were beautiful.

The settlement process is human-scaled. It works better than the development process, but for it to rise again, it requires a very different approach to place-making – it requires the approach found in this book.

Today in Hydra, a Greek island, people have their goods transported by donkey. Hydra is not third world, but an elegant and popular sea-side village where cars are prohibited. The streets are perfect for people, and the place is thriving — elegant and trendy. The no-car decision was probably pragmatic. The buildings reflect a historic past before cars were invented. Knocking these beautiful buildings down to make streets passable by cars would have ruined the village. Instead, visitors come from all over the world to enjoy Hydra. So why can't we intentionally build such places? We don't have to use donkeys for transport, but we can have narrow, human scaled streets. It makes life more interesting, more social.

What to do

when you realize the system's broke,

won't take care of you,

and you want to live

in a wonderful, thriving place.

Taken from the window of the Amtrack train somewhere on the route from New York to Baltimore

Beware the tapeworm economy. Coined by the former head Dillon Reed, of a major Wall Street bank, and then a high ranking official in the first Bush Administration, investment banker Catherine Austin Fitts says "a tapeworm gives off a chemical that makes you crave things that are good for the tapeworm, but bad for you." Like the tapeworm, the tapeworm economy uses government, academia, media and other systems to seek policies that are good for it, but bad for people and communities. Such a well-framed caution, giving words to something we sense, but rarely name.

Chapter 1 – Challenge and Solution

Challenge: "When you realize the system's broke…"

Several years ago, we listened to a speech given by Dee Hock, Founder and Chief Executive Officer emeritus of VISA International (Visa credit card) in which he succinctly summed up his views of the systemic failure of major institutions in western society to deliver on their promises:

Today, it is apparent we are in the midst of a global epidemic of institutional failure. Not only failure in the limited sense of collapse, such as the Soviet Union or corporate bankruptcy, but the more common, pernicious form – institutions increasingly unable to achieve the purpose for which they were created yet constantly expanding as they devour resources, destroy the environment and degrade the human spirit. You know what I mean: Unhealthy health-care systems; Communities in which people can't communicate; Welfare systems in which few fare well; Police that can't enforce the law; Judicial systems without justice; Corporations that can't compete or cooperate; Schools that can't teach; Governments that can't govern, and Economies that can't economize.

Think of this systemic condition as a chronic virus – not virulent enough to kill, but ever-present so life is never fully healthy. Is this how we want to live, or do we simply accept it because the aggravation lies just below the threshold of enragement?

Let us start with the economic system. No matter how much people earn in western society, many report stress about their cost of living. When we take a look, we find real reasons why – there are so many parasites in the system that costs are out of control. By parasite, we mean costs that don't actually contribute to the production of wealth and wellbeing.

For an example, let's pick an easy target: lawyers. Lawyers are essential to assure good communications, for example assuring a complex agreement says what it means. However, once their profession is monetized, too many lawyers make a simple agreement complex, thereby creating billable hours for themselves and their opponent's lawyers, and when things then go wrong, engage in litigation where the costs can exceed the damages. This becomes a parasite, or leech on the economy because money that could have gone into better product or lower prices is sucked off into non-productive billings and litigation.

Let's look at another example, more applicable to the VillageTown. When it came time to build in New Zealand, we were shocked at the high price of pre-manufactured building materials. Plywood alone was five times the price it commanded in the United States, even though it was manufactured locally. When we researched it, we found the actual cost of raw timber and the labor costs to make the plywood were in fact lower than the US. The higher cost came in all of the overhead in staffing, offices, marketing and retailing in a market controlled by a few companies having little incentive to cut the fat. Noting this we expanded our review to examine all the costs in house construction from the initial permitting process to the final wall paint, and found hundreds of people in dozens of organizations inflating the cost of construction.

Therefore, we set out to identify both building materials and construction methods that put more money in better buildings, and less in non-essential overhead costs. We only hired subcontractors where the boss came to the job site with tools, ready to swing a hammer. We sought out building systems that had the shortest distance and smallest manufacturing process from raw material to end use. To make the walls, we purchased crushed rock from the local quarry, a rock normally used to build local roads. Semi-skilled laborers mixed it with 10% cement, poured it into square molds and made large bricks that cured on site for 30 days. Walls were built with these foot-thick bricks, giving us beautiful buildings that should last for hundreds of years, and whose thickness provides passive solar heat in the winter and keeps the rooms pleasantly cool in summer. The interior walls were painted with whitewash, about a dollar a gallon. Why don't people use whitewash anymore? Because it is made from ordinary garden store lime with a dollop of glue added – in other words, it's so cheap there is no margin in it to pay for salesmen, advertising, marketing and middlemen.

The upshot was an outstanding, iconic compound of four major buildings for a shell cost more commonly associated with kitset (prefab) garages. The local economy benefited, since most of the money spent was on local labor and materials. The savings enabled the construction of a large hall, frequently used for local cultural events, not to generate revenue, but to make local life more interesting. The common theme? Look local, shorten the distance, simplify, eliminate middleman, avoid complexity, look to what worked before pre-manufactured products were introduced into the construction industry.

Earth Brick Building under construction in 1998

"… and the System won't take care of you"

What do we mean by "the system"?

Our basic needs and discretionary luxuries come from a global consumer market system fueled by fossil fuel, paid for by international currencies, in which these commodities often travel thousands of miles, entirely dependent on an international transport system of inordinate complexity. For many people in western beneficiary societies, basic needs now include not only food, clothing and shelter, but also communications, electricity, medical care and transportation. When you build a way of life in which homes are miles from work and food sources (supermarkets, not fields or gardens), transport becomes essential to survival. In the USA if you stopped the fuel supply, within two weeks millions would be starving.

This beneficiary system is regulated by governments and treaties, often managed by international treaty organizations that increasingly serve the pecuniary interest of large multi-national corporations. All of these things combined – all of the subsystems that operate in western society – can be seen as a single system.

While this global system delivers lower prices for more advanced solutions when it is working, it also is highly vulnerable to insiders' abuse, pursuing power-, fortune- and fame-driven private agendas contrary to the purpose of the system. When this happens, the system fails to deliver on its promise, resulting in outcomes contrary to the purpose of the system. The system's failure then results in hardship, even suffering, on the individual at the receiving end of the promise.

What can we do?

To fix the overall system, very little. The problems are too big, too complex, and they have too many people doing well by those existing systems, people who will regard you as the enemy, and seek in whatever way to thwart your attempts to right their system – and if you prove to be making inroads – to ruin you. However, as we look at the System, we realize it affords many opportunities – freedoms to create local solutions, just as we did in using local raw materials to build our home in New Zealand. We had the right to choose not to use the overpriced systems, but instead to do more homework, more research, to find far more value for our dollars. The secret: ***It's your money.***

Let's look at the capital potential in a village. Let's take the average home price as $250,000 (noting that by the 3rd edition this may be woefully low; it should closer to $400,000 for the average in two places we are looking: California and Auckland). Let's take that as a benchmark, saying that in the VillageTown, the average will be the same. Let's say that 4,000 buildings (housing residential and workplace units) will be built. At an average of 2.5 people per home, this is a reasonable number for a population of 10,000. In the business of real estate development, this is equal to a medium-scale subdivision.

$250,000 x 4,000 = $1 billion (not including the additional value of the industrial park and town center offices)

One billion dollars of your money – not investor's money, not government's money – it's your cash or your good credit. The buck stops with you. Do remember that investors, developers and banks are paid by your earnings or your savings.

There is nothing to stop you from providing for your own collective wellbeing. The key is to start out with that intention from the beginning. Clarify your goals and aspirations, and then seek design solutions that address them. If your intent is to create a self-supporting settlement that provides for your economic security, so you may enjoy a good life with conviviality, citizenship, art, intellect and spirit, make sure these become the fundamental principles guiding the initiative.

Conventional developers generally don't do this because they are in the business of buying, subdividing, building and selling homes, not thinking about your social or economic needs and aspirations. Social issues like alienation of children, families breaking up, old people being thrown away – these things are not in the scope of their job. It's not their business. Sometimes environmental issues get to a point of absurdity. In the middle of the hot dry Arizona desert in the United States, new homes all have electric clothes driers and no place to hang clothing out to dry even though the hot air is free, and electrical generation has negative side effects as well as a higher price tag. The developers don't see this as their problem.

By the time the developers have bought the land, subdivided and built, it's their money – not yours, and we are unfair to criticize them for working within the system. If you don't like what the system is doing, or not doing, find a better way to do it.

There is nothing to stop you creating a different set of principles that includes design specifications that provide for your well-being. If you combine your purchasing power with others, in essence creating a buyers market, you become attractive to policy makers who must give permission and professionals who can build what you seek. By creating a market force, you make their job easier. The key is to be organized, coherent and to negotiate from a position of power. If you are a developer or investor who loves the idea, there is nothing to stop you from leading it. You just need to redefine your job so that it makes paramount the needs and aspirations of the people who will live with the results, rather than your pecuniary interest

…And you want to live in a wonderful, thriving place

New Zealand has an interesting law that governs real estate development. It defines its purpose as sustainable management of resources, and it goes on to say this means to "enable people and communities to provide for their social, cultural and economic wellbeing, health and safety while [protecting the environment]".

> Resource Management Act 1991
> PART 2 – PURPOSE AND PRINCIPLES
> 5.   Purpose—
> (1) The purpose of this Act is to promote the sustainable management of natural and physical resources.
> (2) In this Act, "sustainable management" means managing the use, development, and protection of natural and physical resources in a way, or at a rate, which enables people and communities to provide for their social, economic, and cultural wellbeing and for their health and safety while —
>   (a) Sustaining the potential of natural and physical resources (excluding minerals) to meet the reasonably foreseeable needs of future generations; and
>   (b) Safeguarding the life supporting capacity of air, water, soil, and ecosystems; and
>   (c) Avoiding, remedying, or mitigating any adverse effects of activities on the environment

What does it mean to enable people and communities?
How do we enable people and communities to provide for their wellbeing?
What is social, economic and cultural wellbeing? What does it look and feel like? How does it function?

In answer: that is what this book is about. It is about using the existing system, the existing laws and regulations, to produce a very different outcome: one in which the details, or what Christopher Alexander calls a "pattern language", uplift the human spirit, and provide a higher level of social and economic security to enable people to enjoy what Aristotle calls a good life.

The underlying idea is that while the world may have many problems right now, many of them come about because of how we structure life. Change the structure, and the problems are not solved; instead they vanish. For example, we can burn less fuel by investing billions in new car engines that are cleaner and more efficient. That helps solve the pollution and oil price problems. Or we can move our destinations so we don't need cars or mass transit in day-to-day life. For us, the car problem vanishes. We no longer need oil to get around. Miles per gallon or liters per hundred kilometers no longer matter to us. We now buy nice shoes.

Solution: Build a VillageTown

Let us first build an image in our mind of what is possible.

From the image, create a force, a compelling vision that inspires others, and silences professional naysayers. Create a constituency of people who want to host or to live in the VillageTown, who want to make the vision manifest. The piece of land selected to become a VillageTown becomes the object of their vision. In doing this we create a new paradigm. In the industry, the usual relationship is a contest between pecuniary interest (developers) and the guardians of the common good (sometimes elected, sometimes local groups of vocal activists). We introduce a new relationship, that of host and settler. The host wants a new settlement, usually to bring jobs and prosperity. The settler is not someone looking to turn a buck, but a community of people seeking to create a new community in which to live – they are the common good.

The naysayer then asks, "Is this realistic or a pipe dream?"

The short answer is that the market will decide. It will either sell or not. For the long answer, if we look at history, we find that major changes came about not because of some monolithic system, but often because of a few inspired individuals with vision, passion and will. As mentioned elsewhere in this book, I grew up in Baltimore and witnessed a handful of men and women change the face of their city, and then inspired other cities to do the same. When they began, they were not famous, had no training in what they were about to do, and they were not raving radicals. They felt improvements could be made and set about pursuing them. They painted a vision and enrolled others. They put a stake in the ground. They spoke out. They put their heart in it and most importantly – they got started.

What you need to succeed are:

- People who want to live in it, and are prepared to call it into being
- A strong economic plan to assure it can be paid for and prosper for many generations
- Available and appropriate land

Alternatively, if you prefer sound-bites: People, Prosperity and Place.

Many of us have a self-censoring voice in our subconscious, which may inhibit us from calling a VillageTown into being. We may need to override that subconscious voice with fully conscious intent. This is best done by connecting with others whose strengths are different from our own. If we are good at stating the vision, connect with people good at delivering the goods and others with organizational and people skills.

It's about People

Let us not forget what is most important – the people. The physical form of the village, the organizations and industries it operates all exist for the higher purpose of contributing to the growth and wellbeing of people living in a balanced way with our planet. Primarily, we are not consumers, not workers, not even citizens; we are individuals, families and communities finding our purpose and our place to stand.

When we think of people, let us think of many generations, a place where people find long-term fulfillment, a place that provides more than security. We can make our village inspired – never boring; we can make our village radiant – never oppressive. Plan for seven generations to come.

It's about Prosperity

Prosperity means everyone is doing well, appreciating that different people need different things to do well. Visit a prosperous place and one can feel the spirit. It's not about conspicuous consumption. Rather it is about human activity, people engaged in their own wealth-creating activity that causes them and (by local purchasing) their neighbors to thrive. Prosperity gives time to play with the children, to sing, to plant and tend flowers, to excel at some sport or talent or just to enjoy doing it, and to make ones home and community beautiful. Prosperity reduces tension; generosity becomes the norm.

It's about Land

Once the host political jurisdiction has agreed to the terms under which zoning and planning approval will work, find the land. To motivate people have them stand on the land that will become the VillageTown. Carry poles and stake them where the village gate is to be, plant flags to set out the main plazas. Land makes the vision feel real, it gives meaning. If it is possible, secure the land early in the process, but not before the politicians agree to the VillageTown Settlement planning process.

It's about Action

Yes, you can build a VillageTown. No, you don't need to be a professional in the industry – such people will show up when they are needed. If you are one, great, but if not, don't let that stop you. If you need permission to build a VillageTown, this book gives it to you. Everything required to build a VillageTown has already been done before. It's not rocket science. It's not like going to the moon. The steps set out in this book should make it easier.

Every journey begins with a vision and a first step. Each of us is on an evolutionary path. Each of us is given a multitude of directions we can take – a choice of probable futures. When we walk our life, we must choose one of those futures, and if we listen to our heart, we know which suits us best.

If you decide to build your village, then you will find others join you on the path. It is important then that you remember who you are, not yielding responsibility to the others that join you – they have their part to play, not yours. Building a VillageTown for many generations to come is a tremendous thing to do with ones life.

If this inspires you, then get on with it... the time is now.

Art is not dead. But where it seems dead, life is less wonderful.

Editorial: It's not your fault

As politicians, pundits and bureaucrats jump on the Global Warming bandwagon, we witness vilification of behaviors that were sold to us as good decades ago. When suburbs were designed, they were specifically intended to require that the mundane tasks of daily life be accessed by car using gasoline. Now we read in our morning paper that motorists are bad, and we should expect to pay for our sins of owning and using cars. This shift in dogma came fast – primarily the result of many influential people watching former U. S. Vice President Al Gore's film An Inconvenient Truth in 2006. It's interesting to note that in the 1950's, Al Gore's father, U.S. Senator Albert Gore Sr. introduced American legislation to create the interstate highway system. The father wanted high-speed transport for the good of the country. His son wants to save the world from its adverse effects.

How utterly unfair of our world's leaders to blame the good citizen for a lifestyle that was packaged and approved by their same governments, industry and academia. The solutions proposed are higher taxes to change people's behavior – make it more painful. While this will result in people driving less, cutting out discretionary travel and buying more fuel efficient cars when their current model is due for replacement, it fundamentally is based on wealth conversion – taking money from the citizen for a conduct previously sanctioned, indeed legislated by (through zoning), the very same tax collector.

It took almost a century to get to the point where most people must get around by car. The real, and wealth-creating solution is obvious. Shift how we live so people do not need a car for their day-to-day lives. This is called rezoning.

Local government should ban any subdivision proposal or any zoning plan that fails to integrate residence, work, shopping, primary and secondary education, recreation and entertainment so that all are within a ten minute walk: the walking home-range.
- No new shopping malls or big-block mega-stores surrounded by acres of pavement to park the cars.
- No new suburban bedroom subdivisions where people have to drive to shop, get to work, or go to school.
- No new industrial parks, large office complexes requiring four lane highways to transport the workers in.
- No new regional schools requiring vehicles to get to class.

Begin immediately. Demand subdivision plans that combine all activities in a single place.

What about existing subdivisions? On a case by case review, look at each suburb to see how all activities could be integrated into what is now residential only zones, and be done well. It's not as easy, but it is possible. Rewrite zoning laws.

Of course, that is what this book is all about, so perhaps I am biased. However, this book was being written before this latest Global Warming dogma took over, before Al Gore became a controversial figure. The challenge writing the book faced was primarily about people and quality of life – using architecture and design to address the social, economic and cultural problems western societies. The environmental aspect came as a way to avoid unintended negative side effects.

Global warming is flavor of the month. Policy makers and pundits looking at global warming say the solution is to penalise carbon-generating citizens. Yes, we need to assure Nature is not subject to systematically increasing concentrations of substances extracted from the Earth's crust, but we can do this in a way that engenders a higher quality of life for all. In VillageTowns, cars are banned not to earn carbon credits, but because they ruin local quality of life. View this as an opportunity, not a calamity.

Chapter 2 – The Big Picture – *Imagine*

Imagine living in a place surrounded by natural beauty – by the sea, the mountains or among beautiful countryside dotted with farms. Imagine those farms growing delicious foods brought in daily for home cooking or served in the cafés on the plazas that define the life of your village. Imagine a small town of perhaps five or ten thousand people, a town made of ten or twenty villages. How is it possible to build in a place of such natural beauty? Answer: it brings its own local economy with it. It does not need to be the next ring of an expanding, sprawling economic region. By developing its own local economy and an excellent telecommunications and transport link to the globe, its Founders can chose a location based on quality of life.

Imagine a socially-enriched quality of life. The VillageTown is defined by its villages, twenty in a 10,000 population community, connected by people-filled streets to provide patterns of activity and quieter lanes providing patterns of tranquility. The public life, the theater of the VillageTown unfolds on its plazas. Each one is different – with different architecture, different

culture, a different feeling. Social enrichment comes from proximity without an appointment. The VillageTown is a declared *slow food* community, meaning many tables, many chairs and many hours to enjoy wonderful local food and drink, good company and diversity to keep it interesting.

Where does one get the free time for slow food? Answer: by not having to commute; not having to drive to accomplish the mundane chores of daily life – shopping, taking children to schools or to play with their friends. Your walking home-range is local, all within a ten-minute walk, and the VillageTown is safe for children to walk alone – for a start, they won't be run over playing in the streets, for there are no cars or trucks in the VillageTown.

Imagine a place culturally enriched. On many of the plazas one of the prominent buildings is the Artist Guild Hall – on one plaza the actor's guild, on another the sculptors or perhaps musicians' guild. The guild halls were funded through the savings of not needing wide roads.

Normally a community of 10,000 people also must provide for 6,000 cars with wide streets, on and off-street parking and lots of wasted land. This costs the developer a lot of money – money not recovered through sales. By building a settlement where people do not need cars for day-to-day chores, both land and money are freed up. If there is no developer extracting the additional profits, some of these savings go into enriching the culture: attracting artists, musicians, actors, poets, filmmakers, dancers, writers – all those many people of the creative class who transform the culture of a place from a backwater to the center of the universe. They require a critical mass – there must be enough of them and suddenly the place comes alive. By having guild halls with nearby artists' homes provided only to guild members, the artists become permanent stakeholders, never to be gentrified out because of housing prices or rents.

Imagine a place that never gets boring. Again, critical mass and diversity in the villages becomes the key. For some, the pleasure of an evening walk is a daily ritual. Thus, in planning the VillageTown, the streets, lanes and footpaths going to the villages are designed so one may walk for an hour or two, from one plaza to another without much backtracking. The VillageTown may only cover one or two hundred acres, but it is laid out in a tight series of irregular patterns to keep it interesting – no

grid – a surveyor's nightmare and a resident's joy. In founding it, future residents become involved, and they are encouraged to cluster around different villages. If a country has different ethnic groups or significant numbers of immigrants from particular countries, they will be encouraged to create a village reflecting their traditions, their foods, their architecture and their culture. If your nation has Italian immigrants, especially those skilled in design and food, actively recruit them, for in our research we found many of the archetypes and patterns in Italy – when it comes to quality of life, they have mastered many aspects.

Imagine a place to raise a family where the pressures on the nuclear family are supplanted by that over-worn aphorism *it takes a village to raise the child*. Let us estimate 20% of the population will be school-age children. In a 10,000 person VillageTown, two thousand will be between the ages of 6 and 18. The VillageTown is built for children, beginning with its car-free streets and with plazas where children run free under the watchful eyes of the many adults working in the surrounding offices, shops and workplaces, or relaxing in the cafés or plaza seating. The plazas are carefully designed so play zones do not conflict with the adults. The plazas are designed to offer activities for children more interesting than sitting at home watching television or playing computer games.

The VillageTown becomes the campus. Why isolate students, wasting many

acres for buildings and land used 15% of the year (200 days / six hours a day)? Instead, build classrooms on the plazas, where children walk with their teachers from classrooms to workshops or the playing fields.

The guild halls include classrooms, where the room walls have pull-out cavities. During school, the teacher pulls out the sliding wall with white boards, posters and all the paraphernalia teachers and students tack to classroom walls. At the end of the class, these are slid back into the cavity, and the room instantly becomes available for other community use. Sports fields are VillageTown owned, just outside the village gates. Where in the suburbs families pack more entertainment inside each home, in the VillageTown, the children find their entertainment outside. Families share the burden of raising children, assisted by older people happy to help.

Imagine a place where graduating youth come into their own without feeling they must leave. In the suburbs when one finishes school, it is time to pack up and go to the city. Often the parents then sell up, for suburbs are no place for old people, especially when they lose their drivers license. In the VillageTown, the local economy operates with thousands of jobs,

mostly small businesses, in which the young may find opportunity –especially as their future employers don't need to conduct a job interview; they've known the applicant since childhood. To make it possible for these young adults, affordable housing and a *youth cluster* becomes important. Affordable youth housing provides very small homes designed for people under age 26 with a restriction that when sold, the buyer must be under 26. Placing such housing in a youth zone or village creates the social critical mass that forms the second component of assuring young adults have a place in the

VillageTown. The youth zone may be a village, or it may be a street, but it will be noisier. It may have a bandstand for dancing in the streets; perhaps a university-type pub and it might even have an outdoor climbing wall. Youth Founders will set out its design – and like the artists guild halls – with general initiative funds set aside to be invested in youth amenities.

Imagine a place of visitors. What visitors travel to suburbs as a destination? Who travels the world to visit a shopping mall with the same franchises as back home? The VillageTown begins by making a clear distinction between tourist and visitor, and carefully designs for the latter. Tourists come in high season expecting to pay to be entertained – tourists can be utterly exhausting to locals and tourism tends to create a boom-bust seasonal economy. In contrast, visitors come all year round for a particular, pre-planned experience – perhaps they come for the culture of the artists guilds, the slow food locally grown, or they come to visit one of the many businesses and industries that give the local economy its vitality. No motels in the VillageTown, instead visitors stay in travelers inns – places where meals are served on long tables with benches, and locals come and sit with travelers who sometimes become friends.

Travelers are like flowing water, they keep the place refreshed and clear. Some villages may choose to sponsor a tertiary level academic institution, perhaps a branch campus for an overseas university (by the time students do their year abroad, they are past the offensive and outrageous stage). Alternatively, imagine a village where Founders included a film maker who

Imagine a place both kind to and honoring of old people – yourself sooner or later. Because the VillageTown needs no cars, old people do not experience a traumatic shock when they no longer can drive.

The VillageTown provides for three stages of eldership. The first stage is the free-market big house, the one large enough for visiting family and a lifetime of collected stuff. The second stage is about downsizing, simplifying: a one or two room cottage on the ground floor less than fifty paces to the plaza; specifically designed for elders with no steps or stoops, with a sensor that shuts off the stove when the pot burns. Finally, the third stage offers six to ten bed nursing facilities on many of the plazas. Should you become infirm, your trauma is not compounded by the social deprivation of being removed from your community and the people who know and love you.

During eldership, some will choose to occupy a plaza workplace for settled work – finally getting to do the work they love – blacksmith, toymaker or baker of seasonal deserts. I inherited a wonderful recipe for Dresden stöllen passed down from my grandmother for whoever wants to open the bakery in my village – it takes three days to make, so can only be made for love (or a supplemental retirement income), not practical for staff paid an hourly wage.

Imagine a place where all experience freedom from want, freedom from fear, safety for all, pursuit of good health, conviviality, a place of creativity, a place balancing privacy and public life, a place where one walks with a light environmental footprint to leave a better world for future generations, a place with a wonderful spirit and a prosperous future.

Finally, imagine what happens when a dozen or so such VillageTowns are built in a country. Imagine how they may contribute to the character of the nation. Imagine the farming regions surrounding the VillageTowns devoted to growing slow food – high quality local foods. Imagine how the VillageTowns may influence on what may have been a struggling rural regional economy. Imagine VillageTowns becoming centers of creativity where the arts become a destination for more than just the locals. Imagine as such VillageTowns emerge and establish connection with other VillageTowns, both in their own country and others around the world. Imagine what happens when a community of VillageTowns emerges, sharing a value of quality of life, and sharing their knowledge and understanding of how to build a VillageTown.

Now having begun the journey in your imagination, let us begin the adventure of making it manifest. Turn the page so we may begin to explore the elements and patterns that can call it into reality.

Catherine Fitts' Popsicle Index: How many parents in this room would feel comfortable letting their six-year-old child walk alone to the corner store to buy a popsicle? When she asked this in a large lecture hall, only a few people put their hands up. All of them lived on Waiheke Island, NZ. In the VillageTown every parent should raise their hand (only hopefully not to buy flavored iced sugar-water).

Chapter 3 – VillageTown Layout

Begin with the boundaries.

Know your boundaries. Build a historic district. Once built, do not sprawl. Build nothing more for at least 50 years.

Of utmost importance is that once the VillageTown boundary is set, it is kept. This is common practice in Europe, where the demarcation of village and country is both clear and permanent. In contrast, the United States has so blurred its boundaries that they have merged into one incoherent mess – with an accompanying decline the quality of life. At one time, America had its boundaries. Then with the advent of the car, developers persuaded local authorities to let them put in a new subdivision on the edge of town, or a drive-in burger joint. Then a car dealership was added and then a discount shopping mall with big box stores. The same thing was happening in the next town, and fifty years later, the only memory of the demarcation is a road sign telling drivers they have gone from one town to the next. Later, other countries adopted this American approach to sprawl.

Each site will be different, but in many cases, acquiring additional land for a greenbelt is important. It prevents cross-boundary conflicts (such as new residents complaining about farm smells and noise) and gives the villagers an experience of real Nature, not an artificial city park. In addition, the VillageTown should consider various ways to ensure the surrounding

As much as we all love the hilltop towns of Italy, when people ask about building them as VillageTowns, do consider that it will be a challenge enough to ask people to get out of their cars and walk everywhere. Those grandmothers dressed in black who can walk to the top of the town every day are tough; they have been doing that walk all their life. There are good reasons to build on hilltops – the air usually stays warmer in the evening than in the valley, and the better farmland is down the slope. But until there is a strong market for a hilltop town, best to look for flatter land.

farmland remains as farms. Ironically, the very presence of the VillageTown will encourage developers to buy surrounding farms to convert to suburban sprawl. Buy the development rights or use protective legislation to ensure farms remain farms.

To protect the Greenbelt, we strongly recommend that the urban core is surrounded by a high wall, constructed to keep domestic animals, wandering toddlers and disoriented seniors within. Build many gates and archways in the village walls to enable people to walk beyond the urban core. Make gate latches too high for toddlers and too difficult for the senile.

The pattern of village walls runs deep into ancient human memory, creating a sense of enclosure. Walls can block wind, absorb and hold the heat of sunlight, and create a warmer micro climate in winter when the sun is low. They enable a measure of control of domestic pets who otherwise can wreak havoc on native birds, animals and plants beyond the urban walls. Walls provide security, and they make a strong statement that there will be no sprawl. Settlements work best when their boundary is clear, fixed and permanent.

The wall in some towns will be built of a solid aggregate – stone, formed concrete, perhaps adobe. In others, it may be a hedgerow, a living wall of trees, vines and bushes. In any case, make it beautiful and low maintenance. The VillageTown rules should permit some of its boundary walls to be built into the back of VillageTown houses, although it is recommended that the exterior wall remain the property of the VillageTown.

In setting out village walls, avoid the surveyor's temptation to make it perfectly straight. Nature rarely follows a straight line. The best way to set out the village boundary is with a number of people walking the land with pegs and stakes. Let the proposed boundary line undulate with the hills, let it move out to enclose a tree or in so the tree sits outside the wall (don't cut the tree just because it is in the way). Don't forget the children's caves – build small recesses in the walls that form enclosures for their fantasy world of children. Outside the wall build large gardens, sports fields, an equestrian center and paddocks for farm animals, and of course, the motorpool and the shipping depot. For rural VillageTowns, 50% or more Greenbelt is the best.

In some places, where the nearby buildings are public, make the wall wide enough to walk upon with lovely wrought iron railings. In other places, build a recess in the top, filled with topsoil and planted with cascading vines and flowering plants.

If you have the luxury of falling water, consider even using the wall as a Roman aqueduct to transport the water to the right place for a plaza fountain. In some places, leave the wall natural. In others, coat it with brilliant white whitewash or clay-tinted slurry that develops a patina over time as different tints are applied and eventually wear through.

Nature in the Greenbelt

The ideal VillageTown will have about 4-600 acres of land, including a large, surrounding *greenbelt*. The greenbelt buffers cross-boundary conflicts, keeps the neighbors happy, and provides people with access to Nature on her turf. If not there already, plant fields of flowers, stands of native trees, places to walk, run and ride horses. Build a cemetery and provide sacred space. Part of the greenbelt should be sports fields, used by schools as well as by the community.

If the land is available, consider setting aside a reserve where Nature is primary and humans her guests. Consult with experts to identify what the ecosystem would have looked like before humans altered it; seek to replicate this, as one would plant a garden and stock it with native fauna. It is important that people know what Nature is like before mankind reshaped her.

Next the Plazas

Set out the plazas – they are the public stage, the social destination without an appointment. In our research, we found a town works best made of many villages – each with its own lively plaza. In each village, the plaza becomes the social connector. Plazas provide the antidote to boredom, the bane of any small community. If you need inspiration, go to the old Spanish, Italian or Greek villages to see how they capture the feeling and provide a wonderful experience, something often found lacking in developments. The secret is to make them living, active places.

Multiple plazas create destinations for walking. Connect plazas by varying-width streets and footpaths. Some must be wide to build the homes. Alleys can be green-streets forming back-door neighborhoods with the public street allowing private gardens. Straight streets are not necessary unless there is a design reason such as a view shaft. Pay attention to wind channels – block the wind where it may be uncomfortable. Plan a circulation plan so residents can walk for an hour from plaza to plaza, and never repeat the same street or plaza. If you do this, you will find that daily walks become a part of VillageTown life.

Because each village is designed by its settlers, it is expected each will have its own character reflecting its founder. The villagers will decide about their cafes, taverns and restaurants and the features of their plaza. In the photo below, the plaza was designed to provide a place for children to play and parents to gather without disturbing the surrounding cafes.

In these photos of plazas and streets, you will see carefully selected trees and plants. The trees provide shade from the hot summer sun, but they do not dominate. Plants in Mediterranean countries tend to be grown in pots where they soften the urban landscape, provide color and break up the hard lines of stone buildings and walls.

Greening urban open space requires considerable attention to get right. Too many planners think that anything green is good, producing sad, rarely used places that must be mowed and sprayed. Green space is essential; humans need access to Nature, to green. Some work best as the "secret garden", a magical place of trees, flowers and water. Others provide important views from home and work place windows. Plant a grove of sacred trees rather than treat them as street urinals for dogs. It may be my bias, but I have seen too many city parks that just don't work. Build plazas in the villages; save the parks for the greenbelt.

This plaza in Mallorca is family-oriented. On a sloping site, they built a flat, raised playground for children with walls high enough for parents to sit on and to protect the cafe tables from skateboards and balls. Even on this day of passing showers in summer, it was alive with townfolk of all ages and stages of life.

Reflective Sunlight: *In this lovely town in Mallorca, the walls of the buildings reflect the sunlight, casting a warm glow on the light paver street. Working with sunlight is important.*

The Art of the Plaza

Set out many plazas and do not make them too big. The plazas serve their first function during the planning process – before the VillageTown is built, by allowing the VillageTown Founders to form themselves into villages where each village focuses on an architectural code, theme and flavor for their particular plaza. Please appreciate the importance of this step – it takes some up-front time, but defines the character of each village for many generations. Authenticity comes from citizens implanting their personality in the architecture. Encourage each plaza to be different. If some of your village founders are from a particular ethnic or cultural background, support them to implant their cultural on the design of their plaza. Expect that some people will press for a trendy look, and if their village founders agree that is what they want, give them free reign to do a modern, innovative design for one of the plazas. However, for most of the VillageTown plazas, permit me to suggest that you encourage timeless vernacular.

One may argue that Italy mastered the art of the plaza best. The tables and umbrellas encourage what they call slow food – taking the time to enjoy life. Plants tend not to be in the ground but in pots. If you have freezing winters, the pots can be taken in, marking the passing of the seasons. Plazas need not be large, indeed, it is best to make them smaller than one might think. Their purpose is to provide a gathering place, a place to stroll and to connect. Plazas are places to sit, some with warm outdoor seats to read the paper, others with outdoor cafes. They should have room for children to run without disturbing their elders.

The plazas are the stage upon which public life is played out. We suggest one plaza per village close to its center.

I was in Auckland, dropping off a draft of this book to an architect who is an excellent critic – the book is better for his red pen. On street parking proved impossible, so I circled the block and found a remarkable new urban development. Built in a sparkling finish of stainless steel and white concrete, I noted that the scale was very much in keeping with the VillageTown principles – medium density with open space where we propose plazas. Overall, it was attractive, upscale and sheltered from the bustle of the city. But in character it felt like the opposite of the VillageTown.

There were no people. Actually, there was one woman on a cell phone, and a caretaker with a loud blower chasing designer leaves. Even with the professional offices next door, this glorious potential plaza showed no life. In front of each townhouse a single space for one car. At one time this would have been called a bachelor pad, home to the young upwardly mobile professional.

The computer generated design stood out. Each tree resembling the click and paste of my architect software where you get to choose summer green or autumn red. It's scary when life begins to imitate software.

Right size, right height, looked like fireproof buildings, right scale of open space. Only need to change three things:

- Get rid of the cars and put workplaces, shops, cafes and classrooms on the ground floor
- Encourage each resident to influence the design, to add personality
- Design for all ages, so it is occupied all day long, so it is a complete community

If those three things were done, it would be a completely different feel to the place. Now, I am not criticizing this development. There will always be young, upwardly mobile professionals seeking a clean, trendy look in the city, and places like this serve that market well. The reason for the observation was to note how close we already come to the scale but not the heart of the VillageTown.

The challenge of making trees work in a Plaza

Trees and grass are good, right? Surprisingly, in urban environments, not always so. In this photo, the winning architect proposed a stand of pine trees, but the politically correct decision overrode this and native kauri trees were planted. Good thing for the city government there is not a Society for the Prevention of Cruelty to Trees because the resulting litter-filled effect adds nothing to the plaza. To see the kauri tree in its native habitat, please see the photo on page 56 of this book. It is very different.

Update 2014: The trees are taller, but it still feels cold, dead and sad. It also tends to attract litter, cigarette butts and dogs use it as toilet. We now read a proposal in the news that the trees should be torn out and replaced by another design. Sigh.

When swaths of grass do not work

Here we have an unfortunate outcome with grass on an urban plaza. This plaza was near to lovely paved plazas whose photographs appear elsewhere in this book – plazas and pedestrian streets bustling with people, pumping with life. In contrast, here where we find grass, the result is a sense of poverty. Even with the fountain, the place feels unloved, unwanted. Grass and trees have a place, but it is not in the plaza. Use grass in urban parks, where one walks among trees and flowers set in their appropriate environment. Vegetation on plazas seems to work best when carefully contained in large pots.

When a plaza works. When it doesn't quite make it.

Auckland's Chancery Lane (right) is an attempt at a European plaza, but has a cold and contrived feeling about it. In contrast, Hydra's main plaza (below) on the waterfront has a feeling of authenticity and it is a delight. What makes the difference?

People, design and workmanship.

For the most part, Chancery closes at 6:30; p.m. it's not a community but an outdoor mall trying to imitate a living European plaza. For it to come alive, the upper offices need to be converted into apartments and homes. The gates, which are locked in early evening, need to remain open and it needs to loosen up and allow life to happen. Close to the University of Auckland as well as the central business district, it could become a lively destination, but only if it offers the attractions.

Chancery feels as if one is standing in an architectural rendering out of a designer's head. The pavers are uniform and the pattern is wilful, yet poorly executed – note the lines where the fan pattern is split by a straight line. There is a strong sense of command and control – the opposite of the life of a plaza.

In contrast, in Hydra, the pavers are irregular, the craftsman made the decisions. The environment is less controlled, with more random colors, more individuals stamping their personalities on the decorations. The buildings reflect individual personalities. Most importantly, it's about the people. Auckland's plaza is in the business district, isolated from the community with locking gates to keep out those who might wander down after shopping hours. Hydra's plaza is where everything happens – arriving boats, perhaps a dozen cafes, shops, offices, residents, tourists, business people – and on Hydra, no cars are permitted anywhere. A few delivery donkeys add to the fun. People walk down to meet others – casual social contact not requiring an appointment.

What makes this work? Ostensibly a staircase, but obviously not heavily used, the tables spill over from the restaurant on the plaza. Placement of the plants in pots softens the ambiance, but does not overwhelm. Hand hewn wooden shutters and doors lack the precision of modern security gates, but provide a beauty no powder-coated steel bars can match.

Promenade Streets and Quiet Streets

Connect the plazas with different types of streets and lanes.

Not all homes and workplaces will be on the plazas, some will be on the connecting streets. Family hotels and guest houses are better placed on the quieter streets, nicely lined with potted plants. Shops and store fronts work best on the main pedestrian thoroughfares, and if the VillageTown becomes a shopping destination for the region – yes do expect this to happen – these streets should connect the more public plazas with the motorpool / parking lot area where people leave their cars to walk into the VillageTown.

Finally, appreciate that some people want to hear nothing but birds in the ivy – they want to live on quiet back streets used only by neighbors and those who want a peaceful contemplative walk.

Note that in the three photographs to the right, the street widths are all about the same, yet the feeling of each is entirely different. The paving becomes more irregular and the way rain is channeled is different. The busy street has a raised side walk separating slow moving pedestrians looking in shop windows from fast moving people and cycles.

Encourage high ground floors and permit upper floors to overhang, some with open balconies and others with extended residences. This becomes especially valuable to protect pedestrians from rain. In permitting overhang give careful consideration to winter and summer sun. In climates with a burning sun, shelter in the summer is important. In the winter, orientation so sunlight is on the street and reflecting into windows makes the street welcoming and more comfortable.

Designate at least one main street as the VillageTown Parade, where it becomes possible, literally, to have a parade from the entry to the heart of the town. Design it wide enough to house the whole town and many visitors on the sides. Traditionally in western society, such parades started outside by the main gate and went to the cathedral and town hall in the center, with its large plaza allowing room for gathering and ceremony. In setting out the Parade, pay careful attention to wind patterns and sunshine. If you can, align it with something astronomical, such as the dawn sun shaft on the equinox or solstice.

Primary pedestrian street

Secondary quieter pedestrian street

The Village Parade would be very wide, going direct to the center

Very quiet residential-only lane

Different Destinations in a Small Area

It was amusing to look up boredom on Wikipedia and find "*Boredom is often associated with adolescence, especially in suburbs, small towns, and other isolated areas. A typical teenager's complaint is that there is 'nothing to do'; this statement can have a number of economic and social causes. Younger teens cannot drive, but in many communities are unable to get anywhere without a car possibly due to lack of public transportation. It may also mean that their desired sources of entertainment are too expensive. It could also be a symptom of learned helplessness, possibly related to boredom experienced at school.*"

Boredom is real. In small communities it can become overwhelming. Interesting that in Wikipedia the writer identifies the spreading out of society thus requiring a car as a source of boredom. While this may aggravate the condition, a VillageTown with only one plaza and too much of a monoculture, may be equally as boring to its citizens.

The details in this Mallorcan town include beautiful stone pavers, not black pavement. The pastel wall colors feel warm. The cafe is a welcoming destination.

Many aspects of the VillageTown, such as an arts-enriched population and a diverse local economy, prevent boredom. Another way to make the VillageTown layout interesting is to create many "destinations". The VillageTown should be full of destinations, and each should be both different and in its own way, fulfilling. Reference the design used in films sets. More than architects or landscape architects, film set designers focus on the details that create mood, which engage people. Observe the details, not to be slavishly copied, but to inspire a dialogue about details that work. However, do not imitate the faux-build techniques of film set designers; we want the buildings to last for centuries – make them real.

To understand what this means, if you want an interesting homework assignment, go to the real Venice (lower left) then go to Venice Las Vegas style (lower right). Venice is about passion, design detail that seems to be the birthright of its people. Las Vegas is about imitation (even the sky was fake). Real has grit, defects, the variable hanging potted plants cared for by their owners. In the beginning, your place may look too new, but have no fear, Mother Nature will paint her patina on it soon enough.

Venice and Las Vegas are both tourist destinations. The appeal of Venice is its authenticity. It was built at a time when the city was a trading city-state. Vegas is fake, a stage-set in the desert. The water is clean and dead as a swimming pool. The purpose of everything in Vegas is to get tourists to spend.

Different feelings to an outdoor VillageTown destination
Lively
- Promenade – To see and be seen; with teen spaces separate from adult promenades
- Cafe connection – To meet others, join for a drink, spend time talking – conviviality and citizenship
- Water – a fountain of walk-in water jets for children (and everyone else)
- Entertainment – Street theater, musicians, artists, chess tables
- Indigenous or ethnic–- food, shops, architectural ambiance
- Partying – Youth zone
- Industrial – Work zone including wharf and well-designed industrial areas
- Academic – Higher education institute (variation on Cafe connection – think cafe dialogue and debate)

Tranquil
- Peace and Quiet – a walled garden designed for walking among flowers and trees
- Grove – a stand of large, old trees reserved only for walking and sitting – no bikes, horses or dogs
- Water – flowing, riverside, natural pools, Zen pond, seaside, wharf, waterfall
- Outlook – a high place to look far in the distance (also sunset/sunrise)
- Pastoral – paddocks, livestock, nature
- Sacred – natural site or man-made religious including cemeteries
- Academic – Feeling of a Library or enclosed college where all is quiet

The street or path to get there
Lively
- Relatively smooth streets wide enough for numerous people, bicycles, prams and the occasional VillageTown vehicle
- Should have shops or workplaces facing the street frontage

Tranquil
- Narrow lanes or paths leading to a quiet neighborhood and infrequently accessed destinations. Paving can be more irregular, have outdoor stairs and more verticality.
- Should have private homes facing the street frontage – no commercial shops or active offices.

Imagine what it would feel like to walk from your home to the different destinations, described above. Imagine the people you would meet, what you would do – meet a friend, stop for a bite or drink, jumping into activity or seeking solitude. Imagine it for all, including the young and the elderly. Then let your imagination travel beyond these outdoor places. Visualize walking to indoor activities at each of these very different plazas and destinations. Done right most residents will find it is never boring.

Lucca, Italy

Framing Gateways to Mark Transitions

Between villages consider a gateway building in which the ground floor is the public street, but above it part of a home. Use the gateway as a frame. Make a different architectural style and different type of activity on the other side of the gateway.

If wind or noise is a concern, build the gateway so it can easily be closed, with a smaller, human sized doorway off to the side or in the middle of the wind wall door. Build large, thick, sliding pocket doors; avoid the sail effect of a hinged door.

The Town Plaza

Designate one plaza for the Town Hall, and make it bigger – big enough to hold the population of the VillageTown. Design it in such a way that it functions as an open market with stalls that can be easily set up. For this reason, this plaza should have direct access to the widest street, the Parade to fit incoming vendors driving trucks and trailers. The buildings surrounding this plaza should have upper floor balconies and flat roofs, suitable for viewing the activities in the plaza. They may also be higher, 4 story, with larger building lots for grander buildings, including detached mansions. Provide for a stage and a band-stand. One building, probably the Town Hall should have provision for a drop down wall-sized projection screen for watching outdoor films – best built into an overhanging eve, so the screen is entirely hidden and protected when not in use.

Integrate School Classrooms, Playgrounds and Meeting Spaces

In the chapter on education, we discuss VillageTown education, recommending that instead of commandeering large swaths of land to be reserved for the inwardly focused school campus, we make each village plaza the campus, and operate it in a decentralized manner to provide for checks and balances. We recommend:

- Class size small, 10 to 15 students each, never more than 20
- Classrooms clustered – no more than 3 or 4 in one place
- Classrooms with pull-out walls to allow flexible room size (one large room or two smaller rooms).
- Design classroom for school use during the day and community use when not reserved for school. This involves extra design detail such as surface wall that slide into pockets – when used as a classroom the wall shows whiteboards, corkboards with students' drawings, educational aides like the alphabet or period chart. When the class is over, the teacher slides the teaching wall into the pocket, hiding it.

Integrating the school needs with those of the community demands careful planning. We recommend:

- On each plaza set aside public space for multi-purpose classrooms and home-rooms
- The VillageTown subsidized guild halls have a school component (e.g.: music classes)
- Sports fields, equestrian areas, playgrounds and gardens have a school component
- Public halls, theaters and gymnasia have a school component

With a statistical estimate that 20% of the population is school aged (6-18), planning both places and routes for the young will do much both to enhance their life in the community, and make it easier on adults, especially elders. Routes from class to class should be on main streets, not back streets. Weather should be taken into consideration. Design school routes that have overhanging balconies over the pedestrian walkway.

The 2,500 year old stadium at Delphi, and what do children do? They run – architecture inspires behaviors

Chapter 4 – Landscape Architecture – Plants

The approach to the VillageTown makes a statement as strong as the buildings and plazas within the walls. While the VillageTown is to be built in a matter of months or years, if it is done well, it may stand for centuries. In planning for future generations, include a carefully thought-out landscape planting program on the approach to the VillageTown.

I was driving in Italy to another destination when I came upon this tree-lined route. With the sunlight filtering through, the magic of it caused me to stop, park, then stand in the middle of the road to take a photograph. It made a strong statement about the values of the people in that region, as clearly the planting was intended and the people were willing to wait decades.

Drive to New Zealand's Northland and for the most part en route the vegetation is olive drab in color. Come into Kerikeri and the landscape architecture changes; thanks to the foresight of settlers in the 1920's who had a vision of creating a citrus industry in what was a relatively barren land.

Plant fruit trees along the rural roads; make the fruit free for anyone passing by. Plant heritage apples and peaches, quince trees and figs. If the climate will support it, plant all sorts of citrus trees. Seed collectors now are gathering older species of fruit trees, ones that do not need spraying, which may have wide variations in flavor, but which are not popular with commercial growers for irrelevant reasons, (they don't last as long in storage or do well with long-distance shipping). Consider setting aside part of the annual VillageTown budget for maintenance of these trees and plants. If possible, don't hire a maintenance staff. Instead, have the VillageTown sponsor a volunteer club to tend the plants, providing them with the tools and materials.

Plant flowering trees and trees with different colored leaves, to make the approach to the VillageTown more beautiful. Selectively, plant both native and exotic trees. In selecting native plants, remember how Nature defines a garden – a collaboration between humans and nature. Native plants need to be carefully positioned with understanding of how they mature. Too often native plantings look politically correct, dominated by the will of the landscape architect rather than reflecting the inherent beauty that is found in their natural setting.

Along the roads that have high visibility approaching the VillageTown, work with local farmers to select crops that enhance the visual amenity. We live in a valley called Church Bay, which became transformed – dressed – when a number of vineyards went in. It became one of the most attractive parts of the region.

If your VillageTown site has enough land to support a greenbelt (about half of a 500± acre [200± ha] property), make it a place both to experience the outdoors and Nature. In the greenbelt, build sports fields, exercise parks, equestrian and dog-walking lands. Plant gardens, both food and flower, and make them an attractive part of the landscape. Include horticulture in the local school curriculum, and make some of the classrooms part of the gardens. Plant fields of flowers, and if the region happens to be blessed with a stand of beautiful old growth trees or even a full forest, consider the VillageTown securing the conservation rights to vest them in a heritage trust for permanent preservation.

Finally, approach plantings within the urban core with great care. Just because its green doesn't mean it will work. Choose plants that don't constantly shed, that don't aggravate allergies, and which don't overgrow so they become disproportionate with the buildings. If grass is planted, treat it as the Oxford colleges do – with great respect and with hand (quiet) mowing. If it is too much to hand mow or graze with sheep, don't plant it.

Oxford hand cut lawn

The vineyards that transformed Church Bay, New Zealand

8,000 BC +/-

When technology shifts, the definition of wealth changes.

For nomads, wealth was cattle and sheep and the hierarchy tribal – an extended family ruled by patriarchs and matriarchs.

1,500 BC +/-

When primitive technology shifted to horse-riding warriors, nomads stopped moving and built walls to protect themselves. Over time, wealth became land and the hierarchy became landed aristocracy. – the king owned the land and granted titles to vassals.

1500 AD +/-

When early science and technology introduced machining to produce things like navigation aides and guns, it became possible for Europe to trade with the East, hence wealth shifted to that which is transportable in ships… gold, silks, spices and their medium of credit redeemable in gold and silver coin. The hierarchy evolved into merchants, bankers and industrialists.

2000 AD

Now we witness a new shift in technology: instant global communications. What will be the new definition of wealth? It's looking like it will be quality of life. Unlike inequitable wealth of history, with quality of life, I cannot be wealthy if my neighbor is poor. With the world made local through broadband the poorest person in the world is my neighbor. To enjoy quality of life, all must live well.

Chapter 5 – The Local Economy

Introduction

After I wrote the first edition of this book, the world witnessed a catastrophic failure of the global economic system that brought it to the brink of disaster. It was man-made, spawned by removal of checks and balances, opportunism and greed. It makes it clear that trusting such systems is unwise. By the time I wrote the second edition, gold hit at an all time high because what were once considered reserve currencies became distrusted by too many people. We are told inflation is about rising prices, but this is a misnomer. In fact, purchasing power of major currencies, including the dollar, pound and euro is dropping.

In such troubled times, the recommended investment is in tangibles, yet most tangibles, be they precious metals or commodities are only mediums of exchange – they do nothing until you sell them to buy things you need, want or love. The best tangible is one that provides for a good life while it offers economic security. A VillageTown is one of the best good-life tangibles an ordinary family or individual will find. It enables its citizens to maintain a higher level of control over their wealth, their security and their lives. Before the economy crashed, the same principles held; now the argument is more compelling.

Unlike a conventional development that relies on the growth of the regional economy to sell new homes and offices, a VillageTown settlement focuses on the creation of a local economy not dependent on the region. Its citizens bring their jobs and businesses with them, and the settlement focuses on lowering their cost of living. By eliminating the need to drive, the average family saves about 15% of their income. By cutting food and utilities prices, the cost of living is further reduced. By setting up a wholesale buying group that uses the VillageTown's intranet, a wide range of goods and services cost less. Entertainment costs less because the community is culturally enriched. Combined purchasing power lowers the cost to live.

To leverage this purchasing power, we recommend that in the investment stage that the VillageTown establish what is in name, or in effect, a bank to process the estimated billion dollars in mortgages taken out by the 4,000 families and individuals buying homes. The bank finances construction, but when the VillageTown is complete, the stock held in trust is called in and new stock is issued, one share per house-title. In this way, the citizens gain ownership not only of their home, but a strong asset base including a thriving bank, where the profits benefit them and keep money turning locally.

The benefits of controlling ones own local economy are numerous, especially when it can take advantage of advanced technology that supports strong local money-turn. The local economy is essential to the success of the VillageTown.

The Local Economy

When a developer plans a subdivision, little consideration is given to a local economy. A growing regional economy drives the demand for more housing – more jobs means people need more homes, roads, shopping centers, schools – and, on the down side, when the economy collapses, the developer crashes. The developer responds to the economy. The fundamentals for a VillageTown are entirely different. Planning for a local economy in the VillageTown is essential to its success.

The core economic principal that distinguishes the VillageTown is this concept of self-supporting. It is for this reason that a VillageTown can be placed as much as two hours from a city (or one hour by commuter air). A local economy is one that generates wealth and then *turns* that wealth internally – at least five times before it goes back out. In today's global economy, the local economy will sell to the global and at least 20% of the VillageTown income needs to come in from the outside. The local economy is layered, built on a foundation that provides the basic needs independent of the global economy – if it melts down the Villagers will survive. The local economy is diversified. It shuns monocultures. A one company town is a bad idea, especially in these modern times when owners and investors have little loyalty to the workers and families dependent on the company's jobs. The local economy must provide conditions that encourage a wide diversity of businesses and offices to operate. Then when some collapse or move away, the local economy only suffers a bit – overall it remains healthy.

In providing for these local economic conditions, the late 20th century measurement of pecuniary-interest-over-all is toxic. We say *late 20th century* because before then business had a significant ethical foundation, predominantly set out by the church, which expected they make decisions that considered the morality of the time. While predation occurred, it was not until the late 20th century that new generations of business leaders were trained by business schools that the sole measure was profit and legal predation was legitimate. We are finding this is proving to be a very bad instruction as predation and its subsets poverty and pollution wreak havoc. Some fear catastrophic damage may be pending because of how we have conducted our business affairs. As a friend quipped the other day, *How's it been going now that businessmen have been running the world for 400 years?*

To properly evaluate business decision making and action, we hear of the 3-P's:

People: how decisions impact people – their employees, their subcontractors and suppliers, their customers
Planet: how actions impact the planet – global warming, pollution and ecosystems
Profits: is the business healthy? Are its investors getting a good return? Is it rewarding initiative and hard work?

To this, we suggest three more "P's" need to be added:

Public: More than just the workers and the customers. How does a business impact the public, the community?
Place: More than the impact on the planet, what impacts our common locality? In this, we need to do more than just avoid or mitigate adverse effects. How does business success make our VillageTown better, more beautiful?
Prosperity: how the outcomes create wealth, in contrast to converting wealth from others. Is the business contributing to the common wealth of the VillageTown and its surrounding region? When a place has a large divide between abject poverty and affluence, the community cannot be healthy. The wealthy must imprison themselves behind security gates and video surveillance. In extreme cases, they employ armed guards and the freedom of their children to be normal kids having the run of the community and nature beyond is utterly curtailed. This is not prosperity.

New economic conditions are supportive of village economies

In the late 19th century, with the rise of industrialization and concentration of business in the cities, the economy of villages weakened. In many places villages went into decline as the young moved away to find work in the factories and offices which required many people in one office or factory building in order to pay for the massive machinery required to make profits. Some villages became ghost towns; others remained home mostly to the elderly and the weak, struggling to get by.

With the onset of global telecommunications and transport, with the invention of automated systems that no longer require people live near their work, for many the opportunity to return to village life becomes a viable economic proposition. For this to happen, one cannot simply set out roads and buildings. A well thought out local economy plan is a necessity.

The bank, the BMW and the Peanut Seller

The fundamentals of a strong local economy

In normal economies, at least 20% of the income should come from outside. Sell local to global.

$$$: Make decisions that are good for people
$$$: Make decisions that are good for place
$$$: Make decisions that are good for the planet
$$$: Plan for diversity in local businesses and jobs.
$$$: Each dollar should turn at least 5 times; 20 is better
$$$: Invest in info-systems; track number of turns.
$$$: It costs less to save a dollar than it does to earn one
$$$: Control your own food & energy locally
$$$: Control your money; own your own bank
$$$: Combine your purchasing power
$$$: Don't waste water, it is essential to your survival
$$$: Don't mortgage your children's future
$$$: Make things; do not lose your skill base or tools
$$$: Plan for three economic states – bad, normal, boom
$$$: Pay attention to unanticipated negative side effects

Outside Income and Earnings

Sell local to global (L2G). At least 20% of the gross income and earnings in the VillageTown should come from outside the VillageTown. Broadband technology enables people to meet remotely, to run machines and robotics. L2G includes retired persons on pensions, businesses that buy in raw materials and resell them as finished goods and other normal participants in the wider economy. The VillageTown plan cannot dictate such income producing activities, but it can provide the design to attract such people, such as a 50 acre (20 ha.) industrial park. As my grandfather said "build a birdhouse and the birds will come."

Pay careful attention to the kinds of activities you seek to attract. Do not overly depend on the global economy – it is too volatile and often does things that are good for some of its proponents but bad for the VillageTown and its citizens.

The Theory of Unanticipated Negative Side Effects

Side effects are omnidirectional, but evaluation tends to unidirectional – think bomb versus rifle shot. Evaluators focus attention on the target, not on the side effects. This is also called tunnel vision or wearing blinders (blinkers in UK).

Side effects range from very good to very bad. The evaluator concentrates on the good direct effects to justify the product or process. The somewhat good side-effects are typically picked up by marketing departments seeking to create good press. The very bad effects (like a hand grenade with a 100 meter/yard lethal range) are observed by the experts and if not mitigated, the product or service is not introduced into the marketplace. The danger comes in the middle, the marginally negative side effects; the ones that:

- Take longer than normal human observation to have an obvious effect
- Involve complex interaction with other forces, so the cause is not obvious
- The not-noticeable ones, and/or
- The noticeable but inconvenient ones that have adverse effects on the career or earnings of the evaluator or expert if they speak up.

Unanticipated negative side effects are cumulative – slowly corroding quality of life. Communities and nations that seem worn out, damaged, tired or suffering malaise are often victims of unanticipated negative side effects.

Before introducing any technology or processes into the VillageTown or its local economy, pay careful attention to any and all negative side effects that will have an adverse impact on the wellbeing of the VillageTown and its people. The side effects will not be printed on the package.

Money Turn (also known as the multiplier effect)

At present, some great financial minds in the world are working on the idea of alternative currencies. This is not a new idea, except that in the past it often would be used by a local community when the national currency suffered crippling inflation and was no longer functional. While some VillageTowns may want to experiment with such concepts, my sense is that this is too radical and will attracted unwanted attention from powerful vested interests. In examining alternative currencies, it appears one of the prime principles behind such alternatives is the concept of "turn" – how often the money is spent locally.

There may be a better way to support money-turn: education and information. If the citizens understand that their local economy benefits when they patronize local businesses, most of them will act out of enlightened self-interest. To do this, they need information… what is the local content of the transaction they are about to make. If the community owns its own bank, and most transactions are run using its intranet, a database can be built that separates transactions that are paid internally and externally. Over time this will grow a record of the local content of any product, which can be displayed on the cash register at time of purchase. It won't be precise, but it should be good enough. This approach favors informed choice over compulsion.

It's cheaper to save a dollar than earn one

It's cheaper to save a dollar than to earn one

Think about it… to earn a dollar you must work for and pay tax on it. But if you save a dollar, you neither work nor pay. A central theme in VillageTown design is to cut out unnecessary costs while increasing quality of life. In its construction, the walls cost less to build and insulate better, saving both one-time and ongoing costs. Cut out the middleman on food, and you can buy better, healthier food for less. Remove the need to drive every day, and you save on average 15% of your income. Common sense.

The other day I visited a Canadian who moved to New Zealand and opened a business importing a better solar panel. As an advertising feature, he drives around in this vehicle. For some peculiar reason, NZ classifies it as a mobility vehicle which means it requires no drivers license, registration, inspection or insurance. Most remarkably however, is the solar panel on its roof means that they have not refueled it in the two years they have been driving it. They leave it outside (it has weatherproof doors for the winter or on rainy days) and the sun recharges the lead-acid batteries. They tried more expensive lithium batteries but found the extra weight of lead-acid lowered the center of gravity. They get local transport where their only cost was the US$7,000 capital outlay. In the VillageTown such a vehicle would have its controller set for low-speed, although it can go 50 kph.

At present, such products are cheapest sourced in China. But with the rapid advances in 3-D printing, a slow-speed vehicle that does not need freeway levels of safety will be able to be manufactured in the VillageTown industrial park. Do not underestimate the changes that are coming.

Is it good for the community?

Most people have the capacity to ask, "Is this good for me and my community?" Will it engender prosperity and wellbeing? It is a remarkably simple question, but once one begins to ask it, spending decisions changes.

In a VillageTown, financial decisions that are bad for the people and community are avoided. In the 19th century, business embraced Darwin's theory of evolution, because it gave scientific cover for business decisions that were good for the proponent at the expense of the general good. Predation was natural, and therefore OK. Now science is telling us two things. First, that Darwin was wrong – indeed, in mature ecosystems the natural world cooperates. As the evolution biologist, Dr. Elisabet Sahtouris commented, "If we ran our bodies the way we run our global economy, our brains and stomach would get all the nutrients and our fingers and toes would fall off – imagine, a spot market for blood!" Second, science is telling us that our 20th century Darwinian exploitation of the earth is beginning to bite back. Unless we return resources to balance, quality of life may decline precipitously, even catastrophically.

Provide for diverse industries and jobs

Nature teaches us the importance of diversity – when environmental conditions turn harsh, not all plants and animals die – thus life goes on. With many different plants and animals in a mature ecosystem, nature also teaches us the importance of self-interested cooperation – bees pollinate flowers to get food, yet the way they do it assures both that the flowers will seed new plants and the bees will continue to have a food source. If we study nature carefully, we shall find in it most of the lessons we need to establish a thriving and durable local economy.

In the 20th Century, we threw quality of life out of balance by teaching our best and brightest that what matters in life is winning and that profits are the measure of winning. This has created perhaps the most aggressive economic system the world has ever known. Even the most conservative scientists now tell us its side effects may be hazardous for our health – our more radical scientists tell us catastrophic failure of earth's systems may occur in our lifetime or that of our children.

Coins tell stories.

Collapse – The 100 mark brass alloy *Notgeld* coin on the left is a local currency struck in 1922 by the Province of Westfalia in Germany when post WW-I rampant inflation had destroyed the value of the German national currency. The economy had collapsed and the seeds were being sown for the rise of Nazism. Germans were starving – a condition hard for those born after WW-II to imagine. The metal of the coin was not representative of its value, like today's money, it represents an agreement on value.

Normal – At the same time Germany was in crisis, the British domestic economy was in a stable condition, as represented by this 1923 silver half crown. France and Great Britain paid the price for this inequity two decades later when Germany struck back.

Boom – This 1915 gold Sovereign of the British Empire represents a time of economic boom (for some). It marked the pinnacle of a three century boom in which the British Sovereign was minted in Australia, Canada, India and South Africa as well as at the London Mint, as Britain's Empire covered 20% of the world's land mass.

So how do we create a local economy that is both in balance with our social, cultural and environmental wellbeing, and at the same time is structured to be durable in three economic conditions:

- Bust – The economy will collapse
- Normal – Things will remain pretty much as they are now
- Boom – The economy will expand

Normal – Most economic planning presumes conditions will remain as they are now. This is the easiest form of planning, as we know what conditions to expect, and to plan for. Yet too often, this represents the limit of economic planning, and even planning within "normal" conditions demands care. The economic impact of 9-11 where the travel industry saw flights curtailed literally overnight, or the almost-lockup of the global financial system are examples of normal conditions that can severely damage the local economy of a community too dependent on the global economy on or part thereof.

Boom – Booms are different from the gradual increase in global prosperity to which we have become accustomed (thanks to technology and cheap oil). Economic booms are usually caused by some change in policy that releases access to credit to stimulate a national economy. After WW-II, the USA made a conscious decision to keep the boom effects of the wartime economy going, and they did so by inventing the suburb. This book shows how those policies destroyed a sense of community in much of America, replacing the extended family with the nuclear, and produced a host of social and environmental challenges that seem to get worse, not better. Margaret Thatcher changed the rules in the U.K. and the economy boomed. However, the same adverse effects occurred. Communities saw the rise of sprawling subdivisions, the roads became clogged and the young moved away from their community in search of employment.

Bust – The Westphalia coin in the photograph reminds us that economies can collapse and first-world people can starve if systems fail. We have now built a food system almost entirely dependent on diesel-fuelled tractors, diesel delivery trucks and a long-distance supermarket distribution system. More recently, we shifted to an economic and communication system entirely dependent on computers – a system that only runs if the electrical grid supplies power. In the Great Depression in the USA, poor people say they hardly noticed – because in those days they kept gardens in an America that was predominantly rural and village. Today it would be different, all would suffer. The potential for economic collapse always looms, especially as the global economic system becomes more complex and vulnerable. Prudence dictates that in planning for a local economy, include provisions to assure the VillageTown sustained its people, and those of the surrounding region, in such adverse conditions.

The challenge is to maintain a direct rural and farm connection for local, good food, and establish an underlying local economy that can operate independent of the larger economy and which can put unemployed people to work in hard times. In boom times, we need an attractive and prosperous enough local economy to keep the VillageTown's citizens and youth from packing up and heading for the promises of streets paved with gold that beckons. A strong local economy and high quality of life will protect the VillageTown.

Diversity

Avoid creating a company town, or a one-industry village. The purpose of having independently-owned work places surrounding the plazas and on some of the main pedestrian streets is to foster economic diversity. Industrial centralization killed village economies when stronger profits could be realized by moving people to large factories and offices. Now, the western economies are becoming Broadband economies, meaning much of the work may be done using computers, telecommunications and other related tools. One now can even run a manufacturing system where the machine is in one continent, and the controls are in another. Distance no longer means what it once meant. Replacing distance with the speed of light – telecommunications – gives life and potential to the re-emergence of VillageTowns. Plan for many smaller businesses.

Avoid franchises and chain store operations. They extract most of the money spent there, only circulating low-wage salaries. They tend to be bland, lacking in character, and the authentic aspect of the owner-operated business is often missing.

The Creative Class

The VillageTown will naturally attract a significant number of both independent, self-employed electronically-linked workers and telecommuters who may be employed by large companies happy to have workers live where they want as long as they remain in contact and can be productive. The VillageTown infrastructure must serve them well both now and for the future – this means excellent, future-proofed telecommunications, good freight delivery and direct connection to national and international transport systems when needed.

If we read Richard Florida's books on the Creative Class, we find he points us to an economic engine not defined as an industry, but a class of people. By creative, he refers not just to the artists, but also to scientists, engineers, architects, designers, researchers, filmmakers and a host of professionals whose day-to-day work involves thinking stuff up – inventing, improving or designing new goods, new ideas and new services. Allied with these primary creators, he identifies secondary creators, those lateral thinking investors, financiers, lawyers and other professional support people who assist making the primary creators effective in their work.

Florida identifies the Creative Class as making a major contribution to economic wellbeing. Savvy governments around the world have picked up on his message to attract these creators to their nations and their local communities. Florida observes that the traditional attractions – the big sports stadium, convention center or casino do nothing for these people. Instead, a key influencing criteria for their selection of place to live comes in personal quality of life: conviviality, citizenship, art, intellect, spirit.

In creating an attractive environment that will draw these important contributors to the local economy, look to fostering an enriched local cultural experience. Attracting and supporting the creative and performing arts – musicians, actors, painters, dancers and so on, even if low income, sets the stage for a far

more interesting community life. Excellence in the arts does not come from a large population base but from a community design that pays careful attention to the artists' needs. In an uncontrolled environment this produces gentrification – the artists arrive, make the place trendy, then the money-making moves in to rub shoulders and ends up jacking the price of housing up so high the artists leave. In a planned environment, the artists are attracted, but then protected so they can afford to stay, and also so they want to stay.

Of course, arts is not the only criteria. Site selection that offers outdoor activity becomes a draw card as well. Richard Florida observes that traditional workers who engage in hard physical labor prefer passive entertainment after hours, while Creative Class workers who may spend their work time at a desk or in a chair want to get on a bike, go for a hike or kayak a river when the work day is over. For them a sports field is a flat piece of ground where a pick-up game of tag rugby or soccer can be played, not a multi-million dollar stadium to passively watch professionals. In addition to the outdoors, they are attracted by a safe place to raise children, clean air and water, an amenable climate and a diverse and interesting social network.

Having identified the Creative Class as an economic engine that contributes significantly to a local economy, it becomes important not solely to create an attraction for this one economic group. For a start, it would create an elitist community. Worse, on its own it is vulnerable to global economic downturn or systems failure especially telecommunications systems. If they fail, the flow of information and money could bring the western economy to a halt within hours. Best to have a diverse economy of which the Creative Class is one part.

The Local Food Economy

At a fundamental economic level, the VillageTown Plan must think local, especially about the basics. Traditionally food, clothing and shelter were the three basic requirements for civilized life, to which we added refrigerators, stoves, washing machines and heating... plus cars, telephones, money and stores to purchase these essential goods. It is a commentary on our civilization that if we take away these latter essentials, millions would face crisis in short order.

Beginning with food, the benefits of an organized economic system should be a primary design consideration in setting out the framework of the VillageTown.

It involves three key parts:
- Establish a computer-based purchasing system, so families can centralize orders for food, enabling a VillageTown food coordinator to negotiate wholesale orders with local farmers in advance of the growing season.
- Establish a food-banking system where families can

Organic wine grown locally on Waiheke Island

- deposit funds in a VillageTown Food Bank from which farmers borrow money to plant the crops, so the interest stays in the local economy.
- Require all residences have a Food Box next to the Mail Box, so the delivery systems runs from farmer to depot to customer, not require the customer be at home.

The benefits of this system are multiple:

- The food will cost less, and saving money costs less than making money (Remember: it's cheaper to save a dollar than earn one – the easiest way to make you and your community wealthier is to cut expenses).
- Local food can taste better. The VillageTown may seek to become a Slow Food Community, where the quality and character of food becomes an important part not just of the economy, but also of the social and cultural wellbeing of the community. Food becomes integral to conviviality– an art mastered by the French and Italians centuries ago.
- In the event global systems breakdown due to war, climate change, energy costs, global depression, economic crash or something else unimaginable, the local food source is protected with a closed loop system. This is especially true the extent to which the farming can be less dependent on petroleum. As transport costs go up, local foods place less demand for diesel. From an environment perspective, this also means less pollution.
- Local food markets support local farmers going organic. Most chemical farming is done to increase yield, not to make food healthier for the people who eat the chemically treated food. Chemical applications are about risk management where the government establishes a standard of what risk level is acceptable – how many people may get sick or die before the risk is deemed unacceptable. Why do we have to eat risk assessed food when for all time up until the last century, all food was organic? Why experiment with our health and wellbeing, especially when the alternative is affordable and needs no risk assessment? With a farmer-to-customer direct food system, the farmer can see steady and comfortable earnings on non-chemical foods and the customers will still pay less than for conventional food because all the middlemen, packaging, processing and long-distance transport costs are removed.

The Industrial Park

If the scale of the VillageTown permits, plan for a walk-to industrial park. Put it next to the motorpool and the freight depot. Locate it the noisy end of the noise overlay map, near some of the youth housing villages and noisy sculptors. If a natural feature such as a port forms part of the geography, look to placing the industrial activities close to the port, but design it in a way that villagers walk over to observe industrial activity with sufficient physical separation –perhaps multiple levels – to assure safety for both workers and observers. In classical times, industrial sites, especially ports, were the stage for much human activity. It's fascinating to watch, so make it safe and permitted. It is entirely possible to design with safety regulations. In doing so the character of the VillageTown is enriched. In setting out the Industrial Zone, therefore, make it a multi-level design, with industrial manufacturing, shipping and storing on the ground levels, but provide for elevated pedestrian observation areas including provision for cafes, factory shops and even residences for some industrial workers.

Industrial Capital Investment Plan

VillageTown industry can be divided into two major groups – sell local to local and local to global. Because the VillageTown plan envisions a major capital investment both in VillageTown infrastructure and in individuals building homes and workplaces, the industrial opportunities can include those which begin by selling local to build the village, and then when the VillageTown is built, to transform into selling similar products to the national and global markets.

The most difficult part for many businesses is getting established – finding the customers and building the business. With immediate, local demand created by the construction of the VillageTown, the business plan need not focus on finding first customers, but instead get right into the business of making the products – the first customers will be the VillageTown Civitas Corporation (the ViTo) and the settlers building homes, work places and building the VillageTown infrastructure. This pays for tooling and capital investment. This is best accomplished if the VillageTown Plan includes industrial economic wealth-creation as an essential part of the plan, just as it does in building streets, utilities and public spaces.

The VillageTown Plan may elect to form stock holding ventures, with the customers investing in the small businesses from whom they will purchase. Typically small business operators are good at product, but generally not as strong in the skills

Read carefully, makes sense when you think about it. Found in Cornwall, UK

of running a profitable business. If the VillageTown Plan includes establishing these ventures with professional management to ensure success and profitability, all win. This is sometimes referred to as Community Capitalism.

Some of the seed capital for industrial development can actually come from the VillageTown Capital Investment Fund. In building a normal subdivision, a significant investment is required for roads. Because the VillageTown saves on much of this investment, it frees capital for other purposes, and some of the freed capital should go into a local capital investment fund to provide seed capital for the local industries, especially the initial industries focused on building the village.

The Building and Building Ornament Industries

The first industry to start in the VillageTown is the building and building-ornament industries, which need to be in place when construction begins. The VillageTown may require several thousand buildings, which may represent an investment of half to a billion dollars or more. Rather than spend this money on pre-manufactured products imported from other places, many of these elements can be manufactured on site – at a lower cost, with better quality.

This market includes construction material, such as the manufacturing of mineral based thick-wall blocks, structural columns and other building components of the industry. Next, make local joinery – doors and windows, and ornament such as lintels (which can become a high art of carving), wrought iron and gutters. 4,000 homes need about 100,000 doors and windows. Make them in the industrial park.

The next layer of construction components come in cabinets where the cost of shipping boxes made mostly of empty space argues for locally made goods. In addition, the industry has become notorious for making poor quality goods of what is, in effect, glued sawdust panels that warp when a pipe leaks and that too often break down prematurely. Higher quality raw materials can still provide affordable products if the manufacturer is local and sells direct to the end user.

Once the VillageTown is built, there is no reason these industries cannot continue. They may find their products in demand elsewhere, provided transport remains affordable. Some may branch out into other new VillageTowns, opening subsidiary businesses. The plan should include business plans for these independent businesses, so from the day they open their doors, they have in place their transition plan from selling to local markets to marketing globally.

A 4,000 building VillageTown will need over 100,000 doors and windows. Two or three companies can be started in the Industrial Park and capitalize all their tooling and start-up investment with such an order. Photo taken in Poundbury. These windows may be higher maintenance.

This stool is made from leather-covered plywood nailed on some firewood. The leather and its foam padding was affixed with copper boat nails. The stools withstand great abuse by children and teens.

The Four Hour Chair

As an experiment in working with low income people who would save money building a home, but then incur thousands of dollars in furniture store debt, we made the 4-hour chair – a tutorial for people who had used tools but never made furniture. We then found it was a useful training exercise for everyone.

The challenge in making a chair comes in ensuring that all four legs solidly stand on the floor; that it is comfortable and won't come loose or fall apart after years of daily use.

Much of the time spent in making a normal chair comes from precise measuring to assure the wood fits together – mastery of the tape measure for precise lengths and protractor for precise angles. This requires years of apprenticeship to get right. We began by tossing out the tape measure and protractor.

Instead we set out a flat piece of 3/4 inch plywood upon which the four legs were screwed from the underneath. This assured all four chair legs were cut square and would sit solidly on the floor. After we screwed down the first leg, we placed the cushion on the plywood to identify where the other three legs should go. We let the cushion determine the seat size, rather than take measurements.

Next the seat frame was made – the size of the cushion, less any overlap on the front. The seat frame was a simple rectangle, 2x4's screwed together with readily available, self-drilling, self-countersinking deck screws which, because of their design, hold firm after years of use. A top was then affixed to the seat frame. The top can be thin plywood, saddle leather, upholstery webbing or rope. No measuring – match the cushion.

The seat frame front was then affixed to the front chair legs with a single strong screw through each leg. For the next step two volunteers were needed. The cushioned seat was rested on stacked phone books until the front height felt right, and the front of the seat frame was single-screwed to the front legs at that height to create a pivot point. Then one volunteer carefully sat on the front-fixed cushioned seat while the other (strong) volunteer held and lifted the rear part until the sitter pronounced the angle just right. Then the chair maker screwed in the rear screws, thus fixing the perfect angle. No geometry – fly by seat of your pants.

The same process was repeated for the seat back and for setting the arm height to tailor the chair to the body. The first chair took two hours to assemble, and when done, produced a perfectly comfortable, rather ugly and heavy chair made out of 2x4 (50x100) timber. The remaining two hours were then spent with an angle grinder and sander cutting away over 50% of the timber, shaping the square angles into a unified sculpted piece of furniture. Human scaled design - faster, easier, great outcome, wealth produced.

In the 20th century business schools taught us that two major ways to generate new wealth were:
(1) a shift in technology [case study: IBM] and
(2) organize a disorganized business [case study: McDonalds].

In the case of the 4 hour chair, the shift in technology was the lowly deck screw. A self-countersinking, self-drilling screw with a square head shape to make it harder to strip, it has a very sharp, narrow point, so drilling a pilot hole is unnecessary, especially in soft wood. Its unique shank design means it propels into place with shallower thread to spread out the force, so the screw takes less energy to put in, but is difficult to pull out or work loose over time. After ten years, the 4-hour chairs are still solid, with no glue, only the screws holding the timber together.

The second way to generating new wealth – organizing a disorganized business, is found in the 4 hour chair by abandoning time-consuming skill of precutting wood parts to match up. Grinding then sanding two pieces of wood already fastened to each other is faster, and the best way to determine if an angle is comfortable is to sit on it.

This lesson in chair making has two tangible benefits for Village building.
1) It shows how untrained people can rapidly master vernacular processes
2) It gives them something to sit on.

Hard and Soft Furnishings Industries

The next logical industries are those related to furnishing the several thousand homes, offices, shops and public buildings. Hard furnishings include chairs, tables, sofas and bed frames. The hard furnishing industry can be a natural outgrowth of the cabinets especially if this is set out in the Plan. When building a new home, often old furnishings don't work – wrong size or wrong style. With several thousand customers at hand the local market opportunity is both large and enables the new businesses to overcome the hardest part of any business – start-up.

Soft furnishings include curtains, rugs, bedspreads, table clothes, towels and other fabrics. Two particular good industrial models stand out in this area: toile and woven durable fabrics.

Perhaps one of the best examples of an intentional industry in this area comes from France when in the 18th century Louis XIV began supporting the local manufacture of brightly-colored, block-printed cotton fabrics that were light-weight and washable. Known as Toile, the origins are from India, where in the 15th century Portuguese ships brought such fabrics from India to France. By the 18th century, manufacturing was in France, and the designs shifted to the fields, flowers and rural scenes of France. The industry now offers a complete French Country style popular in many countries. Products go beyond fabric to include dishes, picture frames, clothing and wallpaper. Curiously though because the origins of the process was block print, it hasn't seemed to translate effectively to woven products such as rugs, blankets, hangings and upholstery.

For woven products, we find art merging into industry with indigenous cultures such as the Navajo and Zapotec Native American tribes. Once again, just as with the India-inspired French Country style, we find the Navajo product in fact is derivative – cross-cultural in its origin. Navaho did not make rugs until the American traders established a market for them, often recommending colors, patterns and designs. Some of the best 19th C. rugs are called Germantown because the yarn came from the Germantown factory in Pennsylvania, some 2,000 miles east. Not all Navajo patterns come from traditional native designs. Traders provided the weavers with Oriental rug patterns to appeal to the taste of US East Coast city customers. A century later, this design has become the American Western style, and like the French Country style has expanded to a wide range of furnishings. This can happen in the VillageTown, and with the Internet, the market becomes global.

Such industries provide good earnings for their producers. Over time, the products established a reputation where authenticity becomes the selling point, thus protecting them from cheap imitations made in low-labor cost manufacturing countries. Navaho rugs began as market driven products and only later emerged as collectable folk art.

The opportunity to establish such a regional industry comes from the initial market of several thousand new homes and commercial establishments being built in several years. While not all residents will want to purchase a local vernacular theme, many may choose so, both as part of the process of defining the identity of the community, and even more so if they become investors in local capitalism. Once established, and especially in the early VillageTowns, when their point of difference gains substantial international publicity, the "Village style" may become a sought after product line, one easier marketed thanks to the Internet.

The Cobbler

Know your banker, know your farmer and know your cobbler is a good slogan for the VillageTown. Instead of spending $25,000 on a new car, spend a lot less on a custom-fitted pair of shoes.

In Europe there still are cobblers that sell life-time shoes. People who buy them say they are the most comfortable one can imagine, and when they need work the cobbler refurbishes them. Go to those old towns where people still walk and bike to work, and look at what they wear on their feet. Have a look at the photograph just before the table of contents in this book. The shoes and bicycles are classically elegant and you can be assured they are comfortable. Instead of buying a €20,000 car, they buy elegant Italian-made shoes and bicycles.

You will be walking everywhere; shoes become the symbol of VillageTown life. Perhaps the purchase price of a new home should include three free pairs of locally-made, life-time shoes.

Retirement Income as a Part of the Local Economy

Presently, government pensions and private retirement funds provide substantial outside income for a local community. We say at present because there is some concern among the financial industry that with the baby boom retiring we may find payout exceeds income for too long, thus bankrupting the retirement and pension funds. However, it is unlikely that all pensions will dry up, and while it is important to have strong provisions for local support of elders – including lowering the cost of living – the income flow from pensions and retirement benefits does form a significant income stream for the local economy. The more that income stream, which comes from outside the village, can be "money-turned" in the VillageTown, the better.

The Visitor (but not the Tourist) Industry

Tourism has been sold as a "clean and green" industry, but in practice, too often it proves to be destructive to social, cultural, economic and environmental wellbeing. The problem comes when people arrive in a small community expecting to pay to be entertained. They tend to produce a boom-bust economy, as they arrive in large numbers when the weather is good or on holidays, and the local economy suffers during the off season when they stay at home. Employment tends to be at the bottom end of the scale – too often wages that won't support purchase of a local home – tour drivers, dishwashers, shop clerks in T-shirt shops. The social interaction tends to be answering the same questions and hearing the same jokes to the point where locals

> Reminder: "Turn" is the number of times a dollar gets spent locally. A pension dollar that goes to pay a non-local bank mortgage comes in and goes out. A pension dollar that buys local food from a farmer who uses it to pay the local food-bank loan has turned twice. If the local food bank investor then spends the dollar on a night at the local theater, which pays the actors, the dollar has turned four times. The higher the turn, the wealthier the community. Turn works best when people get feedback on the turns their dollars do.

wish the tourists would send their money but stay at home. Even eco-tourism is problematic as tourists come to see the natural environment find their very presence in large numbers tends to harm fragile attractions they came to see – they love it to death.

The Visitor Industry may look similar, but is entirely different, both in character and in its effect on community wellbeing. Visitors are people who come individually or in very small groups for a particular predetermined purpose and a particular prearranged destination. They come seven days a week, they come year-round, and they disperse, so their effect is not as great on the prime areas of attraction. Their interaction with locals tends to be more give and take. The locals are left feeling refreshed, not exhausted, and often both visitor and host leave having learned something new.

Developing a Visitor Industry requires an intention built into the VillageTown Plan. Create reasons why visitors would come, and include the visitor experience in the VillageTown master plan. The creative and performing arts is always a good draw, and has the additional benefit of enabling artists to make a living on their art, rather than holding down a day job to pay the bills. If the primary manufacturing of building materials, hard and soft housing goods is developed, this is certain to generate

We were on the island of Santorini, taking photographs for this book. We got a room on the worker's side of the island, not the tourist places. Outside our window were women harvesting beans. When we ordered dinner from a local place, the beans on the plate came from that garden.

Oxford: A man in a top hat lead a group of visitors, and from time to time he would stop, set up his ladder and tell a story of that place.

visitors who come both to buy, but also to establish a closer connection to what they are purchasing. In designing the work places for these industries, include visitor safety in the plan, so safety regulations permit visitors to observe. For example, in a fabric workshop where it is deemed unsafe to have visitors on the shop floor, design a mezzanine walk above where visitors can watch but not disturb or build a glass wall to separate work space from visitor space.

For the first VillageTowns, a great opportunity exists to create a VillageTown Institute to train visitors wishing to learn how to build VillageTowns in other places. There are so many elements – only briefly covered in a book such as this one – which can form the core of a curriculum for a professional certificate in village building. In addition to in-depth programs, where visitors may stay for months, the opportunity to create short workshops can make a substantial contribution to the local economy.

In accommodating visitors, give attention to timeless patterns such as the Travelers' Inn instead of the modern motel or hotel. Too often modern travel is characterized by isolation, by getting a bed for the night, and eating alone or with the people with whom one is travelling. Until the 20th century, travelers stayed in inns, real inns. The inns had a there a large public hall where locals and travelers would mingle. Tables tended to be long with bench seating, so people would not isolate themselves but strike up a conversation. Sadly, in the 20th century, most of the remaining such inns tend to be drinking holes for old locals, often with a sour or damp smell, and decidedly unwelcome for visitors. Such a fate is unnecessary especially if the master plan provides for Travelers Inns and does not encourage motels or hotels that isolate people from the community. Visitors add more than income to a community. They bring perspective, stories and sometimes friendship.

Students

Perhaps the archetypal successful student industry is found in England's Oxford/Cambridge where, for over a thousand years, the primary local economy is based on academia. Unlike modern mega-universities, "Ox-Bridge" managed to keep the atmosphere, the utter delight of the aesthetic experience, in addition to superior scholarship. University buildings sit next to private residences, shops and restaurants, and bicycles serve as primary transport for students and professors alike. In examining the potential for an academic component to the VillageTown Plan, elements of the Ox-Bridge model should be integrated into VillageTown design, high-density yet with enclosed greens to provide a sense of peace and tranquility.

The VillageTown Plan may wish to consider forming an alliance with an existing university to offer a branch campus to add this economic and cultural component to VillageTown life. The existing university need not even be in the same country,

Oxford Students

What began as a bookstore for local students became a national institution

as many top universities seek to establish overseas campuses for their senior and graduate students.

From an economic basis, this provides employment for scholars, support staff and income opportunity for services catering to students. The VillageTown should focus on upper level students. They tend to be better behaved as the party animals tend to get flushed out of the system by the first or second year.

Advanced education when mixed with a rich cultural life can make a five to ten thousand population community remarkably rich. For example, a university presence supports real bookstores, not just the best-seller industry. The students and faculty enrich the local culture keeping it fresh, as new people come for their term of study or visiting role as a lecturer or professor. Of course, such a presence provides direct employment, but it also provides a labor pool of lower-paid student workers. Entry-level jobs become harder to fill as a community becomes desirable. Students are always grateful for the jobs.

Regional Asset Opportunities

The VillageTown is not an island, nor is it a colony imposed on a host region; it is not a gated community. Rather it is an economic engine for the host region and it is important that while the VillageTown citizens (current and for the foreseeable needs of future generations) are its shareholders; the people and communities of the host region are its stakeholders.

If the host region already has a working food system, don't create a competitor, ask the host to expand its expertise. If there is a local bank, credit union or other financial institution, explore how they can marry with the VillageTown to embrace the Legacy Fund, the savings of 10,000 citizens and the impact of hundreds of millions in new money coming into the region.

If the profits are large enough, the VillageTown should invest in the host region. For example, in one candidate site, the rural areas lack broadband and the service providers have no interest in serving those areas because there is not enough business to justify it. If the VillageTown defines its economic catchment area as the whole region (in that case, the county), it then invests in that broadband backbone so that it can engage those rural areas in its economic community. For example, the food systems should support small-scale farming which includes say a chicken farmer who supplies 10-50 dozen eggs a week. The food computer system coordinates order entry so a carton of eggs from egg-farm A is tagged as going to customers A, B & C. The food collection truck collects those eggs on its daily run (dropping off the egg cartons used last week) and the tablet in the truck keeps track of where those eggs go. As soon as the eggs are collected, ownership moves from the farm to the consumer, and the computer system pays the farmer. The eggs arrive at the VillageTown freight depot, and again the computer system tells the driver which house to drop off each carton of eggs. Each house has a chilled food box next to the mailbox, so that the cost of the eggs has virtually no middleman charges other than the transport. All the rest of the transaction is in software.

Celebration of regional qualities: In terms of regional opportunities, we are noticing that many of our prime candidates for settlements are in wine districts: good climate, great lifestyle, very beautiful. While not everyone drinks wine, such regional amenities may serve as regional asset opportunities with their own festivals celebrated in the VillageTown.

VillageTown Services and Shops

Except for local food, the economic opportunities discussed so far focus on wealth building from the outside. Even the primary construction and furnishing industries to build the village involve money from outside, since most if not all VillageTown Founders will come from somewhere else. Once the VillageTown becomes settled, the "Turn Businesses" make a substantial contribution to the economic wellbeing of the VillageTown.

The core public life of the village happens on the plaza. This means the plaza needs local businesses such as the cafe and the village shops. The primary income these local businesses earn will come from other residents. The challenge to the VillageTown Plan is to set a very high goal as to the average number of turns a dollar makes before it leaves the VillageTown (including the outlying farms that must be considered as part of the local area for the purpose of economic wellbeing). If a cafe serves peppermint tea from plants grown on a nearby farm, economic wellbeing of the community is higher than if the money is spent on an overseas company that ships the boxes of tea to the VillageTown.

As mentioned briefly above, of utmost importance is that most, if not all of these shops and services are owner-operated, not franchises or chains. Community character and quality of life comes from the proprietor standing behind the counter, ready to be of assistance, making decisions based on the pulse of his local community. The outcome of franchised branding is blanding. The chain or franchise makes money, but it is bland, characterless, and adds nothing to the sense of place or community. By having the VillageTown own the underlying land on a leasehold basis, a VillageTown can begin with a policy of *No;* thus attempts by chains or franchises to break in begin on the back foot. By endowing the VillageTown with a substantial litigation fund, it can fight off aggressive attempts to crack the town. Of course, once operational the VillageTown may, by referendum majority vote, let a franchise in. But best to start with No.

Credit Unions, Farm Banks and Local Banks

Banks are in the business of money. They take in money, loan out money, cover their expenses and make a profit on the difference. Because the VillageTown involves thousands of buildings constructed at the same time, substantial capital is involved – the total value could be in the range of one-to-two billion dollars or more. Add to that perhaps 65%+ of the VillageTown population employed or self-employed (the rest mostly children and elders) and we are talking about real money. How does the VillageTown Plan incorporate financial institutions to manage the flows of money and keep the profits local?

The Mega-Million Dollar Legacy Fund

What happens when 4,000 home buyers pre-identify and commit to their new home at the same time? The price of construction benefits by efficiencies of scale – a lot of money is saved. But if those savings were passed on to the individual buyers, too many would take a quick profit, which does nothing for the community. Besides, they are not entitled to it because it was the group commitment that made it possible, not the individual. Instead, those net profits should be retained by the organizing company and then, when the job is done, the company should be recast as a VillageTown operating company – including the potentially hundreds of millions of dollars in the VillageTown bank. Let's say that 4,000 people buy homes at an average (meaning some are priced higher and some lower) of $250,000 for a total of a billion dollars. Let's say that the savings from efficiencies of scale amounted to $100 million.

The idea is that the organizing company establishes a Legacy Fund with that $100 million that is owned by the citizens of the VillageTown. The Legacy Fund is managed by skilled fund managers whose instructions include a fundamental instruction that the planning should be for no less than seven generations (about 175 years). This means that it cannot be paid as a rebate or dividend to the initial buyers of the homes, or used to reduce their normal ongoing fees in a way that would deplete the capital. However, it can and should be used to invest in the local economy.

The VillageTown will attract Small to Medium Enterprises, sometimes called SME, who by virtue of their size find it difficult to compete with big business. The Legacy Fund can level the playing field by employing experts who can provide big-business quality advice to the SME as well as unify them to achieve economies of scale in purchasing goods and services. Further, it can make direct investment or loans in such SMEs. If the VillageTown operating company owns the Industrial Park and leases out space, it could even provide below market lease rates for desired SME tenants to enable them to be more cost competitive in the national or global market.

This concept of *VillageTown Inc.* is paramount. For it to be most effective, it becomes important to start out with cash that normally does not exist when a new community is founded. This cash enables the people and businesses of the VillageTown to take change of their future. It is of the utmost importance that it be protected during the development stage when greedy opportunists bring a sense of entitlement that the cash should be theirs. It is not their money; it belongs to the people who committed their life savings and perhaps 30 years of indebtedness to a mortgage. It then is equally important that it be protected on an ongoing basis. Smartly invested, it should grow, exceed the pace of true inflation, and enable SME private enterprise to grow the wealth of the community.

The fund managers may also invest some of the fund in starting other VillageTowns. The VillageTown Stewards & Company collect a 10% reinvestment premium through the organizing company to provide seed capital, but there will be need for more funds. One VillageTown can start another, and in the process get a new trading partner.

The core of this question is to remember, that at the beginning, it's your money or your good credit. Large financial institutions may try to convince you to give your money to them, but you have to ask how much such a move benefits them, versus how much it benefits you, your family and your local community.

Large institutions may present themselves as sources of capital, but often they tend to be middlemen. The largest sources of democratic capital are insurance and pension funds. By democratic, we mean the funds come from a wide range of ordinary people, not a few from the rich list. Such funds look for long-term stable investments. A community financial institution based on thousands of people living in a VillageTown is perhaps as stable as one can get. Indeed some of the longest lasting institutions in the world are local communities, with some villages and towns operating for thousands of years and still going strong.

The challenge of the VillageTown Plan becomes one of how to structure these local financial institutions so they support and enhance local community wellbeing in a manner that is sustainable over the long term.

Farm banks bring the farmer and customer together. With a large-scale local food purchasing and distribution system, the next logical step is for the customers who have discretionary savings to place their capital in a "Farm Bank". A Farm Bank is a professionally managed fund where farmers borrow money to plant next season's crops from bank deposits made by their customers. Because banks take a spread as profit, a direct relationship can eliminate that and split the difference, eliminating third party profits that leave the community. Farmers get lower cost loans and customers get higher interest. All the customers, even those who could not afford to deposit into the Farm Bank, realize a slight savings if the farmer passes on some of the savings in the form of lower food prices.

The VillageTown Bank – Think about it. In a 10,000 population VillageTown, there will be about 4,000 homes and most will be financed through mortgages. The financing package could easily be in the billion dollar range. Why give this business away? One approach to funding a VillageTown is to establish your own bank. Because it is important that the future villagers are known before the village is built, the most effective way to finance the construction is on an individual basis – each family or individual borrowing their conventional construction loan for their home or workplace. These loans are qualified and processed by a finance organization owned by the ViTo. This mortgage bank or credit union qualifies the mortgage applicants following standard industry practice, and then it then packages those mortgages into prime mortgage backed securities that it sells to investors, primarily pension and insurance funds. After the

construction loans are rolled into long-term mortgages, the bank provides the retail servicing of those mortgages, giving it a secure income stream that enables it to offer a full range of secure-intranet connected community banking services.

Because risk is carried by the investors, the stewards hold this bank during VillageTown construction. When the buildings receive their permits to occupy, the investors are paid off, and under this plan, the assets shift to the villagers. The stewardship stock in the ViTo is called in, the ViTo is recast as a VillageTown council to reflect its new role, and new shares are issued: one per title, permanently attached that title. In this way, the community gains ownership of its local bank and its profits can be used to lower the cost of living, most notably through offsetting taxes and operating costs. This has many additional benefits in how the community and individuals manage their money.

For example, in times of high inflation and low interest rates, the bank could provide mutual funds that apportion individual ownership of tangible investments that hold their value regardless of the declining value of currencies. With the

community intranet, local citizens would be able to buy and sell in their nation's currency, but instantly convert it to their tangible assets held in this chattel funds. The bank computer would track and transfer ownership of the assets. Mutual funds in chattel is not a new idea, but instant, zero-commission sale of them is a new idea made possible by new technology.

Corporatism

We live in an era where corporate law grows stronger while public law, condo law and NGO law weakens. This is called corporatism. It is the dominant *ism* of our time. In some ways corporatism resembles feudalism more than democracy: Real power is still held by the chief (CEO), but he does battle using lawyers instead of knights, and his cash reserves replace swords as the source of his power.

Local governments have limited powers and homeowner associations have even less. Why start out with weakness?

To benefit from the powers accorded by the state to corporations, create one. To make it democratic, make its sole stockholders the VillageTown citizens. To give it powers, issue one share per building title and one vote per citizen. Spell out its authority in the accompanying title or deed to the property. To assure powers are not centralized, use checks and balances. Set up both for-profit (tax paying) and non-profit (tax exempt or tax loss) subsidiaries to benefit its stockholders (the citizens of the VillageTown). and stakeholders (the citizens of the host region). From initial property sales, establish it with a multimillion dollar litigation fund to reduce bullying by private corporations or government. Vest ownership of the for-profit bank, motor-pool car rental, waste reuse systems and other profitable businesses. Charge it with operation and maintenance of the infrastructure, using profits to offset what normally would be charged as local fees. We call this organization a *civitas corporation* (the ViTo).

Summary

When several villages have come together to become self-supporting or nearly so... is how Aristotle began in talking about the purpose of the city-state. In forming the VillageTown it becomes especially important that the local economy follow a similar pattern. Of course, there are great differences between then and now. A VillageTown exists within the context of a national and global economy. It does not field its own army. Instead of soldiers, it has lawyers. Instead of a slave class, it has technology. Humanity has evolved in many ways over the past two thousand years. But the core economic principle remains as valid today as it did in 300 BC: *Look after your own local economy.*

Reduce the cost of living, control your money, own your bank, use your collective purchasing power. Pay especial attention to attracting a wide range of businesses, jobs and entrepreneurial industries to keep the overall local economy strong and resilient even in hard times. Do not presume overseas goods will always be cheap – make things. Maintain a skill-base with a walk-to industrial park. Provide employment for citizens at all ages and stages of life, especially entry level jobs for youth and settled work for elders. Redefine retirement; don't count on government pensions. Run your own health care. Keep your food sources nearby and protected; grow for health and flavor. In initial construction, take advantage of efficiencies of scale. Use some of the savings to make homes affordable, but also invest in a low-maintenance, high-quality infrastructure and governance structure. Start the VillageTown out with a substantial asset base both in cash and in public property owned by the citizens. Use both private and public sector law, tools and powers to serve the interests of the citizens. Buy good shoes, you will be spending most of your day in them.

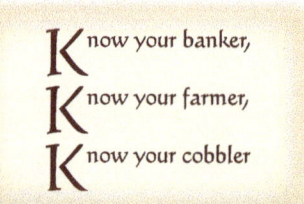

Know your banker,
Know your farmer,
Know your cobbler

Local Economy Checklist

- ☐ Commit to having a strong economic plan for the VillageTown
- ☐ Define the shareholders as the VillageTown citizens & the stakeholders as the surrounding host region
- ☐ Establish an economic planning committee with experts in required fields
- ☐ Establish standards for economic opportunity that provide for a good life and protect the environment
- ☐ Plan for boom, bust and normal economic conditions. Protect the local economy.
- ☐ Identify local resources and regional elements that may strengthen a local economy
- ☐ Identify your food source and create an economic plan for local, year-round food
- ☐ Identify business opportunities in building the VillageTown, and capitalize them to support local industry
- ☐ Identify how 20% of the VillageTown resident's income will come from outside the VillageTown
- ☐ Identify what is necessary to attract such earners to live in the VillageTown
- ☐ Don't focus on selling houses. Instead focus on attracting head-of-household jobs
- ☐ First seek to attract 3 to 5 medium size (200 employee) anchor businesses that sell local to global
- ☐ Build a walk-to Industrial Park and attract businesses that manufacture things using skilled labor
- ☐ Identify business opportunities in furnishing the VillageTown, as above
- ☐ Identify what kinds of amenities will attract members of the Creative Class and build accordingly
- ☐ Provide an ultra-high speed Broadband network link to the VillageTown, and within a separate unlinked intranet.
- ☐ Provide excellent freight and transport links to the region and beyond. Consider owning your commuter airline.
- ☐ Investigate the potential for the visitor industry and university-level facilities in the VillageTown
- ☐ Provide for village services and shops and encourage owner-operated businesses
- ☐ Investigate opening a VillageTown bank (citizen owned) to handle mortgage financing and ongoing banking
- ☐ Write the VillageTown's diversified business plan
- ☐ Reality check this plan against the 100:1 scale model - in other words, will it fit with what you plan to build?
- ☐ Subject this plan to aggressive peer review by experts and informed amateurs
- ☐ Set up a strong community owned corporation that has the power to protect its citizens and the community
- ☐ Keep the profits that come from economies of scale in that community owned corporation
- ☐ Invest those profits in a Legacy Fund that plans for seven generations (175 years) investing in the local economy

In a local economy, we are all interdependent

Chapter 6 – Food and Slow Food

We went to a small village in Greece, not a tourist trap, and found a local place for lunch. The food was fresh, local and wonderful. The villagers were taking time to allow themselves the pleasure of their afternoon meal – as people have for centuries until franchises invented fast food.

That Greek lunch stands as one of the most memorable meals in preparation for writing this book – simple, flavorful, long-lasting, affordable, with a local house wine. Nothing particularly elegant about the restaurant – the table cloth was paper, the wine served in basic water glasses. What made it special were the fresh greens, the homemade bread, the tomatoes in season – all local, all fresh from the island, and providing plenty of tables so everyone could enjoy the luxury of a long, slow meal.

In 1986, an Italian, Carlo Petrini, founded the Slow Food Movement to promote "food and wine culture, but also to oppose the standardization of taste, defends the need for consumer information, protects cultural identities tied to food and gastronomic traditions, safeguards foods and cultivation and processing techniques inherited from tradition and defend domestic and wild animal and vegetable species." Three years later, the movement formed into a non-profit organization, which their web site explains: *"Slow Food is a non-profit, eco-gastronomic member-supported organization that was founded in 1989 to counteract fast food and fast life, the disappearance of local food traditions and people's dwindling interest in the food they eat, where it comes from, how it tastes and how our food choices affect the rest of the world."* (See www.slowfood.com for more information.)

Conviviality is one of the elements of a good life. Conviviality is often enjoyed around public dining. No accident that Slow Food as a movement calls its member communities Convivia. Form the VillageTown as a convivium and build an infrastructure that supports a wide range of flavorful, healthy foods affordable by all.

The Cycle of Food

The cycle of food begins with the farmer. Know your farmer, know your food. Know where your food comes from, know what's in it, and assure that what you eat is good for you.

For most of humanity's history, all food was organic, meaning that no laboratory-made chemicals were used to accelerate growth and make the farmer's job easier. However, as science shifted its focus to farmers' fields, early research found that if certain chemicals were added to both plants and animals, the farmer could make more money through greater yield. Some chemicals stimulated growth, others combated disease, others killed weeds, parasites, bugs or affected other parts of the natural processes. Nature has an interdependent ecosystem not set up solely to serve the food needs of human beings.

The problem with this scientific approach is scientific immaturity – despite our high opinion of western science, we have a long way to go. Too often, we focus too narrowly on one problem and the direct way to nail it. We also suffer the unfortunate tendency of university business schools to instruct their students to find the next new big thing by looking over the shoulder of the science and technical departments and turn it into a business. This results in new discoveries being brought over into commercial enterprises before all the ramifications are understood – once again falling afoul of the theory of unanticipated negative side effects. Humans have this remarkable ability to convince themselves and others nothing is wrong when they personally stand to gain. Trouble is that we are doing it at such a large scale now that nature is hitting the tipping point.

The primary push for turning farms into toxic hazardous material sites is to get higher yields per acre – more food and, in theory, higher profits. Proponents of chemical farming claim that without adding chemicals billions would starve. While this may or may not be true, it simply is not relevant for a developed society of the sort that will build a VillageTown.

The primary push for GE food is about patents – royalties on food. Genetic engineering would have unfolded very differently without royalties. One day humanity's ability to use science to evolve life may prove of the utmost value, indeed may evolve human beings to a higher level. However, at present science is being pushed by business to generate products that can be patented. Some of these products are being released into nature without any idea of the potential ramifications. Not smart.

When all the middlemen, the long distance delivery and all the other attendant costs are taken out of local food serving the

VillageTown, it can afford to pay the farmer more money and still find their food costs less. With that extra money, the farmer can back off on intensification whose sole purpose is to get the highest yield for the land available. If not using tons of pesticides and fertilizers means less food per acre, it won't matter. The game is not about squeezing the maximum out of the land, it's about great tasting, healthy food in a stable town/farm economy.

Higher return for the farmer:

In 1950, the average US farmer received 44% of the consumer's plate. Today, it is under 16%. The middleman takes over 80%. When food is grown locally and with computerized order/direct delivery, it's possible to pay the farmer 44%, plus 6% for local delivery and the consumer pays half the retail price. For this 2.5x increase to the farmer, the farm would grow food that is healthy, nutritious & flavorful, following Slow Food principles.

See Canning, Patrick. A Revised and Expanded Food Dollar Series: A Better Understanding of Our Food Costs, ERR-114, U.S. Department of Agriculture, Economic Research Service, February 2011.

Health and Food – The human body is made up of trillions of cells working in cooperation to keep us alive for upwards of a hundred years. When our bodies suffer trauma – usually something breaking due to us colliding with something stronger or sharper, modern medicine works wonders in putting us back together. Additionally, modern society protects us from trauma – far fewer people die from falling off a horse or being crushed by an industrial machine.

However, when we look to medicine to fix a body suffering from disease such as cancer, cardiovascular, or other internal malfunction at the cellular level, the track record is not so good. Indeed I recently attended a lecture by biologist Dr. Bruce Lipton, in which he listed the top three killers in the USA:

- Cancer 553,000 a year,
- Cardiovascular 700,000 a year
- Iatrogenic Illness, 784,000 a year (Iatros means Physician, Genic means Induced – together we have a fancy word meaning the medical system can be toxic or fatal)

Our modern systems can be hazardous to our health. The problem we face is the power of pecuniary interest. It was Eisenhower who cautioned us to beware the military-industrial complex. We should also have been cautioned about the pharmaceutical, medical complex that seems to have taken over the role previously held by the Church before the reformation. Doctors are described as performing miracles. When we are sick they give us pills. In countries like the USA, losing ones medical insurance was the modern equivalent of excommunication. The answer is not to toss out modern medicine, but to understand that nature – our bodies, have been working on our health for as long as cells have been evolving, and health comes from a sophisticated immune system properly cared for.

In 1986, the World Health Organization held its first international conference on health promotion in which it proclaimed: "The fundamental conditions and resources for health are peace, shelter, education, food, income, a stable ecosystem, sustainable resources, social justice, and equity."* Sounds like the principles on how to build a VillageTown. As we look at these conditions, we see they can be divided into one internal (food) and eight externals. Peace, education, income, social justice and equity are about people in groups. Shelter and a stable ecosystem are environmental – about the conditions in which we live. Food is the one we put into our bodies to keep our trillion cells working as one.

When we look at food, however, we find reality far more complicated than what we know. Ordinary home grown foods, domesticated over thousands of years but not genetically modified, contain vast numbers and combinations of chemicals that our bodies use to keep us going. When instead we shift our diet to fast food, to processed foods and to the same food eaten often, food laden with chemicals to make it grow faster or to kill off things that might cut production, we find our bodies sometimes begin to break down.

Slow food is about more than the pleasure of long, social meals. It could easily be described as the practical application of the WHO prescription for promoting world-wide health among people.

* http://www.who.int/hpr/NPH/docs/ottawa_charter_hp.pdf

Food Checklist

- ☐ Embrace the principles of Slow Food
- ☐ Consider rooftop greenhouses to commercially grow food.
- ☐ Negotiate long term food purchase agreements with local/regional farmers; with some buy the farm's development rights.
- ☐ Establish local food inspection with higher local standards, not relying on national standards. Best if these people have expertise in food health and flavor, not just quality standards
- ☐ Establish a farmer's bank where farmers borrow from the VillageTown, not an outside bank

- ☐ Provide farm-direct food ordering software system to every home and office
- ☐ Provide a daily food handling facility at the freight depot
- ☐ Provide small electric type VillageTown vehicles with truck beds for VillageTown food delivery
- ☐ Set out a food-smell map for the VillageTown; enhance the aromatic experience through careful placement of food preparation facilities (bakers, coffee roaster, spice maker, restaurants, etc). Control noxious food smells such as hot-oil vent fans so they are not offensive.
- ☐ Have excellent drinking water, with its own pipes and filters. If you have a source of truly fine water, consider glass lined pipes from the source to the VillageTown. Do not chlorinate or fluoridate the water, used advanced purification systems, not chemicals. To avoid tooth rot, avoid sugar and brush your teeth.
- ☐ In subtropical or cooler places, build glass arboretums on some of the plazas that house sitting places, cafes, protected play areas for children and hothouse trees and plants. At every home require food delivery boxes and compost pick-up binsSpecify food standards and provide education for farmers to secure higher quality control

- ☐ Recruit (from overseas if necessary) as permanent VillageTown residents, chefs skilled in traditional, flavorful methods, (the miller, cheese maker, brewer, etc.) for foods other than fresh. Note that the indigenous people may also have food knowledge and wish an entrepreneurial opportunity. If such people exist, engage them and listen with respect.
- ☐ Encourage people from other countries to establish their food traditions on their plaza and to hold their own food festivals.
- ☐ Encourage plaza cafes with inexpensive, very good foods to facilitate social connection over good food.
- ☐ Consider a farmer's market that is weekly, close to the motorpool, or that is next to the VillageTown Gate so trucks can come in with fresh produce. If weather can be inclement, consider permanently-installed, easily-drawn awnings.
- ☐ Consider food harvest festivals.
- ☐ Establish a Seed Savers program and plant Heirloom varieties to enhance diversity
- ☐ Set aside land for small gardens within the village walls – especially pottager gardens
- ☐ Set aside land for larger food plots just outside the village walls for residents use
- ☐ Plant fruit trees everywhere, and make them free to the public
- ☐ Provide food storehouses for lean or emergency times, so VillageTown is not dependent on outside world in case something goes wrong. Best if cooled underground or in caves.

Chapter 7 – Local Transport Area: *A Walking Home-Range*

Lucca

To quote Christopher Alexander's Pattern № 11 "cars turn towns into mincemeat". From a development point of view, cars claim valuable land as homes require land and money for the garage, the driveway, wide streets with on-street parking, mandatory off-street parking for shops and offices, gas/petrol stations, car dealers, muffler/tire/battery drive-stores, inspection stations and all the ancillary businesses required to keep cars on the road. It is dangerous to play in the streets, which are noisy, smelly and get grease stained. Worse, as soon as cars are introduced, people expand their territory, driving miles to shop or work. This limits life for those who cannot drive – children and the elderly, and it claims a significant amount of ones income to purchase and maintain the car. Cars offer wonderful freedom, and this book does not propose a car-less society. However, it acknowledges that one size does not fit all, and the great experiment of the 20th century – a car in every garage – is biting back with a vengeance. Cars offer great freedom, and on the highway, nothing offered by mass transit comes close, but not in town. To understand the theory that underlies this concept, please re-read the section on *The Home Range* found on page vi.

The solution can be found in two places – the historic city "centros" of Italy and in a more limited way, the inside of the modern mega shopping mall (just ignore how folks got there). In both places, cars are kept outside the perimeter. For local government officials having a difficult time imagining approving a car-free VillageTown, imagine the proposal is for a large shopping mall, only without a roof, and in addition to stores, people will live and work there. Of course, we prefer that you imagine the Italian city centro, as the quality of life there offers far more than the prospect of living in a shopping mall on steroids.

The idea is simple. Define the village walls, its perimeter, and keep all cars outside the walls. At one or two places outside the walls build a depot and motorpool. Inside the walls designate what is called a Local Transport Area (LTA). Inside the walls, people walk, ride bicycles and e-bikes, and are permitted to use especially designed low-speed electric vehicles called similar to golf carts. The walking and bicycling part is easy to understand – as a rule of thumb, nothing should further than a ten minute walk. To understand these slow-speed vehicles think electric golf cart, but with extra features and style.

Go to Italy, and you will find all sorts of designs, from the stylish chic design to electric garbage collection micro-trucks. The reason they work is due to range between fill-ups, or to be more precise, between recharging. If a VillageTown is set out with everything in a ten minute walk, this means nothing should be more than half a kilometer away.

Ban Cars – it's that simple. The effects of doing so completely change the character of the VillageTown – restoring local to its people. In the annals of human history, cars are relatively new, and as such, we haven't quite worked out their place. They are such marvelous toys, press your foot and you rocket to speeds unimaginable a century ago. Because of their mass production, the average citizen can afford to own an intricate and sophisticated piece of engineering – the automobile is seductive.

Before embracing such a seduction, let me invite you to turn to the beginning of Chapter 11 and look carefully at the aerial photograph taken of a suburban development in Las Vegas, Nevada. Look how much of the land is taken up by roads and garages – single use land used solely devoted to the motor vehicle. Imagine how life would be if cars were banned. In that Las Vegas residential zone, cars are absolutely necessary. Food is miles away. Employment to pay for the food is a longer drive.

The fundamental problem of the car comes from its intended purpose – it was designed for maximum performance on open highways, where one needs speed, comfort, protection from the elements – all of which point toward a very large, sealed enclosure that separate people and dominates the roads. Cars were not made for closely-packed urban environments like VillageTowns, and cars are entirely inappropriate for such places. The solution that America invented and then exported overseas was to re-invent how we live – to invent the suburbs. Now we are finding that while this is good for the car companies, it's not so good for people or for the long term health of Planet Earth.

In addition to banning cars, ban conventional mopeds. Often using two-stroke motors, they tend to be the vehicle of choice of teenage males seeking to prove their manhood with speed and noise. To experience car-free, travel to the Greek island of Hydra, where all motor vehicles are banned (except for tractors and the municipal garbage truck) – it's quiet. Then travel to any nearby island where mopeds are permitted. The mopeds end up everywhere, and they are utterly invasive. They cannot be easily controlled. The only solution is to ban them entirely, for they serve no purpose. In contrast, we found that similar sized electric mopeds seem to work well – they made no noise, so lacked the teenage testosterone factor. If teens must race, build them a dirt track down in the old quarry where they can't be heard. They'll love it.

In all the various aspects of a VillageTown, we suggest that this is a prime element that must remain non-negotiable. A VillageTown with cars is not a VillageTown, and as soon as they are allowed in, everything necessarily must change. If you find this difficult to imagine, think of an enclosed shopping mall with a car driving inside, on the pedestrian walkway.

Let us be clear – there can be no compromise on cars. Cars cannot be domesticated by design tricks like winding roads with variable widths or speed bumps. Nice idea, but it doesn't work. Place the motorpool and all car parking near the entrance to the VillageTown. Park and walk, or park and transfer your bags to one of the waiting electric carts.

Story: In Prince Charles' village of Poundbury, his master planners tried to domesticate cars by using curves and stone chip road surfaces. When I visited in 2000, young children were playing in the central

In Hydra, all cars and trucks are banned – except for their municipal garbage truck. As it can be seen, the pedestrians are paramount. Indeed even the diners' luggage appears to have priority.

plazas on bicycles – for a while it was working. When I went back in 2006, the stone chip was gone, replaced by conventional paving. Poundbury lost out to cars.

Because the residents could drive cars in the village of Poundbury, they did. In May of 2006, as I sat having a delightful outdoor meal in the village cafe, I marveled as a car slowly mounted the granite curbing blocking off Ashington Street. The driver, careful to not dent his alloy rims, then drove up the sidewalk. Sadly, I did not have enough wits about me to grab my camera and record it for this book before he was gone. Never-the-less, it hammered home the lesson:

Cars and VillageTowns are not compatible. The car cannot be domesticated in local urban areas. As Christopher Alexander writes, they turn towns into mincemeat. The extent to which our living places must be modified to accommodate cars makes no sense in limited-distance places. In a town of 10,000 people, designers must accommodate for more than 6,000 cars that drive over a quarter-million miles every day. Cars blow out the site plan and lay a heavy burden in terms of overall costs, which are ultimately paid for by the villagers. Cars pollute, they are noisy, they are dangerous and they separate people – they are anti-community. Cars must be physically prevented from entering the village – use design, do not rely on rules to keep the cars out.

Having said this, anyone who wants to own a car or three may do so. The resident may buy or lease a parking space in the motorpool garage – no different than city dwellers who keep their car somewhere nearby, but not in their home. The difference is VillageTown residents will not need their car for the mundane chores of daily life.

Understand this: move destinations so people do not need to drive, and their environmental footprint lightens without pain, without tax, without expense and it returns hours of quality time to everyone's daily life.

2000 Poundbury – Gravel discouraged cars

2006 Poundbury – The drivers complained. The cars won.

VillageTown Vehicles

As a rule, in selecting a way forward, planners choose between products on the shelf, and investing in new technology. Having owned companies in the 1980's which wrote software, I appreciate the risks of relying on the optimism of an engineer that a new technology will work out easily. Thus, in looking at appropriate vehicles for local transport areas, it seemed wiser to look for products already available. The internet makes this considerably easier.

The Italians have a wide range of products available for purchase now. In typical Italian fashion, they are well engineered and designed, ranging from stylish to functional. Most of these vehicles run on rechargeable batteries with a range of about 60-100 km (35-60 miles) between charges.

Electric-motor technology is rapidly evolving. In 2013, the stewards travelled to China and visited several factories making ebike motors and batteries. At the Bafang factory, the international sales manager invited me to try a new motor in prototype stage. Mid-mounted so it assisted the rider in driving the chain, it was the first motor I had tried that actually drove the gears, so it could be shifted like a car. Within a few blocks (on a freezing winter day, I should add), I was convinced. Its biggest appeal is that it was designed to bolt on to an existing bicycle. When the motors arrived a few months later, I installed one on a 1951 Raleigh DL-1, one of the finest bikes ever made and another on a Bella Ciao, a new Italian frame/German assembled bike in the classic European style. We are now down to one car at home because we go to town (and to the city on the ferry) on these ebikes. See the photo below of the motor on a Pashley bicycle.

Bafang makes motors for four-wheeled vehicles, and the battery technology is evolving just as fast. The batteries we bought in 2014 were half the weight, half the size and twice the power of the battery we bought in 2013... and the new battery costs less. The batteries are recharged at night; it takes about 2-4 hours, and costs about 3 cents in electricity. In the photo below, the battery is under the basket.

The implications of this for the VillageTown are significant. It means that the VillageTown can establish its own vehicle-making industry of ultra-light delivery and service vehicles as well as operate a fleet of ebikes. In one prospective VillageTown site, we are considering locating the visitor parking lot several miles from the VillageTown in order to help a dying town get a new source of business. Some visitors would ride the electric bus from the parking to the VillageTown, but others would rent ebikes for a pleasant 15 minute ride.

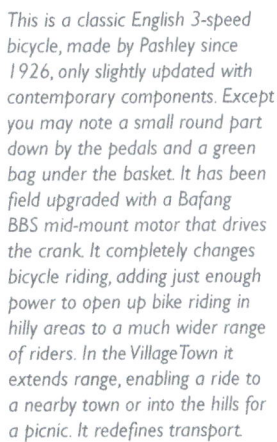

This is a classic English 3-speed bicycle, made by Pashley since 1926, only slightly updated with contemporary components. Except you may note a small round part down by the pedals and a green bag under the basket. It has been field upgraded with a Bafang BBS mid-mount motor that drives the crank. It completely changes bicycle riding, adding just enough power to open up bike riding in hilly areas to a much wider range of riders. In the VillageTown it extends range, enabling a ride to a nearby town or into the hills for a picnic. It redefines transport.

Providing for cars in the suburban landscape requires claiming, paving and maintaining a lot of land. Vast barren lots for cars adds nothing to quality of life. Setting aside land so people must get into a car, drive to their destination and park... and then get out and walk to their destination is not smart. Move the destinations so the distance between home and destination is within a ten-minute walk. The travel to get there is good for health and socially delightful.

Twenty reasons to not want cars inside the VillageTown

1. Homes cost less - no need for families and individuals to pay to build driveways or garages or buy the land for them
2. Workplaces cost less - no need to pay for land, construction, maintenance and taxes to provide off-street parking
3. Village costs less to build - no need for parking meters, parking enforcement or on-street parking lanes, signs or road paint
4. Village needs less land - the roads can be narrower, no need to set aside land allocated for moving or parked cars
5. Destinations closer - walking to destinations is faster because they are closer since intermediate land is not used for cars
6. Roads are cleaner - no dripping oil, no spilled fuel, no tire-tread marks, no debris or fluids from car crashes to clean up
7. Roads last longer - less weight and wear & tear on the streets on a day-to-day basis means they last far longer at lower cost
8. Roads are more attractive - they can be made of paverstones that make road cutting easier (lift pavers - no patches)
9. Buildings and windows remain cleaner as the dust and grit from tires and diesel smoke are eliminated
10. The local air is cleaner and smells better with no tailpipe and fuel tank emissions, no tire and brake dust
11. Teens find other activities - society maintains a higher level of non-invasive supervision
12. People connect - when not cocooned in a steel & glass chamber, people connect better
13. Cafe dining alfresco (outside) along the street becomes far more enjoyable
14. Save money - no need to buy, finance, depreciate, insure, license, park, fuel & fix a car
15. Safety issues around the fuel storage are eliminated (fuel kept only at the motorpool)
16. Children, pets and elders safer - no risk of getting run down by a car
17. Eliminates anonymous predatory behavior enabled by the car; fear is reduced
18. Elders need not move away when they lose their license to drive
19. People live in a quieter environment, no cars passing by, especially late at night
20. No social pressure on status about what kind of car one drives

Note that in this list, there is no mention of peak oil, global warming or any other topics of the fear-based prophets of doom that command headlines today.

It's not that I do or do not believe in these big scientific questions; it's my belief that you cannot build a community based on fear. I have no doubt that polluting the air, water and earth is a bad thing. But even if vast new reserves of fuel were to be discovered and cleaned up, highway sized cars have no use in a local, medium-density community. They are too big, too fast and too costly.

You don't need to require everyone walk or bike. In the historic cities of Italy, you will find very small, elegantly-designed electric vehicles that enable some people to get around inside a weather-protected shell. They must drive at a walking pace, and only a few people seem to use them. More are used as delivery and service vehicles. The cities even provide charging stations for them. Where vehicles are required, these small vehicles make more sense inside the urban core. They do not occupy much land, and when driven on the streets, it is clear that the car is in pedestrian territory and must drive accordingly.

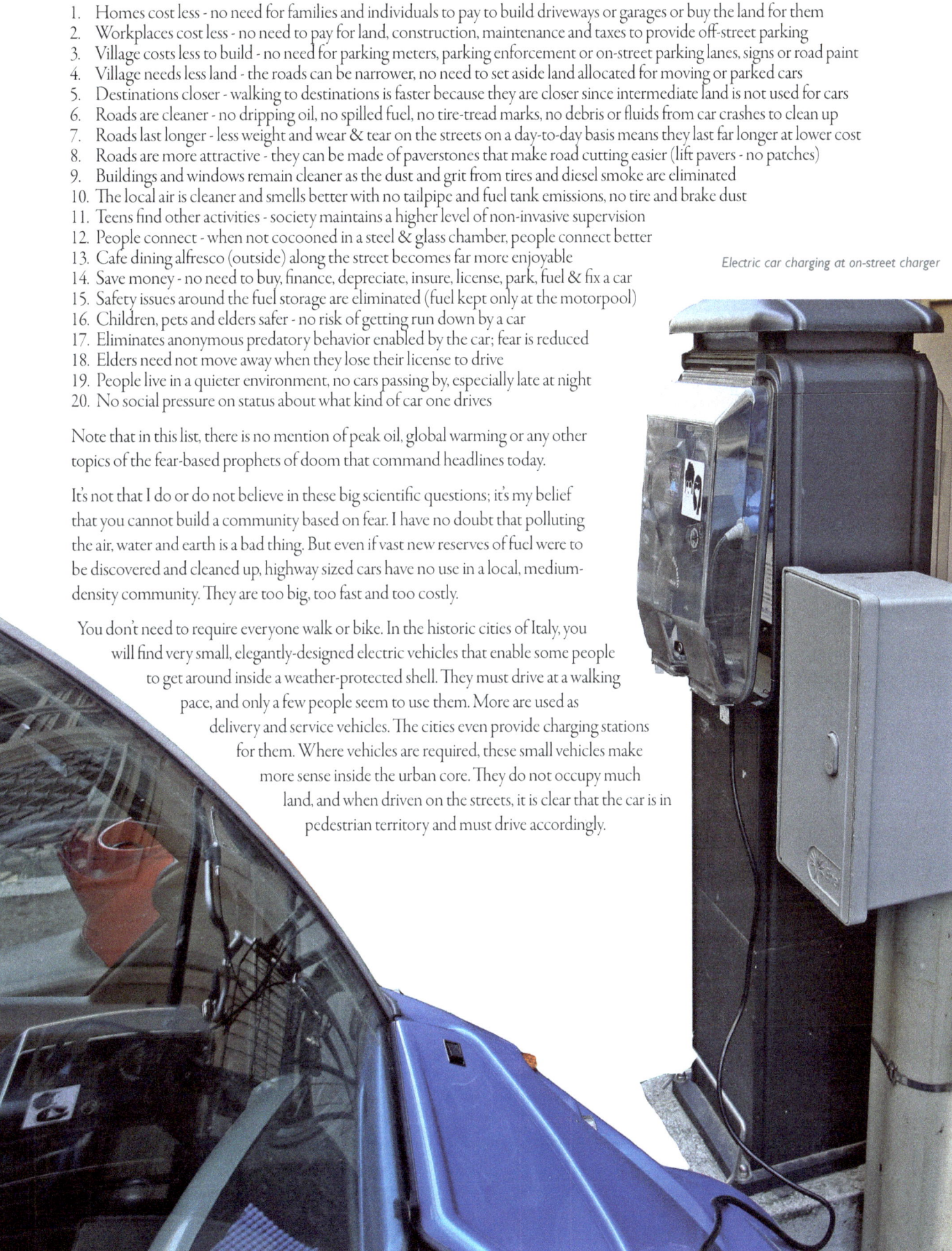

Electric car charging at on-street charger

Chapter 8 – Utilities and Convergent Technology

In the 20th century, municipal governments collected and purified all water going to homes to drinking water standards, even though only 1% was drunk – most went to toilets, bathing and cleaning. Never-the-less the taxpayers paid for unnecessary purification. Then all the toilet and cleaning water was flushed into a sewage pipe where semi-clean (gray) water was mixed with toxic (black) toilet water and out to a treatment plant where more expense was incurred cleaning the water of its pollutants and toxins, again at taxpayer or user expense. As part of the treatment process, it was of the utmost importance that the nutrients in the sewage water be cleaned out before the water went into rivers or wetlands, lest algae blooms kill the natural ecosystems. At the same time, we are told water shortages are coming, and water will be a valuable resource.

In the 20th century, municipal governments collected solid waste – plastic bottles, old tires, food scraps and a host of leftovers from our consuming society that again were mixed into a toxic mess and buried, although toward the end of the century, some were collected and carted off for recycling. It is uncertain how much was collected for recycling and then dumped due to contamination or lack of market demand.

In the 20th century, energy came mostly from petroleum and coal, and it was cheap because the polluting gasses and particles were not included in the cost. The pollutants were invisible, anonymous, and public opinion was captured by slogans like "What's good for General Motors is good for America." Because there was so much money to be made in energy, seemingly rational human beings made decisions that brought them money and power, but were bad for their descendents – a most unusual behavior in the animal kingdom.

In the early 21st century, the message on Global Warming got through, and rather suddenly, pundits and policy makers are looking at the link between energy and a particular type of air pollution known as greenhouse gasses. Among other things, they are saying that if we dig up coal or pump petroleum out of the ground and burn it above ground for energy; we pump chemical compounds into the atmosphere that may be having adverse, unwanted effects on the temperature of the earth. They propose new taxes and making it harder to get around as the solution.

Thus, while the growing awareness of greenhouse gasses is helpful, we need to set a higher standard so we don't create a

new set of problems because we failed to look at the big picture. Let us explore this in more depth:

In 1956 Senator Al Gore (Sr.) sponsored the Interstate Highway Act, the pivotal law that put America on the road, and funded what became known as suburban sprawl. At the time, it seemed like a good idea, and according to Stewart Udall, VillageTowns Stewards & Co.'s Chairman Emeritus, until his death at age 90 in 2010, who was a freshman Congressman at the time, Congress adopted the Act with no debate.

In 2006, Former Vice President Al Gore (Jr.) promoted a documentary *An Inconvenient Truth* that made global warming a mainstream issue. Mr. Gore tells us that if these greenhouse gas emissions are not arrested we could face severe global changes to our environment – changes that could flood our lowlands and change our weather, thus adversely affecting lives, food and ecosystems. The effect was to shift the thinking of world leaders – they finally got it. Or did they? Yes, we have a new awareness, but the proposed solutions may generate new problems. In many cases, their responses suggest humanity needs now to sacrifice, to shift into things like high-density hi-rise apartments (because they require less heat) and to pack ourselves into Tokyo style trains. These purveyors of doom seem to want us to adopt a hair-shirt mentality, to pay for the sins promulgated by our fathers.

In this book, we set out a different vision, a form of human habitation where quality of life is paramount. A low carbon footprint makes sense because it costs less and increases our quality time with family and friends. Yes, it is possible to build a VillageTown with ordinary, non-sustainable technology, but it does not make a lot of sense, now that some of our best scientists and engineers are coming up with better solutions. What we do different is to look at the whole picture, not just the anti-pollution technology. Consider some of the elements we propose should be implemented in contrast to the status quo:

The Status Quo: Securing permission for the conventional subdivision and development

Normally, when a developer approaches the local government seeking approval for the VillageTown subdivision, the officials will tell the developer to provide:

- a plan for treating the water supply with filters and chemicals to meet drinking water standards, with a single water pipe going into each reticulated building;
- plan either to hook up to the municipal sewage system, or to build a new one and to expect to pay a large initial payment and ongoing utility charges for the sewage treatment;
- a plan to haul solid waste to the dump to be recycled or buried, again with attendant fees;
- an agreement with the power company to provide upgraded lines to connect to the grid.

Following this archaic pattern people pay for valuable energy to be thrown away and will pay again for new energy.

It will be of the utmost importance that the local government officials and policy makers who consider an application to build a VillageTown set these 20th century expectations aside, for they are obsolete, expensive and of little benefit to the environment or wellbeing. "You will do it our way because that is the way we have always done it" is not the smartest policy to follow. Instead, it becomes important that integrated thinking become a core process in the application approval process.

Developers will say that half of the job of real estate development is securing the permits. In part this is due to the adversarial character of the process. The developer is seen as being primarily motivated by profit, whereas the permit department either sees its job as protecting the public interest, or in the less enlightened departments – enforcing the rules because they are the rules. The VillageTown comes into the permit department with a different brief, one that will require a change in policy or an enlightened permit department to see that its purpose and the VillageTown's purpose are intentionally aligned.

A better approach: Securing permission for the VillageTown

Because the VillageTown approach views all of its elements as related, these separate utility functions need to be combined into an integrated solution. The principles to be applied are relatively straightforward:

- provide multiple water pipes, so drinking water is provided to the highest drinking water quality but toilet water needs less expensive treatment to do its job properly.
- provide multiple waste-water pipes so washing water can be filtered and reused.
- create a closed-loop sewage system much like the recirculating water in your car's radiator. Then implement extraction systems that remove the sewage part and use its nutrients for production of biofuel (biodiesel and alcohol) and permaculture fertilizers.
- avoid buying solid wastes such as tires, plastics, etc., but for that which is unavoidable invest in a plant that converts their complex hydrocarbons into useful materials.
- invest in advanced sewage treatment systems, perhaps one that generates fuel and fertilizer.
- if the sewage disposal grows biofuel and fertilizer, run it as a joint-venture with the local farmers who grow and deliver VillageTown food.

In following this integrated plan, several outcomes change:

- cost of water treatment is lower and better
- sewage treatment may go from a cost center to a profit center
- many miles of sewage pipes to a distant plant no longer necessary, the sewage biofuel plant is a closed, odorless system near the VillageTown (in the Greenbelt, if it is part of the plan)
- solid waste may go from a cost center to a profit center
- if combined with energy efficiency in building design, upgraded power lines from the grid may not be needed
- cost of electricity may be lower

The VillageTown comes as a package. If the local officials become difficult, and insist on doing the old way and the elected officials do not intervene, consider looking elsewhere. The prospect of turning away a billion dollar sustainable investment in their locality may not bother the officials focused on their own department's problems. However, the upper level officials and the elected representatives may be more willing to negotiate, especially as the intended outcome is for the systems to be more sustainable and better for people and the environment.

Energy 101

For the most part we live in a *material system* that is closed and an *energy system* that is open. In other words, all the matter that will exist on earth is already here, but most of the energy for earth comes from the sun. It is true that from earth we get some energy from nuclear power and from gravity (water dams and geothermal from gravitational pressure), and from the moon we can get energy for tidal power, but most of our energy comes from the sun. Solar energy can be divided into old energy and new.

New energy includes direct heat – warming walls and floors and water tanks on the roof – as well as direct electricity, using photovoltaic cells to make power when the sun shines on the cells. It includes expansion – wind, and evaporation – rain to recharge hydroelectric dams. It includes photosynthesis where plants and algae convert energy into complex molecules – hydrocarbons from which we can get alcohols, biodiesel and synthetic natural gas (syngas) and firewood among others. Solar energy is huge. In 20 days, the solar energy striking the earth (on average 4.2 kW/hr per day for every square meter of the earth's surface) equals all the known remaining reserves of petroleum, natural gas and coal.

Old energy is dug or pumped out of the earth, and it includes coal, petroleum and natural gas, believed to be originally energy from the sun, old biomass under the ground. The problem with using such resources is the undesirable negative side effects that scientists fear may be the undoing of our civilization. In a word – they are dirty, meaning they give off undesirable gasses, liquids and solids. In addition, it makes little sense to use what appears to be a finite resource infinitely through time, or to use it at a rate faster than it can be regenerated. The great forests of Europe and America were stripped to heat homes – not smart – the people lived, the trees died, and we no longer have the great forests on Earth. See page 177 where we quote the four principles of The Natural Step, an intelligent way to think about how to live on earth smarter and better.

In moving to a more sustainable energy reality, we have solutions we can apply now, and others that will require advanced technology. On the direct side of the list, the most obvious is first to do an audit of how we use energy and determine where it is unnecessary. In the Village Town, we address this first by replacing driving with walking – put most of our daily destinations within walking distance: Using US national averages, this reduces car use by over a quarter million miles a day. Next, we reducing energy demands in our buildings, first through passive means (optimal heat gain in winter, natural cooling in summer) and then through smarter technology – light weight concrete that has higher insulation values.

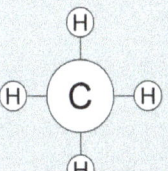

Hydrogen, Carbon & Oxygen

Hydrogen, carbon and sometimes oxygen combine to give us most of our fuels. Methane is: CH.

Glucose is $C_6H_{12}O_6$. Ethanol is (C_2H_5OH). Petroleum and Coal ($C_{240}H_{90}O_4NS$) are more complex.

At the molecular level, these three atoms form the core of our energy needs. Whether we are talking about energy for our bodies or for our cars, the chemistry is remarkably similar. Thus, when we extract the nutrients we need from food, and discharge the balance into the waste stream, it still contains considerable energy.

In understanding fuel, global warming and sewage, appreciate that the chemistry and biology are related and we need to relate our technology accordingly.

Biofuel 101

Biofuel is not new. Indeed you can run older technology diesel engines on olive oil, moonshine or the finest perfume – most any liquid that burns. Yet today in many parts of Europe, Spring means miles of biodiesel rapeseed fields with their brilliant yellow flowers.

Biofuel includes methanol, an alcohol replacement for gasoline and biodiesel that can serve as a 100% replacement for petroleum based diesel. Man has been making biofuel for many centuries in the form of booze. When Henry Ford designed his Model T, he designed it to run on alcohol, not gasoline. His logic was simple... alcohol is a local fuel. As of late the debate over biofuel poses it as a choice between filling the rich person's SUV or feeding hundreds of poor people on grains. This argument tends to be emotive and in fact is misleading. It can be true, but there are smarter ways.

When distilled as a fuel, alcohol is cheap, and the mash can be made from many different plants. For communities near the seaside, kelp farms are especially attractive - they clean the water, and they grow at an astonishing speed (because they do not fight gravity like land based plants). They can be mixed with other Village Town organic waste that would be unsuitable for organic fertilizer, and the resulting brewed and distilled fuel can be used by the farmers who provide the Village Town with their food. One advisor to the Village Stewards suggested a more sophisticated approach in which the mash is fed to Tilapia fish that are grown not for food (since they would be eating sewage), then ground up into a stew where heavy-metal eating bacteria remove the toxins from the sewage, resulting not only in a further energy source for biofuel, but fish-based fertilizer for the farmers.

Biodiesel is made from oils. Used cooking oil, oil-rich plants, algae and even coffee grounds can be used to produce it. In a Village Town setting, surplus waste products should be the source of biodiesel production rather than allocating farm land to grow it. Plants like jatropha may have a high oil content, but as an invasive weed, it is hard to later eradicate.

The biofuel industry is evolving rapidly with new technologies being pursued around the world. The Village Town should become conversant with the latest proven technologies, but also should maintain perspective. The main purpose of biofuel production is to convert waste products that can be used by the farmers supplying the Village Town. In considering technologies for this, do not overlook the oldest one of alcohol distillation.

Greenhouse sewage treatment – In 1997, in response to a very high water table that precluded normal sewage treatment, an American municipal government, Weston, Massachusetts installed a greenhouse to treat their sewage. It had been developed by scientists and engineers who were working in the hydroponics industry and saw how the system might transfer to the process of treating sewage. This is now considered a proven technology, and Weston disposes of 7,000 gallons (26 m³) of raw sewage per day in this manner. The system is gravity fed, includes grinders to take whatever is flushed, and then it goes through several anaerobic and aerobic stages to produce pure, clear water. It can handle up to 25,000 gallons per day.

If you look carefully at the greenhouse photo above, you will note the yellow building in the background. It is the office of local dentist whose building is adjacent to Main Street. There is no odor. You have to be told it is a sewage treatment plant to know it is there.

The president of the private contracting company that designed and operates the greenhouse says that if he were to do it again today, he would not

design a system that strips out all the nutrients (that are bad for the nearby wetlands) but instead would keep it nutrient rich to grow biofuel. In his view, the sewage should end up being an asset where the municipality would make money on it, rather than charge for its disposal. One principle of the VillageTown economy is to make capital investments that reduce the ongoing cost of living for the residents. Eliminating charges for sewage treatment would fall under this principle.

Unlike growing food or flowers, which might engender consumer concern no matter how safe it might actually be, biofuel from sewage offends no one – in order for it to be useful, it must meet purity standards and then be burned. The biofuel would probably best be processed as B100 Biodiesel that will be needed by the regional farmers to run their tractors.

It is important for officials both to appreciate that this greenhouse system is not experimental but also that it is not the only innovative model. In preparation for writing this book, I did an internet search, finding several innovative systems. I chose to look at the Weston greenhouse because Massachusetts is known for having tough wetlands regulations and it was convenient to my flight plan. There are many successful innovations to consider. Do your homework.

Ironically, I arrived from sunny England to be greeted with record rains and flooding in Boston. When they spoke of the high water table, it was decidedly visible. I needed to be careful where I parked the as the water covered much of the parking lot and was rising (the blur in the lower right of the photograph of the greenhouse [top page 106] is floodwater). They say global warming will result in heavier rains falling in shorter time periods. The principal was aptly demonstrated that day in Weston.

Electricity

Environmentalist James Lovelock stirred controversy when he declared the world needs to shift to greater reliance on nuclear power in order to forestall global warming. I am not a scientist, but I hope he is wrong. The idea that we produce hazardous waste that remains highly toxic for tens of thousands of years seems too uncertain for those of us who are concerned about what world we leave future generations. The risk of power plants being damaged by earthquakes or other natural disaster is not the same as it would be for conventional plants. Many such nuclear plants are cooled by water and in the event of a breakdown that releases highly toxic wastes, water can spread that around the world. Do we really need to take such risks?

Having said that, the VillageTown needs electricity. The proposal to create a Local Transport Area in which electric vehicles are used requires power to charge the batteries. Implementing advanced wall-sized, real-time video conferencing so people need not travel to meetings requires electricity. There are a number of solutions, all of which should be considered.

First, use less. Design buildings to use natural light, natural sunlight and natural air. Use only high efficiency electric motors for all appliances and HVAC equipment. Where possible, design homes with integrated heating, cooling, water and refrigeration systems, and design these to use maximum solar gain and heat recovery. Use high efficiency lighting and light less. Darkness at night is better for human beings – it's what our ancestors knew for the first million or so years of human existence and our bodies have day/night rhythms. If we must have street lights make then smart, only turned on when someone walks by, and using advanced lighting like LED's that only light the foot path, not the whole street. Discourage stand-by appliances such as TV's that passively consume electricity*.

Second, realize that if you follow the prescriptions in this book, the cost of building homes should be lower, and their market value higher because of the amenities. Rather than pocket unreasonable profits, or pass those capital gains onto the first buyers of the homes, use these funds for technologies that normally would not be cost justified. Make the energy footprint smaller and cost of living lower. Consider photovoltaic solar cells – a rapidly emerging technology, that may prove feasible by the time your VillageTown is ready to build. Photovoltaics turn sunlight into electricity. Consider them not at the household level but for the whole VillageTown.

It is unlikely that all electrical needs can be provided for by photovoltaics, but the other option is not necessarily to draw all electrical needs from the central grid, which promises to increase prices and from time to time face shortages. One of the more interesting technologies is breaking down biomass into a form of synthetic natural gas that can be burned to run electrical generators. If this biomass plant is linked with a zero waste policy for garbage, it may solve two problems simultaneously.

In some locations wind, tidal and waterpower may provide a good local electrical generation source. The primary drawback to wind (other than the visual amenity) is the power drop when the wind stops blowing. One potential solution may come in using surplus wind generated electricity to drive a hydrogen generation plant that breaks distilled water into hydrogen and oxygen, which is then stored and used to run a generator when the wind stops. This works because the energy in the wind is effectively free, thus the inefficiencies of energy loss less relevant. In all these ideas, seek out the latest technology. A lot is happening and by the time this edition is published, new and better solutions will be out there somewhere in the world.

In summary, the 21st Century demands we reduce our energy demands and use what we need far more efficiently. Look at innovative ways to generate it and efficient ways to use it.

---

* For that matter, discourage television isolation by having community TV like the old theaters where people make TV watching a social event. Do everything you can to make the VillageTown life more interesting than TV. Compete with passivity.

Solar power

The energy from the sun is free. The cost is in the capital cost of the panels to capture the energy. Several years ago, solar energy was a boutique product, more expensive than buying juice from the power company. This is now changing as the engineering gets more efficient. With a $1-2 billion construction budget and a mandate to implement the most sustainable, affordable technologies, solar power can be expected to be a major energy source for the VillageTown. If the VillageTown builds greenhouses on the roof, some of that glass will be solar panel glass, to harvest energy as well as rainwater, but still allow enough -light in for the plants.

This demonstrator panel on a trailer may look like a normal solar panel, but those two hoses at the bottom that go to a water bucket tell a different story.
We are told by solar engineers that only about 15% of the sun's energy that strikes a solar panel is converted into electricity. The rest either reflects away or is converted into heat. Put your hand on a solar panel in the bright sun, and you can feel how hot it gets.
To address that issue, this panel is actually two panels in one. The electrical grid transforms the solar energy into electricity, and then within the panel water pipes capture the thermal energy and use that to directly heat water. The total efficiency of the unit is much higher with the hot water is available to heat radiators, swimming pools, hot water tanks for bath water and so on. Where very high water heat is required, the solar panel feeds medium hot water in, thus reducing the electrical load on the hot water tank.

Water

I live on an island where clean drinking water falls from the sky. It flows from our roofs to large storage tanks, and then is carbon-filtered at the tap. No chemicals, no treatment, just pure filtered water. Showering feels different than city water.

For those who live in cities, the average water consumption per household per day is in the order of 500 liters / 130 gallons. When one considers that the human body needs about 4 liters / quarts a day, it becomes clear that about 99% of the water treated to meet drinking standard is not used for drinking.

The answer is to require additional pipes running into each home – at present, one pipe runs in, and one out. It comes in meeting drinking water standards, and exits as pathogen-ridden black-water, fouled by a relatively small amount of effluent from defecation. Pipes are cheap. Water is precious, and good water is very precious.

Consider a multi-pipe infrastructure:

1. **Rainwater** out: rooftop collection, stored, filtered and back in human intake. Figure 5 gallons per person per day.
2. **Compost** out: a grey-water fed grinder in the kitchen sink collects all food scraps, piped to a central compost system
3. **Shower/dishwasher** out, cleaned, filtered, purified and pumped back in for re-use for washing purposes
4. **Yellow water** out - separate urine at point of capture using special toilets. Segregates antibiotics and birth control
5. **Black water** nutrient extraction system, converts caloric value to biofuel, returns clean toilet water in closed-loop system
6. **No clothes washers**: Provide "free" laundry service that collects and cleans using a closed-loop commercial system. Who likes doing the wash? And it provides jobs. Use a similar closed-loop system for washing cars in the motorpool.

With 150 acres of rooftop rainwater harvesting using greenhouses (100 acres of houses plus 50 acre industrial park), it is estimated that storage of 100 acre/feet (about 123 mega-litres) of rainwater, and 20 acre/feet of constantly-recharged reused water will provide for a 10,000 population VillageTown, which requires annual rainfall of 7.5 inches (19 cm).

The higher investment in pipes adds to the initial cost, but not by much. For most it is amortized in the home mortgage. In the long term it allows far better cost control on what now is an expensive and sometimes problematic public utility. It also means that sewage treatment is no longer a risk utility since it will become a caloric extraction system for what becomes a surplus resource. Of course, all of this could be done with a single pipe system, but it makes the job harder, especially if the antibiotics are fighting the natural biotic systems that break down the effluent into safe by-products.

Storm bombs where inordinate amounts of rain fall in short time frames are becoming more common.

Storm Water

Collecting and Using – Water captured on the streets can be used for food growing, especially noting that in a car free VillageTown, the usual contamination from dripping oil ceases to be a problem. In the VillageTown, such water collection tanks can be underground – under the streets, warehouses and other industrial buildings.

Open Channels – In Pattern № 64 *Pools and Streams* Christopher Alexander writes "Whenever possible, collect rainwater in open gutters and allow it to flow above ground, along pedestrian paths and in front of houses." If the roads are made with a concrete bed, while wet, the concrete can be shaped with a gentle depression that holds a lot of running water, but is not steep enough to twist an ankle or collect rubbish. Where the water moves down a steep slope, embed round stones in the wet concrete, so it makes a rushing sound while aerating the water. Open channels for storm water allow people to connect with water, for children to play in it, and generally they cost less and are easier to maintain than underground pipes. In steep sites, collect some storm water at high places, and then pipe it into a storm-only fountain that shoots upward due to the gravity pressure.

Solid Waste – Zero Waste

Set a design specification of zero waste. Yes – it is possible. Let us first look at handling solid waste:

Construction Waste

One reason for recommending building the VillageTown a single, mineral-based bulk material is the absence of construction waste. Unlike cavity wall, timber-framed, clad construction (which leaves off-cuts of chemically treated timber and sawdust, wall board off-cuts and seemingly endless plastic wrap for everything from the timber to the insulation), variable density aggregate comes in bulk containers (cement should be ordered by the truckload not in bags). Leftover material is mixed into non-structural elements like garden paths or crushed into the road base. Where wood must be used, try to select durable heartwood timbers, not treated pine.

The last job took all our leftover the broken brick, reinforcing steel and stone rubble that we then embedded in an aggregate mix and covered with a mosaic made of off-cut stone. A simple but effective way to dispose of the construction waste from the job site, but only because all our waste was non-toxic and safe to use as a patio foundation.

Food and Food Packaging Waste

An essential design element of the VillageTown, discussed in the food section of this book, requires next to each mail box, a food box. Fresh, locally-grown food is delivered directly using a computerized ordering and delivery system that enables food to go directly from grower to consumer. For this to work well, we recommend going from a weights and measure system to a crate and bottle system. Instead of ordering a 10 kg or 25 pound bag of potatoes, one orders a red box that when filled generally averages 10 kgs or 25 lbs, but is judged visually. If by weight, it is over or under a little bit, in the end it really does not matter, and it makes the delivery system a lot less complicated. Fill the box and deliver it.

For the most part, we recommend liquids be delivered in wide-mouthed reusable glass jars – wide mouth so they are easier to clean. In setting out the kitchen storage requirements for the homes, it becomes a mandatory requirement that each kitchen have adequate storage for food that comes unwrapped, unboxed and unpackaged. In this way, the disposable plastic, glass and paper used in the delivery of food is significantly cut back. While there is a market for certain recyclable plastics, the energy to ship them to a recycling company, then grind and melt them down is less sustainable than reusing a crate or bottle that only needs local cleaning. Using durable, reusable boxes, bottles and crates.

Disposal of food scraps is relatively simple, provided the buildings are built for it. Traditionally people kept compost buckets, but in an urban setting this is complicated and labor-intensive. Better to use a sink garbage disposal fed with grey water that pipes the food scraps to a central collection point outside the villages. This avoids the problems of mold, odors, and the necessity to use high pressure water to regularly clean the slop buckets, and additional collection vehicles on the streets.

A more recent use of food scraps is to produce biofuel, and planners of the VillageTown should investigate the industry at the time the VillageTown is being planned. At the time of this writing, biofuel is an emerging industry with some methodologies being "pseudo sustainable" meaning they appear to be better than the old ways, but when one examines the complete support structure required to produce the product, one finds the real impact to be non-sustainable. As a rule of thumb, the larger the US farm lobby supporting a particular biofuel method, the more questions one should ask. Beware of spin.

Recycling Daily Inorganic Matter

Paper, cardboard, metal and plastic containers, and a host of other goods are recyclable, and while it would be better if they were not consumed, we are speaking about building a VillageTown here, not reinventing the world-wide packaging industry. While we can address local packaging, such as food, other goods come in packaging that we must transform from a cost into a raw material we can use.

The first element for recycling is to make it easy. Design a collection system that segregates the various products at the time of disposal, and design the collection vehicle (a small electric truck) to match the divided bin. Require that the collection point be in the house, directly along the street (another reason to not have setbacks for VillageTown housing). Occupants lift up a door, drop the refuse in the correct bin. The truck extends a receiving divided bin and

the various dry materials are tipped in their respective compartments. The driver inspects the rubbish and instantly bills the occupant for anything they then have to hand sort because it was in the wrong bin.

The next element is to invest in capital equipment to use the recycled materials locally. Crushed glass can be used in certain building materials. Plastics can be used for the food bins. Look around the world and you will find someone has what you need. Be prepared to visit other cultures, as the inventions may be Swedish, German, Italian or Chinese.

Recycling Hard Goods

There was a time when furniture lasted for generations. Now cheap furniture is lucky to last as long as the financing. Expensive furniture can be trendy, and disposed of before it is worn out. Computers are proving to be a major headache as they tend to last about 3 years before something breaks. When they do break they are obsolete and not worth fixing. Home appliances are also items now thrown out when something breaks.

Furniture

The first solution is to establish a furniture making industry when the VillageTown buildings are being constructed. Invest in these businesses just as you do the infrastructure. This can be direct investment, or the ViTo facilitating loans for entrepreneurs to set up business. Either way, establish a VillageTown license to assure production standards and quality are met. To secure the license, set performance terms that assure VillageTown sustainable goals are met. Set the standard of solidly-made, timeless, durable furniture that is easy to maintain. Establish a local upholstery industry, and if talent exists, support local fabric design and manufacture that becomes an identifiable marker for the VillageTown. Expect these industries to both make new and to refurbish. By doing this, the amount of furniture rubbish is cut back. Set up a non-profit trade center, where people donate castoffs – one person's junk is another's treasure. Along with this, set up a local E-bay type auction intranet (local to the VillageTown only) for residents to sell and barter new and used goods, as well as services. If you wish, this can be set up as an alternative currency trading system. All these ideas are proven – the innovation is putting them all together.

Computers

There is little that can be done locally with old computer systems, except to establish a repair center that keeps older machines running, and sells used, refurbished equipment to people who cannot afford, or do not need the latest. Also, give

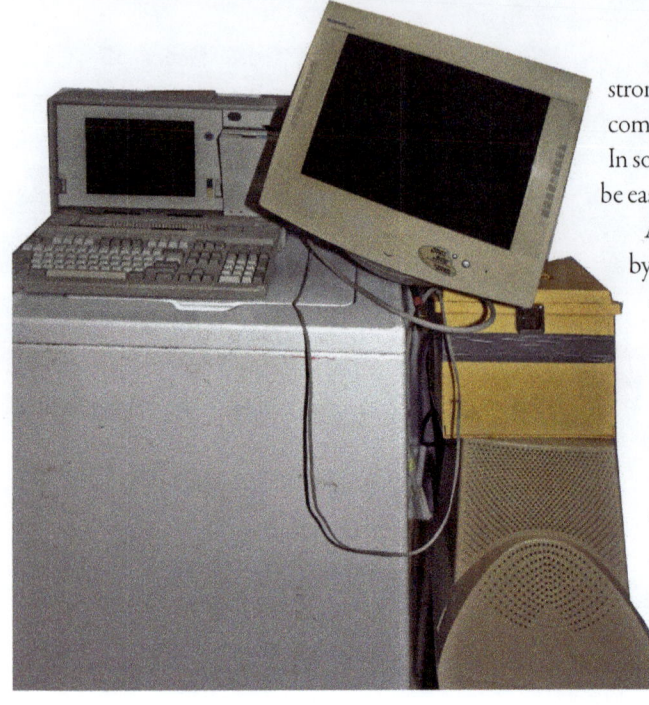

strong consideration to looking at industrial quality computer systems that may be installed VillageTown-wide. In some cases, these systems are designed to last longer and be easily repairable.

At one time, all computer systems were massive, run by central data processing departments – often fully contracted, as in the case of IBM. Then as the radical freedom movement emerged, especially in the San Francisco Bay area, focused on Berkeley, radical techies invented the personal computer to challenge what they saw as the fascist control of information on big mainframe computers. They won. Now we are seeing the internet, again established with biological principles of peer-to-peer cooperation being pressured to become a centralized system where people depend on large corporations for their processing power. While some people use e-mail resident on their own computer, others are taking advantage of centralized free systems such as Hotmail, G-mail and Yahoo. Into this debate about freedom vs control, we add another question – opting for local centralized system. In such a system, some homes may install "dumb terminals" with the computing power in a large system owned and operated by the VillageTown, while others may use a Personal Computer for specialized applications. From a solid waste standpoint, the question turns on the effect of 2,000 homes and offices buying stand-along personal computers vs more than half buying dumb terminals to do the basics. Such a centralized system can also support much more durable and powerful printers – say one on each plaza. There may be as many as 5,000 PC's and as many printers in the VillageTown. Think smart.

Home Appliances

When one looks at home appliances, look at innovation to use less energy. Some of this has to do with feedback, others with design. Imagine if each power point (electrical outlet) had a billing accumulator attached to it, so one could immediately see the effect of leaving the TV or computer in standby mode instead of turning it off. Imagine if one was charged by the actual heat produced by room, instead of paying a monthly bill where one wonders what is chewing up so much money. Such technology is a matter of installing sensors, and when placed in the context of the cost of a building is insignificant.

Challenge your engineers to combine refrigeration, water heating, heat and air conditioning into a single system so that heat is added and removed in the most energy efficient manner. This may result in cool rooms rather than stand-along refrigerators, and depending how energy use is managed, may even result in single systems for whole blocks of buildings in which energy is monitored and charged not at a bulk meter attached to each house, but by actual use.

Finally, the VillageTown through its purchasing cooperative should secure wholesale contracts to bulk purchase appliances that its technical advisory committee recommends as superior in terms of efficiency, engineering, performance and value. In VillageTowns that attract the creative class, one can count on volunteers who will be utterly passionate and proficient in such evaluations and negotiations.

Checklist for VillageTown Services, Technology and Utilities

- ☐ Brief local authorities on convergent technology (send them a copy of this book)
- ☐ Decide which utilities will be VillageTown managed, negotiate agreements
- ☐ If required, include in subdivision application
- ☐ Establish a Convergent Utilities Working Group with local experts
- ☐ Sewage Decisions: Conventional, Greenhouse, Biofuel, Other
- ☐ Water Decisions: Conventional; gray-water multipipe, separate drinking water
- ☐ Storm Water Decisions: Runoff or store
- ☐ Electricity Decisions: Grid, Combination of Solar, Wind, Tidal, or Coal Fired with smokestacks feeding algae biofuel. Rules for efficiency motors, lighting, etc.
- ☐ Heating decisions: Passive Solar, solar hot water, thermal, electrical, Heat Pumps
- ☐ Construction Waste Decisions: Conventional disposal or embed in roads
- ☐ Solid Waste Decisions – Recycle or ban most plastics from shops. Zero waste.
- ☐ License local furniture makers to construct furniture that lasts and produces zero-waste at end of its life.
- ☐ Food Waste – Recycle for compost or for biofuel
- ☐ Computers, whiteware and other large ticket rubbish: Conventional or creative
- ☐ Motorpool Decision: For profit (wholly owned by the VillageTown) or run at cost.
- ☐ Intranet Decision: Conventional services or VillageTown owned Intranet and ISP
- ☐ VillageTown Coop: VillageTown or member owned

Remember to

- Use advances in technology.
- Encourage lateral thinking.
- Encourage integrated thinking.
- Use the Internet to find a place where they have already done it. Visit them. If it provides a better solution than what is on offer locally, bring it in.

Just because it is digital, don't assume the information it provides is right!

Chapter 9 – Education and Culture

Fact: Families move house to get their children into good schools. Create the best educational opportunity they can find. The VillageTown will need new schools. Based on typical demographics, with 10,000 new people moving in, one can reasonably expect two thousand of them will be school-aged children. Traditionally this means needing two or three primary schools and one larger high school. Given that we are building a whole VillageTown, let us subject our schools to the same analysis of first principles, and not just do it the way we always have… by letting the state, encumbered by a myriad of private and political agendas, dictate how to do it. This can be done using public education, as long as we negotiate with strength and clarity.

So, how do we do it?

While I have worked in business for many years, I have a parallel background in education. I sat on the Board of Trustees of a public high school in New Zealand. I hold a Master's Degree in Educational Administration earned at Western Washington University in the USA, where I studied education and then classics for five years under Professor John Bremer – best known for the Parkway Project, the School Without Walls. More recently, in New Zealand I was elected to the local school board.

From an organizational standpoint, there are a few basics.
- The first decision is about control. Will the process be controlled by the VillageTown or the state? Will the VillageTown Founders choose to be public, private or some hybrid of the two? Personally, I prefer public education, and wish to see it reformed rather than abandon it in favor of private education. Seek to make it a model of excellence.
- We recommend forming an establishment board of parents and professionals to make and negotiate these questions.
- The establishment board sets out the values, the principles and the overall policy of the VillageTown education system and then oversees the construction of buildings and hiring of staff for the school or schools.

Socrates taught here in this marketplace not in a classroom

Control

The first question is pivotal. Who controls? We may presume that the VillageTown is sufficiently different in its fundamentals, and sufficiently outside the comfort zone of the educational establishment, that where choice exists, the VillageTown should control the special character of the schools and not turn them over to the state. The education in the VillageTown should reflect the values and character of the VillageTown, and for this reason, the VillageTown should control the establishment of its schools, just as it does the other aspects of social and cultural wellbeing. Even if the public education is not structured to permit this, do it anyway. Ultimately such decisions are political, and the case for excellent education is persuasive. In today's economic climate, many education departments are weak, some almost broke. This may help in negotiations.

The next challenge facing the establishment of the school system lies with the selection of people who will be entrusted with the decision-making in the Establishment Board. How do we select those people?

The core problem that we face is we will have some people who want to take control of the process, get on with it, and get the schools up and running. Others will want to take advantage of the opportunity of the clean slate – and ask the big questions first. Others want to get into the details. What all need to learn is that none of these approaches will work – but all working together should work well. There are assessment tools that can help us identify these four types of volunteers and assure we get a good balance. Two you may want to check out are the four brain types as set out by the Herrmann Brain Dominance Model (HBDI) which is popular in business circles, and Dr. Anthony F. Gregorc's Four Learning Style Types, which is popular in education. We recommend that candidates fill out these assessment tools and the selection of the candidates assure a balanced representation of all four. Further, we recommend that when the Establishment Board first meets, it have a training session to show why they need all four, and how they then need to value each other's skill-set and not regard the others' views as alien.

Principles

At this point, the same challenge facing the VillageTown Founders will face the Establishment Board. We want them to create the framework for the education system, but they may lack the language to do so. For the VillageTown Founders we are lucky, architect Christopher Alexander created *A Pattern Language*. As far as we can see, no educator has created a comparable comprehensive language for education that means we cannot so easily create a system of Pattern Cards for the Establishment Board. Parts exist, but not a template for an establishment board. In its absence, if we are to look for a central principle of the VillageTown let us look to the concept of Integrated Thinking:

Integrated thinking is understanding that everything is connected to everything else, and understanding that the connections and relationships between things can be as important as the things themselves. Once one begins to apply integrated thinking – which includes observing, formulating, decision-making and action, one begins to act intelligently in the best interest of both humanity and planet earth.

Stoa, Athens

The Buildings

In the history of humanity, classrooms are a relatively new invention for the education of the young. They are an effective way to maintain control when one teacher is asked to manage 30 or more students in one room, but we must ask, "what does control have to do with learning?"

Turning to A Pattern Language again, we find several relevant patterns, most notably № 18 *Network of Learning* and № 85 *Shopfront Schools*. Pattern 85 speaks about the relationship of money to student:teacher ratio. "By eliminating the building and the salaries of all those persons who do not directly work with the children, the student/teacher ration can be reduced from something like 35/1 to 10/1. In this one stroke many of the most pressing public school problems can be eliminated at no extra cost to the school or the school district." Alexander recommends, "Instead of building large public schools for children 7 to 12, set up tiny independent schools, one school at a time. Keep the school small, so that its overheads are low and a teacher-student ratio of 1:10 can be maintained. Locate it in the public part of the community, with a shopfront and three or four rooms."

In Pattern № 18 Christopher Alexander writes "Instead of the lock-step of compulsory schooling in a fixed place, work in piecemeal ways to decentralize the process of learning and enrich it through contact with many places and people all over the city: workshops, teachers at home or walking through the city, professionals willing to take on the young as helpers, older children teaching younger children, museums, youth groups travelling, scholarly seminars, industrial workshops, old people and so on. Conceive of all these situations as forming the backbone of the learning process; survey all these situations, describe them, and publish them as the city's "curriculum".

The VillageTown serves as a life-long classroom. By placing workplaces with large windows on the ground floor around the plazas, we provide a host of role models for the young. We envision that some of those workplaces may take on a young apprentice, especially those settled workplaces of elders in semi-retirement. By designing the plazas with places for the young to play and adults to sit, we create safe, natural opportunities for children to learn social skills – far better than learning them from television.

The VillageTown is the classroom. It makes little sense to claim substantial acreage to segregate young learners from the rest of society – especially since school is in session only 15% of the 24/7 year, what a waste of building space.

It also makes very little sense to segregate children by age – indeed in our politically correct societies where the word segregation is now regarded as a sin, age segregation remains institutional practice, from insisting all six year-olds must be in the same grade all the way to insisting people stop working when they hit an arbitrary old age.

In some countries, the law provides for clustering of several grades– something that was essential in a rural country where one-room schoolhouses were common. In France, director Nicolas Philibert made a wonderful documentary of such a school in *To Be and To Have* following a teacher with a two-room primary school showing the older students helping the younger ones. We recommend following this practice, not for lack of same age students, but because in life we need to help each other. If each class has a range of students, in age, ability and with multiple intelligences, we can expect students to develop strong social skills as well as knowledge.

In interviewing an educator I hold in high regard, I asked him what advances have we seen in education since Plato? He replied 'our knowledge of brain development'. We now understand that there are some things one cannot ask of children because their brains have not grown the cells to handle it. Genius is not IQ, but a wide range of different learning styles – and that most children have at least one area of genius. These multiple intelligences can be tested, and he strongly recommended that the VillageTown education system do so. Each class should have a broad mix, the teacher should understand the mix and should encourage the students to understand and collectively work with their own multiple intelligences in the class.

Following this process, we begin to envision a very different set of school buildings.

Home Base and Visiting Work Space

Begin by clustering ten to fifteen students for each teacher. If two teachers want to team up we suggest each cluster keep its own identity. The home base would be a room where the cluster begins the day, their place. It can be a work-place on the plaza, near a garden, or in the Greenbelt. If we have 2,000 students and we aim for a 10:1 ratio, this easily could mean two hundred small rooms or a hundred larger ones with dividers for each cluster, although some will be in the Guild Halls.

Does it make sense to reserve these rooms solely for students, or would it make more sense to design public rooms with a computer tracked booking system? Teachers would have access to many VillageTown resources and the rest of the VillageTown would use the education rooms when not booked out for student learning. If we go with the latter approach, the VillageTown libraries, sports fields, gardens, pools, theaters, lecture and performance rooms, recording and arts studios, even some of the scientific and research laboratories can become part of the students' campus.

This begins to open up other opportunities. In a VillageTown of 10,000 people, especially one that will naturally attract a disproportionately high representation of what Dr. Richard

The walking classroom

Florida calls the Creative Class, we can expect the VillageTown to have many experts in many areas. While following the state curriculum a teacher may find they teach most effectively by taking their students to the workplace of a renowned expert in a particular field who donates time and expertise for the students to learn. Some "teachers" are visitors. During the US war in Iraq, a CBS news producer visited us on his way home from a tour of duty in Baghdad. We arranged with the local high school to invite him to speak to a class – the editor of the local newspaper showed up, and the questions and answers in that classroom were of first rate quality. The teacher became a learner, as did the rest of us. The class, incidentally, was an English class where the curriculum topic was "the language of war."

The Ownership of Buildings

Who should own and maintain the buildings? It depends on who pays for them. We recommend the VillageTown maintain its independence from the dictates of the state education system during start up because we expect the normal bureaucracy of any state system will frustrate the process and flow of the VillageTown initiative. This is not a criticism of any particular bureaucracy, but a factual acknowledgement of how contemporary western systems work. Instead negotiate.

This implies the VillageTown include classrooms as part of the infrastructure, just as it pays for streets, plazas and nursing beds for the elderly infirm. This forgoes the benefit of the state paying for the buildings – and the state can be very generous. In my VillageTown sized community, the Ministry of Education spent over $12 million (NZ) building a school for not more than 260 students, which is almost $50,000 per student seat. If we built a 6 m x 6 m homeroom for ten students and their teacher, at a cost of $3,000 per m², the cost would be about $10,000 per seat. We can probably build them cheaper, better and more flexible.

The Design of School Rooms

Providing space for two thousand students from age 6 to 18 could easily mean the VillageTown takes on a $20 million commitment to build rooms for the education of the young. This is where flexible architecture may come in.

Students have several different needs in their learning. They need:

- Physical space – in essence environmentally controlled space to gather as a group
- Work space using books, paper and more recently computers (desks and chairs)
- Media space with whiteboards, to watch films and educational multimedia
- Applied tool space – art, crafts, technology, science laboratories
- Performance space – theater, music, stage activities
- Exercise and sport space – some outdoor, some indoor

When an architect looks at these needs, it becomes apparent these needs are not solely required for students – they are also places adults would use. If the VillageTown is to allocate valuable and limited land, and possibly fund construction of such spaces, the architect's design brief should include two additional elements: flexible storage and computer scheduling of resources.

Walls might include sliding panels with layers of wall. In the morning, when the students use the room as their homeroom

Given the interest a VillageTown may attract, consider negotiating with state officials to have the state pay for the buildings, but save money by having the VillageTown and its Establishment Board build community-based classrooms to its standards rather than a separate campus.
Also, consider contracting with the VillageTown management to handle the administrative aspects of the education system – especially as it relates to the buildings, their upkeep and day-to-day paperwork.

the walls would have the normal kinds of displays teachers use in classrooms – visual teaching aids, corkboard displays of student work, and so on. When the class leaves the cluster, they slide their wall veneer back into its pocket, so the room is ready for the next group of users. The pocket walls may also be designed so the small 10-person rooms can be opened on one or both ends, to make a larger meeting room.

These rooms also may need flexible furniture, acknowledging the different size needs of children in contrast to adults. The easiest approach is to forego conventional chairs for benches, but whatever method is used, if the furniture is not easily adjustable, then it should have an easy-slide-in closet to put the furniture away every day. Note that traditional Japanese architecture used some of these methods, with sleeping mats stored away every morning.

When we free ourselves from the constriction of a contiguous campus by making the VillageTown the campus, new potential emerges. We find not only do our students get more exercise walking from one place to another, but the layout and public spaces of the VillageTown take on a different and far more interesting character.

Libraries start looking less like a cold institution with long racks of books and more like a place to enjoy books and reading: with desks and reading chairs used both by students and by adults. Indeed, in the section on the importance of attracting and maintaining the creative class, we proposed establishing arts guilds in which affordable, very small artists housing was subsidized by the VillageTown. Each guild would have a large Guild Hall, and it should be part of the design brief to include facilities for school classes – in some cases co-taught by the artists. Integrate the guild system into the education system – part of the subsidy for the creative arts would include a responsibility to work with or at least along side the students.

The same approach would apply to the sports field and gymnasium where the architectural brief would include dual use by students and by adults, although for the most part at separate times, and during school hours, with the school have first access. One of the more worrisome emerging trends in government is what is disparagingly called nanny-state governance. It is based on the fear that children may be compromised by dysfunctional adults. Should this attitude imposes itself in the state expectations under which the VillageTown must operate, then the architectural brief may need to provide for physical separation of changing rooms and the like.

Quality

Traditional schools give children crayons because they are cheap, harmless and well... because we have always given children's crayons. The trouble with crayons is their results look bad when used by older children. Very few artists would use crayons for great works of art, the wax skips on the paper. Somehow, we have developed this idea that children do not merit good tools, not noticing the level of unnecessary frustration this introduces into education. If we incorporate the learning environment into the adult realm, this double standard melts away. Children learning art in an Art Guild building, for example, will see real artists using proper quality materials, as will their teachers. By being exposed to the higher quality standard of those artists, students can be expected to move from the artificial world created by pedagogical segregation into the real world.

Variety

In looking at the homerooms for the students, not all have to look and be the same. First, students are not all the same, and we may find that different interests suggest different locations and functions in the architectural design. For example, some students have an utter passion for horses, and for them the prospect of having their homeroom in the Greenbelt stables would find them wanting to live at school for all their waking hours. Other students may show a strong interest in horticulture, thus the Establishment Board might consider placing the homeroom by the village gardens. This concept can be carried to a higher level by looking at a model developed in the Mt. Edgecumbe High School in Sitka Alaska, where the local Native American Indians called for an applied school to be opened in 1985 based on W. Edward Deming Total Quality Management (TQM) model. The school, which served 88% Native Americans, opened a salmon fish hatchery as part of their applied learning.

The Governance and Management Structure

In countries like New Zealand, a locally elected board of trustees is put in charge of a single school, not a whole school district and the board is given considerable authority over governance. This results in a far more citizen directed governance model that comes with both benefits and risks – the primary risk being lack of talent and understanding of the governance role, as there are only so many qualified volunteers prepared to put their name forward to serve. We think in the VillageTown this would not be expected to be such a major concern.

In such countries, VillageTown Founders have some choices as how to structure both the governance role and the management of their education system. We have some outside-the-box suggestions:

"How many boards?"

Does one have a single board for all the schools, or does one have several that introduce a form of healthy competition? We suggest there should be at least two, perhaps three, but that "schools," as we describe below, have the right to give notice that in the next school year, they wish to be governed by another school board. In this way, checks and balances are introduced, thus encouraging boards to perform to the best of their ability and not become complacent.

"What makes a school?"

If the school's physical campus is decentralized, we may find that schools in fact may be small clusters of two or four teachers, and that we might have as many schools as village plazas. This is the suggestion Christopher

Alexander puts in Pattern № 18 *Network of Learning* and № 85 *Shopfront Schools* where he observes how much of the education budget goes to non-teaching costs, most notably buildings and administrative staff. In small schools, Alexander suggests, this overhead shrinks away, thus leaving more money to lower the student/teacher ratio, which he argues eliminates many of the management costs such as discipline enforcement.

We suggest that these small clusters of classrooms be formed into "schools" and when it comes to pedagogy (the profession of teaching), these smaller clusters carry the authority of a school. It will make an interesting negotiating point with the State on the question of the principal, since the head of the school holds certain specific legal rights. It may turn out that the clusters are considered departments in the eyes of the state, with one or several Principals in the VillageTown schools, or it may be that the state will accept the model akin to the one room school house.

School Management

Prof. John Bremer was fond of using the word *Administrivia* to refer to the endless paperwork that seems to accompany contemporary education. On the first page of this chapter, I placed a photograph of the Agora, where Socrates taught the young, to remind us that great teaching is not about administration, although if you don't cover your tracks, you may be asked to drink hemlock.

At one time, the job title Principal was a truncation of Principal Teacher, which implied an experienced teacher whose leadership in pedagogy was recognized by peers. Now such Principals are lucky to teach one class. Their work is almost entirely consumed with the demands of running a large, complex organization involving both the emerging, challenging personalities of the young and the highly diverse personalities of teachers. Teachers do not select the career because of the good pay and cushy work conditions (although the longer school holidays does appeal); they do it for the love of teaching. Asking the professional teacher to redefine him or herself as a professional administrator does not always yield good results.

Worse, we find that because schools have an administrative staff, the state education department lays more and more reporting requirements on them. This complexity then grows as society looks to the schools to address child rearing issues that used to fall to the family.

For all these reasons, we suggest bifurcation of pedagogy and administration. Because the VillageTown needs an administration to run its affairs, contract out all the paperwork and administrivia to the VillageTown executive department. Unlike the checks and balances recommended for both governance and teaching, the administrative jobs are best done where economies of scale kick in. The same business manager can handle the financial reports for both VillageTown and school, and combining the job means funds are available to compete for personnel that are more qualified.

High Technology

In many cases, students own more advanced technology than their schools. The problem is not just good hardware, but also the right software, which should be easy to use and written for the intended purpose. In understanding how to design an integrated campus in which students use multi-purpose buildings and rooms, schedule coordination becomes essential, and for this nothing will work better than a good software system. The priority of an effective computer system and software should be equal in importance to the construction of buildings and rooms.

Beyond the scheduling software, using software to support pedagogy can make a huge difference in the effectiveness of the teachers and in the quality of management. However, the computer system must not become burdensome. The best systems enable professionals to capture details they need for their work, and then underlying software extracts from that database the information required by senior teachers, management and the state. For example, student attendance can be fully automated using biometric data capture systems that can enable the VillageTown management to know that students are where they are supposed to be, and be alerted if they don't arrive at their next class destination.

This general book on VillageTowns is not, we suggest, the place to explore the details of the software functionality, but do make sure that it is done well.

Curriculum

Why do we have schools? What do schools actually do? Let us start by discussing reality.

One dictionary definition of reality as "a non-derivative experience." Let us examine our education systems, to see how much the schools deal in reality.

We find in the early grades we teach skills – how to recognize letters and numbers, how to read a child's book, how to add and subtract, how to play a simple instrument like a recorder. We experience the reality of symbolism and mastery of instruments such as the pencil and crayon.

As we progress to secondary education, much of what we learn is no longer direct reality but derivative – from someone's text book, or more recently someone's video. We take someone's word that what they are saying, and how they interpret it, is true. Considerable debate burns among adults in this realm, as ideologies and belief systems compete for what to teach. All the while, the students tend to not connect particularly strongly with such derivative experience, and schools find they must engage in frequent testing to keep the students focused. Left to their own devices, the students would focus on reality – playing with their friends, pick-up sports and at the onset of puberty both sexual exploration and self-focus on appearance, possessions and self-definition. To this society has added addictive, pre-packaged derivative experience (i.e. not reality) in the form of television, video, pre-recorded music, computer games, cruising the internet. Society has also invented chemical disruption of natural processes, where illicit drug use seems to be endemic in many communities.

Go to a secondary school and one often finds contained chaos, as underpaid, overworked teachers are isolated with 30 plus students in one hour sessions that run by Pavlovian bells. Some of the students want to learn, some want to please the teacher, some sit in the back and pass their way through. School discipline becomes a major focus of teachers, management, governance and the state school system.

The opportunity for the Establishment Board to establish the character of the VillageTown education system will probably be limited to some extent by the law and state education department's regulations governing curriculum. However, within this framework, generally the law grants considerable latitude to the local community or the families on curriculum delivery.

Two decisions need to be made. The first is on methodology, and the second (in states where choice is permitted) is on qualifications. Two early 20th century alternative methodologies still experiencing strong support are Montessori and Steiner, for example. We recommend that the Establishment Board not adopt either the conventional methodology or century old alternatives. Instead take advantage of the newness of the VillageTown to seek out the best models of education, models that tend to fit the ethos of the VillageTown and its inherent values. Then attract a team of professional educators for whom the opportunity to create a VillageTown form of education is a life's dream.

If there is a key to VillageTown learning, it would be integrated learning, as discussed above. If there is to be an approach to creating a methodology, it would be a community dialogue. Parents are the most natural constituency to approach in a dialogue that asks the questions on how the VillageTown education system should teach. Once the dialogue opens, invite students as well – after all they are the users of the system. Then spread the invitation to other members of the VillageTown – for you will find elders, childless adults and many other people in different walks of life who have much to offer.

While the state generally sets out the required curriculum, teachers and schools have considerable latitude in how they choose to present it. We recommend that the VillageTown becomes the way the curriculum is taught.

Parents Will Move to a New Home to get their Child in a Good School

Good schools are hard to find. When a good school appears, the real estate ads will feature *in the school zone* because the agents know this sells. VillageTowns can and should seek to have the best education on offer in the country. Some will come naturally, by virtue of the structure and character of the community. The rest will come by continually asking *why do we educate?*

Checklist for establishing the schools

- ☐ Brief the public department of educational authorities (send them a copy of this book, perhaps)
- ☐ Which law? (In countries that give a choice between public, semi-public, private)
- ☐ Set up an Establishment Board of Trustees (EBoT) (pick its members very carefully)
- ☐ Open dialogue with the educational authorities, seek alignment of values
- ☐ Decision: [ ] Separate campus or [ ] VillageTown as campus / storefront classrooms (We recommend integrated)
- ☐ Who pays to build and who owns school rooms and buildings?
- ☐ School rooms [ ] Classrooms only or [ ] Multi-purpose community use after school
- ☐ Negotiate arts/sciences rooms and arts/sciences teaching support with Guilds?
- ☐ Who manages paperwork? (We recommend contracting out admin to VillageTown Hall)
- ☐ How many school boards? (We recommend two or three that compete for schools)
- ☐ What is a school? (We recommend they be small clusters of 3-4 teachers of which one is designated Principal who get to decide each year which Board governs them).
- ☐ What technology and resources will be offered to students?
- ☐ What "special characters" will be offered by various schools within the VillageTown?
- ☐ Decide on the curriculum (or multiple) within the parameters of law
- ☐ Draft the Charter for VillageTown Schools setting out philosophy, values, expectations, opportunities, responsibilities and a strategic plan for hired principals.
- ☐ Contract for the design and construction of school buildings
- ☐ Hire principal staff consistent with the Charter
- ☐ Hold elections for school boards
- ☐ If the state does not permit school boards, elect Boards of Influence and command authority.

Intellectual and Artistic Growth: The Guild Hall

Humans create. Creativity opens new worlds, new ways of perceiving, and in doing so enriches our day to day life. With the advent of books, then film, then television and now the internet, it is possible for people to gain access to the creative worlds of art and intellect in locations that otherwise would lack such stimulation. However, media is always a virtual experience.

There is something about live creativity that offers more. Today, for example, we can buy a recording of the world's best symphony orchestra performing one of the great compositions of all time. It will be brilliant, precise and include that special intensity that deeply touches the soul. However, no matter how good the stereo system to reproduce it, the experience will be different than entering a performance hall where there is a symphony orchestra. Not only is the live performance completely different, but afterwards in the cafe or tavern, one chats with the people whose lives are about making music. Those musicians, and other artists, make community life more varied, they add richness to it.

For the VillageTown to provide artistic and intellectual growth, it needs an intentional plan that attracts the Creative Class. To do that, it must provide a physical environment, social milieu and a supportive economy that makes it attractive for them to move there. We see this happening with an investment in both places of higher learning, and in what we call the Artist Guild Hall.

Higher learning is easy. Colleges, universities and research centers already have worked out their economic basis. Some will be amenable to opening a new extension in a VillageTown, so the job of the VillageTown Civitas Corporation (the ViTo) that operates the VillageTown is mostly one of extending invitations and building it. However, the artists and the Creative Class generally are not so well organized or well funded. For them, we must do the organizational work, which is where the Guild Hall comes in.

www.lewenz.net

On each village plaza, the ViTo will build and outfit a large building for an artist guild. Creating a dialogue between the village founders and the artists the ViTo attracts, the guild will self-define, meaning it will determine what it is. We expect several will be musicians, perhaps one classical, another jazz and a third contemporary. Other guilds will encompass the traditional arts of painting, sculpture and

perhaps craft art, such as fine furniture making. Beyond these definitions, we anticipate guilds of inventors, scientists, film and video makers, creative people opening new media using technology, to name but a few.

The ViTo will allocate a portion of the profits from the sale of homes and work places to fund the design and construction of these halls. They will be purpose-built to serve the needs of the guild, and within a reasonable budget (and hopefully a lot of sweat equity invested by the guild members) to provide the tooling, equipment and furniture the guild requires. The ownership of the hall remains with the VillageTown, but its management is vested with the guild. As long as it remains functional and contributing to the cultural enrichment of the community, the guild retains full use of the facilities rent-free. In designing the Guild Hall, the ViTo will include a certain number of short-term hotel or hostel rooms to generate income for the guild to cover its maintenance costs. It may include classrooms for primary and secondary students where guild members may be compensated for teaching classes under the supervision of a licensed teacher. Where the VillageTown builds theaters, museums, concert and performance halls, place them next to the Guild Hall, and put the guild in charge of their management (but leave administrivia to the VillageTown administration).

In addition to the hall, the guild members need to have affordable housing. Their presence in the community promises to make the VillageTown a desirable place to live, to the point where they get priced out of the market. To prevent this, and to lower the cost of living so the members can focus on what they do best, we propose *free-base housing* – a small home or apartment that is provided rent-free to the member. The guild member would have the right either to live in it, or to rent it out and keep the rent if the guild member has, for example, a family and wants to live in a larger village home.

The free-base home solves another architectural challenge. If we build attached housing, yet want the streets to curve, either there has to be wasted space at the turns, or some homes will not be rectangular. Make the free-base buildings trapezoidal. Build one apartment per floor, outfit it with a single bedroom, and provide it to the guild member who covers its maintenance.

Understand that this is not free. People often do not appreciate that which is given free. It is an exchange. The artist's obligation is to pursue their creative or intellectual art, to do what they do best. Under the principle of checks & balances, the village and the VillageTown will retain controls. If the Guild fails to live up to its part of the exchange, the VillageTown can sort it out.

If each Guild has 25 members, and each of the 20 villages has a Guild, that works out to about 5% of the population being supported to enrich the community as a whole. This support comes up front, not out of ongoing fees. In the section on parallel markets, we recommended that 25% of the housing stock be set aside for target populations. One part of that would be for the creative class. Richard Florida demonstrates the business case for this investment. The culturally-enriched communities are economically the strongest.

They also are the most interesting.

Chapter 10 – Governance

> *In our pioneering town of St. John's, we valued education so we called a meeting, and we voted to tax ourselves to build a school and hire a teacher.* So said Stewart Udall over lunch at his house when he was 89 years of age. In this, he captured the essence of democracy. "we valued"; "we voted" "to tax ourselves" "to build" "to hire".

In an ideal world, local government provides services on behalf of the people to improve and maintain quality of life for all while treading lightly on the environment. In the real world people mess it up – what should be simple becomes complex. Thus we find a system of governance must be established not simply to deliver services, but also to curb the tendencies of greed and the cravings for power – to impose ones will on others*. The proposed VillageTown lives in the real world, not the ideal, which means we must both establish systems of service, and systems of restraint.

As observed elsewhere in this book, we are emerging from a historic period driven by non-sustainable practices – that we created an arguably golden era by extracting energy from the earth and dumping its residue in our air, water and land with the unfortunate side effect of creating a more toxic and less enriched natural and human environment. We are now finding the immutable laws of Nature and Earth are beginning to bite back thus we must change how we acquire and use energy.

In this book, we reject retrogressive answers that seem to be currently popular. Instead, we propose a higher quality of life that also walks more gently on the earth. It presumes that most people, and certainly those who want to live in their village, want to change their behavior, to leave the world in better shape than they inherited it, not worse. It also presumes that if they can do so by enjoying better food, better water, a higher level of culture, a safer and happier way to raise children, a kinder way to grow old, a more stimulating work environment and a more beautiful and satisfying physical environment, they would choose this – especially if it costs less that what they currently pay to live less well.

For this reason, the job of VillageTown governance takes on more responsibility than conventional local governance. If the VillageTown installs different systems for energy, transport, water, wastewater, solid waste, telecommunications, care for the weak, the young and the elderly, support for the arts and culture and protection of the environment, then it needs different structures and systems to assure these jobs are done well, for now and for the foreseeable future.

* It is curious that in the English language, we have the explicit word, *greed* to describe the craving of material things, but lack a comparable word for lust for power, the craving to impose ones will over other people and processes that wreaks so much havoc.

By different, we do not necessarily mean new. New comes with risk, thus it makes sense first to look at timeless, proven models and then adapt them for new conditions. The balance of this chapter shall take that approach.

We observe that the systems of governance in many places have become excessively complicated, resulting in conflict, injustice and excessive burdens and costs being placed on law-abiding citizens. We propose a local, simple solution, based on proven western democratic models. While many models of governance have been tried, in western countries, it seems checks and balances representative democracy with separation of powers proves to be the most effective and familiar.

Organizational Structure for Governance - Corporatism

Organize the VillageTown into a legal entity. We recommend using corporate law rather than rely on local government law. If the law permits, you may want to form a new municipal government, but primarily to keep a neighboring government

> Pattern 12 **Community of 7,000** Individuals have no effective voice in any community of more than 5000-10000 persons. People can only have a genuine effect on local government when the units of local government are autonomous, self-governing, self-budgeting communities, which are small enough to create the possibility of an immediate link between the man in the street and his local officials and elected representatives...Give local control to communities of 5,000 to 10,000 persons. Give each community the power to initiate, decide and execute the affairs that concern it closely: land use, housing, maintenance, streets, parks, police, schooling, welfare, neighborhood services. p71 *A Pattern Language* 1977 (written before PC English)

from annexing you so they can collect more taxes, fees or rates. We observe that the power of the private sector – corporate law – is in the ascendency while local government law is becoming more constricting. This is called *Corporatism*. Rather than fight it, use it: form a private, stock-holding corporation. Corporate law allows greater power with less regulation, as long as you pay taxes on your profits. While final decisions will be made by skilled lawyers advising the VillageTown civitas corporation (ViTo), the model we prefer is one where the ViTo is a private corporation owned by all its VillageTown citizens or their homes.

During construction, the ViTo is supported by investors who put up the capital funds and carry the risk. However, when home buyers get their construction loans, investors are paid. When built, the ViTo becomes an asset-rich corporation. Assets include land, its public buildings, the streets, roads, paths and the greenbelt, motorpool, freight depot and businesses such as the bank and the rental car company. We suggest leaving it cash rich with start-up funds and a permanent litigation fund. Pay the investors, call in the ViTo stock, and issue new shares, one per title that cannot be sold separately from the building. Make voting rights by occupancy, not title, so every adult citizen of the VillageTown has one vote. Create two subsidiary divisions, one for-profit, the other either non-profit or a loss-making organization. Run the former for ventures that make money, such as the VillageTown bank. Run the latter as a conventional local government, providing services that cost money, such as cleaning the streets. Some traditional cost centers, such as sewage treatment may end up moving to the for-profit business side.

The ViTo will buy the land for the new community and its greenbelt. We recommend that the ViTo retain ownership, selling title to buildings with the land remaining in leasehold title forever owned by the civitas corporation, the ViTo. This gives the community powers that have been taken away from municipal governments, including the power to ask people to leave if they prove toxic to the community. It also enables the VillageTown to pay a single property tax bill to the surrounding county or regional government, which gives it leverage when it needs cooperation.

Decision, Action, Restraint

So how do we best govern such a hybrid organization? We strongly recommend using time-tested checks and balances systems that proved their worth over centuries. Begin with three branches of local governance – legislative (democratic decision-making), executive (democratic action) and judicial (restraint and fairness). Within these three divisions, be sure to provide checks and balances where the checks "have teeth".

Be sure to design this system to includes professional accountability – hold the individual, be they leaders or employees to personal accountability for their actions so they cannot hide behind bureaucracy. Be sure to include a freedom of information policy in which only the most acutely-sensitive information can be hidden from the public view.

> Utopias fail because their visionaries fail to plan for corruption. Greed, lust for power, ego certainty, vanity and psychic damage are but a few of the human frailties that ruin utopian visions. In free societies, the best answer seems to be a system of checks and balances. Spread the authority out with different responsibilities. In this way when decision making and action cease to provide for the common good, the system has other people capable of correcting it – everyone has to be corrupted before it fails.

Legislative

In a community of ten thousand, representative democratic decision-making proves to be the best system of governance on offer. However, to protect from a clique taking over the governance role and using its power to make decisions that are good for it but bad for the VillageTown, a system of checks and balances is an essential component.

The best system we have seen is a two house legislature where the functions are different, but approval of both is required to pass rules and make resolutions. In traditional societies, the division was between the young, full-of-energy leaders, and the wise, older sages, where the young house came up with the ideas, but they then had to convince the elders of their good value. Keep the numbers small. If there are more than seven people in each, it tends to become cumbersome. In a VillageTown with 20 villages it may make sense to have a group of four villages elect one upper and one lower representative with the other two elected town-wide.

To accomplish the intent, one may consider an upper chamber with representatives appointed by the village councils with a staggered six year term that approves but does not initiate local legislation, and a lower chamber with two year terms that does all the hard work. In addition, one should embed in the constitution or charter of the VillageTown the right to direct referendum if 10% of the adult residents call for such.

The Legislative would make rules that apply to the VillageTown. We suggest:
- It should follow national and state law as much as possible.
- Legislators would be empowered to vote ongoing fees to fund both operations and capital investment.
- Legislators would be empowered to vote resolutions, rules and regulations, and to grant or deny permission for private applications that have a public, VillageTown interest.
- Its elected legislators would not be paid except reimbursement to cover expenses. It's not a job, it's a duty.

In most countries, there are rules of order or standing order forms for such representative bodies, and it would make sense to adopt a proven and familiar model.

Referendum – Active Democracy

Direct democracy offers certain challenges, some of which are logistical. Conventional cost of voting includes ballots, voting places, voting machines and counting votes. In a VillageTown technology can replace all of this. In each home there will be an intranet computer terminal. Intranet means it is not connected to the Internet and it uses a different architecture. Thus, if someone wishes to put forth a referendum on a subject, or to initiate a recall of an elected representative, this can be done with no overhead cost. Rules would be set out to determine when a motion or petition met the criteria to be elevated for a vote and the technology would probably be best to support biometric voting to assure the actual individual registered made the vote. While much debate on such issues will occur in real life on the plazas, the medium does allow for forum and blog debate.

Generally, if the people elected or appointed to govern do a good job, such a power lies dormant. It serves as a powerful check however, because the representatives and administrators know that if they do get out of step with the constituency, the citizens have the power to instantly do something about it.

Village Councils

In addition to the formal structure necessary to govern a 10,000 population community, the VillageTown has the smaller organizational unit of its villages. At this level, simpler democracy like the New England Town Meeting works fine. Each village should have the ability to raise money for local activities, and the right to determine how those funds are spent. The VillageTown Administration will handle the funds to assure probity, but the village will be able to form its own decision-making process to address its own local matters. It is likely that most will develop their own leadership that will speak on their behalf at the town level.

Voting

As noted above the VillageTown intranet will have a local-access computer in every home and workplace. Each citizen will be registered to use any terminal, so that all elections, referendum and snap polls can be held on-line with little or no administrative overhead. Security technology is now sophisticated enough to assure one person, one vote.

The elected officials will find this of use as well, by asking for polls in which they seek guidance. This of course will be in addition to the face-to-face contact that is an important part of small-town democracy. As Christopher Alexander's Pattern Number 12 says "Individuals have no effective voice in any community of more than 5000-10,000 persons." Real democracy occurs in the shops, the streets, anywhere the elected encounters the citizens on a day-to-day basis. The technologies make the democratic process easier and less expensive, but let us remember that democracy is still primarily about human relationships. It is on the streets and in the cafes where democracy will thrive in a VillageTown, not on-line.

Executive Department

Someone has to run the VillageTown. Relying on a pre-existing town, city, county, territorial authority or regional government would likely run into all sorts of problems, as many of the ideas proposed for the VillageTown would be outside the scope of experience and outside the comfort zone of the existing local government. The corporate structure enables this self governing regardless of any outside local government that may have jurisdiction (as long as the corporation owns the land).

Thus, service delivery is best provided by a VillageTown Executive office with paid employees. At the top is the chief executive officer, who can either be elected or appointed by the legislative. I tend to favor it as an elected position.

Elected vs appointed – the risk of empire building looms large in local government. The benefit of *electing* a CEO comes in the clear accountability of winning a vote of confidence. The risk comes in getting a politician not a skilled manager. The benefit of *appointing* a manager comes in the skill certainty. The risk is the CEO ending up running the show, with amateur legislators yielding to the CEO. It's a hard choice especially when people must put their own name forward for election.

Big corporations like IBM engaged in frequent reorganization because they long ago saw the natural tendency of managers to transform the job into a comfortable position for themselves – good for them, but not necessarily in the best interest of the company or stockholders. In one way or another, the VillageTown needs to keep its executive and workers focused on the reason they are employed – to keep the VillageTown running harmoniously, effectively, efficiently and let us not forget – delightfully. When communities get a great manager, this is not a problem, but plans are rarely needed for best case.

If hired, the CEO should serve at the discretion of the Legislative or the people, with no tenure, except perhaps for a budgeted reserve of, say, up to six months pay in the event of early termination without good cause.

Working with the CEO, senior management ought to serve at the discretion of the CEO. Nothing is worse for an organization's operational health than dysfunctional senior management protected by hard-to-terminate employment contracts. We suggest all other employees work under fixed contracts that would expire six months after the election or appointment of the CEO. This would give the CEO sufficient time to get to know the employed staff, but not then clog up the system with ineffective employees. Then, in consultation with the Legislative branch, the CEO would have the right to not renew employment contracts. As a matter of checks and balances, we suggest that a decision to not-hire might be reviewed by an Ombudsman to assure the reasons were in the best interest of the citizens and community.

At a minimum, the Executive branch of VillageTown governance, under the same CEO, should have two subsidiaries – one non-profit and the other for-profit. The conventional services of local government should be provided as non-profit or as a tax-loss, but some of the innovative services, especially where the private sector might claim unfair competition, would be best run as tax-paying, for profit businesses in which the profits become ordinary revenue for the VillageTown budget. For example, as the VillageTown discovered that sewage treatment ceases to be a cost center, and becomes a profit center producing biofuel, it would be shifted to a profit-making venture owned and operated by the VillageTown on behalf of its citizens. Another example might be the motorpool with its rental car business. Without a doubt, the bank would be run for profit.

Ombudsman

There are two lesser offices outside the three primary (Legislative, Executive and Judicial) that are important to checks and balances. These are the offices of Ombudsman and Prosecutor. Let us begin with the Ombudsman. To assure internal checks and balances in the delivery of VillageTown services by the Executive, we recommend electing an Ombudsman who has the right to investigate and hold accountable both the Executive, and individual employees for their performance. It should include the powers to record reprimands against their personnel file that must be taken into consideration for ongoing employment and compensation. This may sound harsh, but we have observed atrocious judgment, errors and omissions by local government personnel where, due to the institutional structure, the employee is not held to account and continues to do damage to the wellbeing of the community. Additionally the Ombudsman should have the right to speak in court on behalf of defendants.

VillageTown Prosecutor

In a separate office from the Executive or Ombudsman, the VillageTown will elect or the Legislature will appoint a qualified lawyer to serve as the Prosecutor. While the Ombudsman speaks for the individual, the Prosecutor speaks for the community. The prosecutor has both investigative powers to form a case, and prosecuting powers to make charges and bring evidence before the VillageTown Court, discussed below.

Restorative Justice

The anticipated judicial process is formal, and for the most part, is intended to follow the time-honored traditions of the western judicial systems. However, it is not the only method, and sometimes it is cumbersome and costly. In New Zealand, an indigenous process called Restorative Justice has emerged from Maori culture and now is mainstream in New Zealand and of significant interest to other nations. It is especially effective with first-time and youth offenders. In the VillageTown, the local village council is the natural place for it to be used, and in certain offences, the village council may ask the prosecutor to refer the matter to them rather than bring it before the Court. We recommend this be investigated and adopted by the VillageTown.

Judicial

The third arm of a checks and balances system is that of the Judiciary; known locally as the VillageTown Court. We recommend the Judicial follow the normal legal system of the country. For example, in New Zealand, this would mean using qualified Justices of the Peace (JP) paid an honorarium. In New Zealand such JPs routinely hear misdemeanor cases.

Private corporations have such a function, although typically it is a legal committee of the Board of Directors. We recommend in the VillageTown that it be more formal and work at arms length. It works using contract and corporate law, rather than municipal law. The powers are granted in the founding documents of the VillageTown. If you buy a property, you accept the obligations that come with the title. By having the underlying property held in leasehold title, the VillageTown may in some states or countries use landlord powers, whereas in others it may use corporate powers.

Essentially, the founding documents must include certain powers when things work as they should and additional powers when go wrong. The Executive must have the right to collect revenue from the property owners on an ongoing basis. Called fees, rates, rent or taxes this revenue is collected when things are operating normally. However, when things go wrong, an additional system needs to be in place.

We anticipate two different types of transgressions. The first relates to conduct. A community needs to protect itself when an individual begins to tear the fabric of the community. As VillageTowns Stewards' Chairman Emeritus, Stewart Udall commented, "[When I was young] small communities were very intolerant of crime." But today in many places those small communities have no power to protect themselves, thus we witness their degradation.

We recommend the VillageTown Court be empowered in its founding documents with four forms of punishment: fines, community service, restorative justice (service to the victim), and eviction backed by the right to order public auction of the offender's home and secure a restraining, trespass or protection order barring the offender from the land of the VillageTown. The eviction right would be a required clause in every rental or lease document, so that if a tenant was found to be offending, their landlord would be required to evict them, or face auction of the landlord's building.

We recommend that within this class of transgression, the VillageTown legislature resolve that violation of certain state or national laws would result in an instant judgment rather than a separate local trial or hearing. For example, being convicted of a murder charge might trigger an instant VillageTown judgment of eviction by the Court with no VillageTown trial required. The judgment of the state would be deemed a sufficient evidence of risk to the community.

The second class of transgression relates to cheating – an unqualified person buying a parallel market home when they are not eligible to do so. To explain: we recommend that approximately 25% of the homes in the VillageTown be set aside for target sectors of the population that are deemed important to the community, but whose purchasing power would not match the open market demand for VillageTown housing. In essence, the ViTo sells a home to a family or individual that meets the target criteria, where the ViTo subsidizes the sale price. That subsidy remains in perpetuity and the ViTo is obligated to protect it, although it may vary the qualifications for parallel homes as the needs of the town and society change.

The intent is to keep this process in the private sector rather than create a bureaucracy to manage it. The owner of a subsidized parallel market home would have the right to sell it at any price to any buyer who met the qualifications of the target market. The potential for abuse comes with a buyer who deceives, or a buyer and seller who collude, where in fact the buyer was not of the target market and therefore reduces the parallel housing stock. If this happens, in the Villager will know about it, and ask that it will be investigated. If it is found to be a breach, the matter would be brought before the VillageTown Court.

At that point, it is essential that the underlying documents empower the Court to act absolutely, with no right of appeal to the state court system; or if the right exists in law that cannot be waived by contract or deed restriction, that it would receive summary judgement. The Court must have the power to order the buyer to sell the property to a qualified buyer, and to set a time limit. At the end of that time limit, the Court must have the power to order the Executive to auction the property off to the highest qualified bidder (qualified meaning 'of the parallel market), or that the ViTo may lease the building at a parallel market rate until a buyer is found.

A comment about this judicial right: The buyer may secure a mortgage for the property, and the lienholder would have reservations about loaning money where there is a risk of the house being auctioned, especially to a limited market. This will have to be resolved by the ViTo at the onset. It may require a clear flag on the property title to signal to the mortgage company they must require the Prosecutor sign off on the applicant to assure the VillageTown is satisfied with the qualifications. If the VillageTown runs its own bank, where all mortgages are managed on behalf of the mortgage backed security holders, this may prove easier to manage.

An explanation

In making these recommendations, we looked carefully at various governance models both traditional and experimental. We found that experimental models often produced unanticipated negative side effects, most notably far greater energy consumed – long meetings, drawn out process that in some cases wore out the community to the point of collapse. We found that when we looked at the judicial role of restraint, communities and citizens need certainty – if you do this, the consequence will be that –and a system that takes too long or is too convoluted becomes inherently unjust.

Living in a small community, I personally observed that in severe cases, a dysfunctional resident can tear apart the very fabric of a community – sometimes deriving bizarre satisfaction from doing so, and modern society lacks effective means for dealing with such behavior. Proposing a resolution such as eviction to protect the community may cause controversy – indeed, in reviewing this book, one might expect critics to unduly focus upon this single idea; however, it would be unlikely such critics would have lived for any length of time in small communities of five to ten thousand people.

In villages and small towns, such nefarious people can become utterly destructive, and the community is simply not equipped to deal with them. It's a fine line between the gadfly and the injurious resident, but communities need to protect themselves from offensive, abusive and dangerous residents. The incident in my community involved a condo owner who filed numerous complaints against a nearby cafe, involving officials, police and hearings that ran on for years. There was nothing the state could do to end what the community saw as legal bullying. Finally, the community became fed up, staged a protest parade down the main street in front of his condo with placards demanding he stop. It was only then that the complainant realized the extent to which he was damaging the community. He moved on to a place more suitable for his temperament. With this in mind, we introduce the concept of public auction as a more suitable resolution than protest marches or vigilante justice.

In doing so, we see it as most important that due process of law be embedded at the same time. The basis of such a drastic enforcement mechanism must be clear and justified. It must not be used to get rid of someone people find annoying. The most significant example of breaching this line is Socrates, who was tried and executed by his peers for the crime of corrupting the young, because he taught them how to ask questions that embarrassed the establishment. The VillageTown needs its gadflies. The rules proposed herein must never be used to get rid of annoying people, but only those who threaten the integrity and fundamental wellbeing of the VillageTown.

Public Works

Within the VillageTown boundaries, the Executive would take responsibility for streets, water, sewer, telecommunications, electricity and other parts of the infrastructure, which if there is a larger territorial authority normally holding such responsibility, would become a subject of negotiation.

In part, we recommend this because the infrastructure will be different. When one bans cars, the streets are maintained differently. If an advanced sewage treatment and gray-water system is installed, the VillageTown will have different operating and maintenance processes. The same differences may hold true for other parts of the village, and it would seem logical for the ViTo to hold responsibility for their operation. This also would then result in targeted parallel housing for such maintenance employees. This has the additional benefit such staff are local, so they can keep an eye on operations even when off-duty – much better than phoning a call center located in a remote location and trying to explain the problem.

For Profit Operations

While most people accept fees as a given, in fact smart operation of local governance can generate income from its activities that can be used to keep the cost of living down for the residents. Some of these operations may be run as non-profit, but tax authorities may find others must operate as tax paying for-profit organizations. So pay the tax and be free to act.

The bank is an obvious for-profit business.

The motor pool is a probable for-profit venture. VillageTown owned and operated, it would consist of a covered garage similar to airport car rentals. Residents reserve the car of their choice using the intranet and then walk (or drive their e-cart) to the motorpool, where they would shift bags to the waiting car, insert their cash-card and drive away. Such an operation would involve purchasing or leasing capital equipment, employing clerks, cleaners and mechanics, and purchase of fuels and maintenance goods. The motor pool would also earn money leasing parking spaces for privately owned cars.

In our research on sewage treatment and solid waste, we find the potential that these areas may prove not to be cost centers, but profit centers, especially if the energy components can be extracted and converted into energy products or supplies. For example, waste water can be treated to remove pathogens, but not its nitrogen content. The wastewater would then be piped to make biofuel – with the biofuel sold to the Motorpool for running some of the fleet. The same opportunity may stand for solid waste disposal – again containing potential energy that can be extracted into liquid or syngas form.

A major for-profit VillageTown operation may be in running the food cooperative. As a design element, each home would have a food box next to the mailbox. The VillageTown's Intranet computer system would include food-ordering software, so the coop becomes the wholesale buyer of food. Such a system, with up to 10,000 residents, may find that it becomes a major business, especially if it then expands into wholesale buying of consumer goods in addition to food.

Non Profit Operations

We feature the nursing facilities on the plazas as an important aspect of caring for our elders and infirm, with the fundamental premise that this cost is paid for by a universal VillageTown self-insurance plan – with property fees paying for its ongoing operation. Eldercare would be a good example of a non-profit operation run by the VillageTown. Initially the capital cost would be paid for by the ViTo, in the same class as the streets, plazas, halls and infrastructure.

The village might consider a non-profit local transport system consisting of free bicycles throughout the village, or even VillageTown owned low speed electric vehicles and run by inserting ones pre-approved bank card in a slot to start it.

All these decisions are made by the people who live there. It's your money, it's your life, it's your village.

Law Enforcement

Rules, laws and boundary conditions are not written for people who behave. 85% of society must behave if the society is to not fall into chaos. It is when a small minority of the population breaches the peace of the community that criminal law becomes important. In many areas, law enforcement will be provided by state or regional authorities, but the VillageTown organizers would be well advised to set aside rental homes, or parallel market homes specifically for the local constable or cop on the beat, and ask that the job be long term so the law enforcement officer gets to know the people. It is unlikely that the VillageTown would run its own police department, but it important that law enforcement be personal yet professional.

VillageTowns intend to return to the kind of community that has a low tolerance for crime. It intends for law to be obeyed, especially because the adults will be present to keep an eye on all the children.

Perhaps the most difficult challenges facing the VillageTown will be those related to drug abuse, especially dealers of illicit drugs targeting the young. The difficulty will come if some of the Founders, otherwise law-abiding citizens, use illegal drugs at home. In some countries, drug abuse among adults is so rampant that it has become mainstream. This does not mean it is healthy or good, but that it is present. Clear statements of how the VillageTown intends to respond to such conduct are best set out in the very beginning, so that those with what the villages deem anti-social life styles will look elsewhere to live.

Governance and VillageTown Management Checklist

VillageTown Mandate for governance (decide on one)
- ☐ Legally constituted local government under corporate law
- ☐ Freehold title with deed conferring permanent governing powers to VillageTown
- ☐ Leasehold title with deed conferring permanent governing powers
- ☐ Other legal form conferring permanent governing powers

Organizational structure
- ☐ Elected legislative / governance body
- ☐ Chief Administrator [__] elected [__] appointed by legislative/governance
- ☐ VillageTown prosecutor (legal training required) [__] elected [__] appointed
- ☐ Ombudsman [__] elected [__] appointed
- ☐ Judicial (legal training required) [__] elected [__] appointed
- ☐ Right of public referendum (use VillageTown intranet)
- ☐ Local village councils

Choose how administration is delivered
- ☐ Conventional – staff reports to Chief Administrator
- ☐ Competitive – two different delivery services that compete for contracts

Legal Enforcement mechanisms
- ☐ Agreements with nation/state/local law enforcement
- ☐ Right of VillageTown Court to assess fines and enforceable injunctions
- ☐ Right of VillageTown Court to order auction of deed to property and evict

Services (decide which are-for-profit and which are not-for-profit)
- ☐ VillageTown service delivery staffing
- ☐ Administrative contract with schools for administrivia
- ☐ Roads, plazas, walls, parks, sports fields, gardens, cemetery, etc.
- ☐ Buildings: Village Halls, Town Hall, Guild Halls, Nursing Hospices
- ☐ VillageTown school buildings
- ☐ Utilities – water, sewage, electricity, biofuel, telecommunications
- ☐ Motor Pool
- ☐ Food and delivery Goods Depot
- ☐ Farmers Bank, Food Cooperative
- ☐ Consumer Goods Buyers Cooperative
- ☐ Credit Union or VillageTown Bank
- ☐ Nursing Hospice Services
- ☐ ISP (Internet service provider)
- ☐ Visitor information and booking services

The American Dream – Las Vegas Style (2006)

Chapter 11 – The Design Brief

Normally, when a subdivision is first proposed, a design brief is established by the customer. Usually that customer is an investor or an investor-developer who borrows the money to buy the land, secure subdivision approval, and either develop it or sell it off to a developer-builder. Very early on in the process, the design brief is established.

☞ *This marks the place where we shift the process.*

> On the front book flap of architect Christopher Alexander's *A Pattern Language*, he writes "....people should design for themselves their own houses, streets and communities. This idea may be radical (it implies a radical transformation of the architectural profession) but it comes simply from the observation that most of the wonderful places of the world were not made by architects but by the people."
> We ask "How can we enable people to do their own design within the context of building a ten thousand population community with thousands of homes, offices, shops and public buildings?" Answer: model train set. Build that over-the-top train set that someone's dad built in the basement. Don't put in trains or tracks, but build a 100:1 scale model of the VillageTown. Make the buildings movable. Move them around in a collaborative dialogue until the design looks right. Then reduce it to paper – that becomes the brief and the master plan for zoning approval. Keep the architects in the room, their skills and expertise is essential to a project of this magnitude. As Christopher Alexander suggests this will radically transform their profession.

The design brief as a vernacular process.

Under normal circumstances, authority for the design brief lies with the developer. In many cases the architect or master planner drives the design brief by holding a series of meetings with the developer, listening to the developer's ideas, going away to make drawings, and coming back with new ones until the developer finally agrees and signs off. In high-profile jobs, architects may seek to plant their artistic stamp on the initiative, convincing the developer to accept a design brief that the architect hopes will be prize winning. With the normal time pressures of business, and especially of borrowed money, the parameters considered when creating the design brief are often truncated.

We propose that the design brief process take longer with a primary role for the villager. It embraces the purpose of securing a strong local economy and the pursuit of a good life (conviviality, citizenship, art, intellect, spirit) for its citizens. We create tools for the people who will actually live in the VillageTown – that enable them to provide for their own collective well being. We propose this to give the VillageTown a true sense of authenticity (see page 35-37 for a discussion of authenticity).

Because these villagers are not professionals, we create *Vernacular Tools*. In testing various tools, we found some non-professionals have difficulty reading architectural drawings or visualizing computer generated renditions. The same information placed on a 100:1 scale model, with three-dimensional scale model buildings, streets and open space becomes easily accessible to almost all. We then take timeless patterns and reduce them to business card sized fridge-magnets, printed on an ordinary ink-jet printer, and have the non-professionals work with them on large magnetic white boards (see p 152). With these two simple tools, we enable non-professional people to create the design brief for their community. Not by themselves, of course – we draw upon all the professional expertise any major development project would. It's just that as a settlement rather than a development project, we change the working relationship between the professionals and the people who will live in the VillageTown.

When we provide a tool set for the villager to develop a design brief, the first thing that changes is the relationship between the professionals, who receive the design brief, and the real client: the people who will live there; who will live with the results. To make this process clearer, we name these future residents as "Founders" and we group all the professionals, be they architects, planners, engineers, designers, bankers, and the like, with the name of "Mentors"

> How to become a Founder: To participate as a Founder in the design process you must have signed a letter of intent that you wish to buy into the Village, and you must have provided evidence of ability to pay for your property – a financial statement or mortgage qualification approval letter.

Example of a 100:1 scale model. This model is of Delphi, and is probably more detailed than needed for planning a VillageTown.

To illustrate this relationship we present a diagram (below). The Founders stand closest to the village model than the Mentors and Regulators because the Founders are the ones who live with the result. The professionals symbolically stand behind the Founders to make illustrate the working relationship of the participants; mentors always stand behind. The aerial photograph in the middle shows a 100:1 scale model that was actually used in one test initiative of the 100:1 modeling we conducted in 2005.

If we do our job right, long after the Mentors have gone to other jobs, indeed long after the Founders have all died of old age, the village will remain with a thriving economy, vibrant social life, rich culture and a healthy environment.

In addition to these two groups* standing around what will become the model of the land, we have a third circle of people who stands beside but not around the circle – the Regulators.

The Role of the Regulators

The Regulators are the local government officials who regulate the permit process. Typically, they review the proposed plan for the new VillageTown that is generally then passed on to an Approval Board (the normal authority for the jurisdiction), often elected officials, who will grant, deny or offer limited approval for the plan, including its subdivision and development conditions.

The Regulators must not be *vested* in the process and for this reason they stand in the room, but outside the settlement circle. This distinction must be maintained so the process does not compromise the independent role of the local government that must represent the people and broader communities when it comes time to approve or disapprove the proposed plan for a new VillageTown.

However, at all important times, they are ***in the room*** and ***dynamically engaged*** with the process. Their role is to identify ideas

---

* Note: In some cases, the VillageTown may deem it wise to invite potentially-affected parties to join in the process as *observers*. Observers would be invited to raise any concerns they might have, especially focused on aspects which may adversely affect them, with an intent to address reasonable ones dynamically.

that may run into difficulty when the master plan is presented for local government approval, and to seek resolution of these conflicts in real-time. **Real-time resolution** is one of those acceleration tools by identifying and resolving a conflict when it is first put forward, rather than wait until it is embedded in the final plan, where upon a three-minute discussion blows up into a protracted back-and-forth, sometimes not getting resolved until a Judge starts banging heads.

One way to easily understand this is the three card system: Green, Yellow and Red.

Red is the Regulators' signal that the proposed idea will run into strong opposition by them (for good reasons as given), and if it remains Red will most likely send the whole proposed plan to Court, something that takes years and requires expensive lawyers and expert witnesses. Because time is of the essence in this process, and the objective is to seek cooperation, not confrontation, this red card condition is also known as a *Drop Dead*. Forget it, try another approach.

On giving a red card, the Regulator then offers the group some alternatives that might earn a Green Card, or at least a Yellow, and the Founders and Mentors receive that information and immediately begin to seek innovative solutions to earn a Green or Yellow Card. This resembles the court ordered resolution process just before a trial begins.

In this process, let us make it clear, the Regulator is not telling the people what to do, but is seeking to identify and resolve conflicts dynamically. For the Regulator, maintaining this distinction is mandatory. Most people in such positions are skilled professionals – able to handle it.

If an idea gets a Green Card, it is then considered provisionally acceptable and it is signed by the Regulator. If it gets a Yellow Card, the Regulator is signaling that this will have to receive a provisional judgment call from the Approval Board.

The Yellow Card brings in another system of negotiation. This may require a special decision by the approving authorities (either the Approval Board or the territorial authority) prior to the process beginning.

We presume that the local authorities find the prospect of a new highly sustainable community with an assessed valuation in the range of a billion dollars to be of substantial public interest. Instead of waiting until the plan is complete before they get a chance to look at it, we strongly recommend that they set up a formal procedure allowing the VillageTown design process to secure interim, provisional decisions on elements that the Regulators determine need a policy level (or political) decision. If such a procedure is authorized, then the Yellow Card would signal to the Founders when they have hit such an issue. Sometimes the Founders will modify it to earn a Green, but other times, go for the provisional ruling.

On getting a yellow card, a delegation contacts the approval board and asks for an interim ruling. If given, it becomes a judgment call, and later the approval board would have to accept it, or provide a compelling reason why in the larger context of the final plan, it no longer stands as a good way to go. In this way, major obstacles are overcome quickly. If everyone is working in good faith and paying attention, the final plan should be approved with no further changes.

How people think – How people relate

As we proceed with the process of the design brief, we then introduce a tool to make a four-part distinction in how people use their brains – how they see and relate to the world. This particular model is called the Herrmann Brain Dominance Instrument™ or HBDI™ and it can be found at www.hbdi.com.

Of all the many similar models, we found this one most useful in the design brief process because it both helps give people language to understand why there are other people at the table with whom they find great difficulty relating, and then shows them why they need those people at the table. These four quadrants (Big Picture [yellow], People Person [red], Analytical [blue] & Process [green]), are color coded and the text describes some of their characteristics. In the work process, we suggest people first identify which of the four quadrants they identify with as most dominant (they may actually use the HBDI instrument if they so choose), and then to so color-code their name tag and at the beginning of the workshop stand in that position around the circle. While many people are dominant in more than one quadrant, (successful CEO's are often strong in all four, which might explain they got to the top job), we find this is an effective way to establish communication and facilitate team-work.

Problem Solver
Mathematical
Rational
Logical
Analyzer
Technical
Realistic

Conceptualise
Experimental
Imaginative
Synthesiser
Strategic
Visionary
Holistic

Safekeeping
Implements
Controlled
Conservative
Planner
Organizational
Administrative
Establishes procedure
Gets things done

Feeling
People
Talker
Emotional
Expressive
Supportive
Interpersonal
Become involved
Build teams

The HBDI™ Brain Dominance Model finds we have four predominant ways we use our brains and people need all four represented if we are to work as effective group.

Build the Workshop – Having the right space to work is important. If a large room is not available, build a temporary one. Make it large enough to hold several hundred people working around multiple tables. The building should be comfortable and well lit. It should be reserved for the process, not permitting other groups to come in and take down the work tables. If possible, a catwalk should be installed overhead to permit top view photographs of the work, and moving spotlights to replicate seasonal solar arc. The scale model will be aligned with true north, and the spotlight arc able to show sunrise to sunset any day of the year, so people see the shadow effect. Each village will start with its own table showing a scale model containing non-negotiable street connections and proposed local streets and plaza. The Founders will lay out their homes, their streets and specify their design code.

Provide power for computer equipment, and an outside or ventilated area to make scale models (especially if using a hot knife on polystyrene foam blocks to cut model buildings). Document the process with still and video cameras.

Beginning the process of creating the Design Brief

Once you have sorted out the working relationships between people, you then turn attention to the subject matter at hand, the design brief.

So where do we start?

We start with land.

You will use a scale model of the land, but be sure to walk the land first and often.

Land selection may be easy – let us presume it's selected, the ownership structure is right, the projected land use as a VillageTown ideal, the locals support it, and its characteristics

are excellent. If you have not found land yet, choose a big site and avoid ruining good farmland.

On the table, we place a 100:1 scale model of the land. If you can secure an aerial photograph with contour levels, boundaries and demarcation of important characteristics such as wetlands, this is best. If not, a contoured survey map set to 100:1 scale will work, but it is most helpful if it also shows locations of trees, buildings, streets and other markers, so the Founders can orient themselves. This model becomes one of the most important tools.

We find this 100:1 display works best mounted on lightweight rigid timber supported by moving legs at table height, so that it can be wheeled apart to get access to middle parts. Each village is a jigsaw puzzle piece. When done all should fit together.

For this, you will need a meeting place reserved for the duration the workshop process without having to break the display down. When you consider this is a billion dollar initiative, allocating semi-permanent work space should be a priority. In the best of worlds, the workshop would be placed on the land, in a prominent location that can oversee much of the land to be transformed into a VillageTown.

If the land is highly contoured, such as in the example (below right), slicing the aerial photograph along the contour lines and then making layers will greatly aid in developing a more accurate design brief. It's no use to design for morning sunlight, only to find in real life the hill blocks the sun until 10 am. If you use metric measurements, this can be easily done by purchasing 10 mm thick polystyrene insulation panels and slicing them along the contour lines. In this photo the contour edges have not yet been sanded.

Alternatively, seek out computer driven routing machine that accurately cuts a 100:1 scale model in three dimensions. Various densities of foam can be specified, it can even be painted with the actual landform details. Do chose a type of foam that is easy to carve and fill, as you will find the design process will cut into the land in some places, and raise it up in others.

Begin with the VillageTown Walls

We begin by setting out the village walls, this always comes first. The Latin word *Urbis*, from which we get urban, meant a walled Village or Town. Walls are not just for security, they are a fundamental defining quality of interchange, marking the boundary condition. Suburban sprawl happens because planners fail to respect boundary conditions. While boundaries can be set out with signs and laws, real walls feel better, they define the VillageTown in a way no sign can.

There are two types of boundaries. The VillageTown walls are real walls that surround the VillageTown on the outer perimeter of the urban core. The second wall may not be a wall at all, but some sort of demarcation that marks the boundary between one village and the next. It may be a low wall, or open land, or it too may be a real wall. It's up to the Founders.

Inside the VillageTown wall, density is high, outside no residences at all. Inside there are no cars or trucks. Just outside the walls, touching them, we place the VillageTown Gate (where important visitors are formally received, and where parades begin or pass through), the 300 acre Greenbelt, and on about 50 acres, the Motorpool, Freight Depot, and the walk-to Industrial Park. Outside the walls, the Greenbelt is rural. Bleed-out of buildings is prohibited, none of the sort of sprawl that ruins a sense of place. Beyond the walls, the Greenbelt is home to sports fields, equestrian paddocks, the sewage processing plant, food and flower gardens, and protected natural preserves, especially of any nearby old-growth stands of timber or wetlands.

The walls should be proper height, which is usually about 8 feet (2.4 meters) and they should encircle the VillageTown except where natural landscape would dictate otherwise. They should have multiple entrances, some for pedestrian traffic and others for access by trucks on special permit. They should be thick, made of stone or use the variable density aggregate in soft form or of hedgerow. They should never be designed with rigid, straight lines lest it feel like a prison. They should be designed to make it difficult for cats and dogs to hunt the rural land.

Walls offer many benefits. They offer security, not the least of which is assuring that a lost child or a disoriented elder is more likely to be in the VillageTown than have wandered off. They offer a sense of enclosure, which is a fundamental human need. Properly designed they can control winds, create microclimates and if covered in climbing plants can form an exquisite backdrop to the VillageTown edge. They also clearly demarcate car-free zones, and make a much safer environment for children. The boundary walls may be determined by the available land or a natural feature. They must be beautiful. As the VillageTown becomes more popular, they serve as a clear reminder that the VillageTown is a historic district. Once built, no sprawl.

In setting out where the wall is to be placed, expect this to be a primary negotiations point with the approving officials. The wall will determine how many buildings fit inside, based on reasonable density of two and three story buildings, streets, plazas and gardens. Remember that in the 100:1 process, nothing is fixed. On the scale model, the walls can and should be moved as part of the negotiation in designing the VillageTown.

Consider the Prominent Buildings

> The tiniest hamlets have a dominating landmark – usually the church tower. Great cities have hundreds of them. The instinct to build these towers is certainly not mere Christian; the same thing happens in different cultures and religions, all over the world. Persian villages have pigeon towers; Turkey, its minarets; San Gimignano, its houses in the form of towers; castles their lookouts; Athens, its Acropolis; Rio, its rock.
>
> Pattern No. 62 High Places *A Pattern Language*

In recent times in many places, the pendulum of planning profession has swung toward hiding human activity, and indeed given some of the excessive, trophy homes built on prominent sites by private citizens; this restraint on the part of local government approving officials is to be commended. However, humans are not hobbits living in hills. In setting out the design brief for the VillageTown, serious consideration needs to be given early in the process to the landmark(s) which defines the VillageTown, that to which people not only look up – but then climb.

Such landmarks demand careful consideration of form, function and appearance. Most likely they would be a public building; a building over which the VillageTown maintained some control, to assure the community interest was maintained… perhaps a school of higher learning, a visitor center and meeting place or a performing arts center. In the dialogue on this key part of the VillageTown design brief, also consider details such as wind, sunlight and shadow. In Auckland, New Zealand, some trophy skyscrapers were erected that created wind tunnels, ruining the human enjoyment of plazas below.

In determining the landmark, avoid trendy like the plague. As of this writing, the buzzword among artists and architects alike is "quirky" as if this is an excuse for banality that is new and different. If it is a building, think in terms of seven generations to come – will it serve them? Prominent is not the same as in-your-face. Expect that this is an area where egos will emerge, especially among the design professions. Be firm and do it right.

Historic District

Even though the VillageTown will be new, once it is built, the intent is that it gets the same designation as a historic district. By doing so, a whole book of rules designed by the local government to control bad future development becomes unnecessary. What you see is what you get. This is an essential trade-off if we seek to secure rapid approval within the Dynamic Engagement Design process. The building shells are designed to be built at one time, after which they will remain as built. To allow for future expansion, and because the proposed building system produces very inexpensive walls, we encourage people to build a two or three story house in which the upper floors are not finished if the budget or need is not there. Then expand within the shell. By doing this the community does not suffer the effect that at all time, some building is wrapped in scaffolding up with a new addition or tear down underway. Future expansion is done within a sound-proof building with all noise and dust self-contained.

Identify the formal entrance and reception area within the village walls

When people arrive at the VillageTown, a human-scaled entry is entirely different from the big sign put up by the highway department saying *Welcome – Speed Cameras in Use*. A human scaled portal provides a clear gateway – a practical gateway that also offers protection from rain. Traditionally an honor accorded visitors was to be handed keys to the village gate. In many countries, we have lost this form of acknowledgement, in part because our planners no longer design for it. The closest we get is the security gate in which we talk to a squawk box and our host buzzes us in. Having a formal ceremonial gate becomes an important part of ritual. The tradition of being given keys to the city makes little sense in the modern city penetrated by a ten lane highway that clogs during rush hour. Such a formal reception will work in the VillageTown, as guests leave their car in the motorpool and walk to the gate.

We recommend you consider the village gate as part of the design brief. As discussed above, we also recommend you consider providing the perimeter of the VillageTown with solid, beautiful aggregate walls. Walls provide a sense of enclosure – they mark where the VillageTown ends and the countryside begins. The primary village gate becomes the focal point of the village walls, they work as one. This pattern of boundary conditions and entrances becomes an important part in defining the design brief, and needs to come early in the process.

In testing an earlier draft of this manuscript on two Italian architects, otherwise enthusiastic about the VillageTown, they expressed reservations about a walled VillageTown. In Europe, they explained, walls were about war, not a pattern they wished to repeat. I note this, but offer a different view. War now comes as fire from the sky, not hoards battering down the main gate. The front door and walls of our homes are about entrance and enclosure. They offer protection from harsh winds, and make a demarcation passing from open space to enclosed. People have an innate need for enclosure, so does the VillageTown.

Village walls provide a sense of enclosure. They also provide a level of personal security from crime that is an unfortunate reality in many places. While it is hoped that VillageTowns will reduce crime, walls and gates offer security. If security requires people at the village gates, please hire very hospitable people to receive visitors– if they need the work, consider employing actors to play the part as they are guaranteed to make it an entertaining part of VillageTown life.

Festival Photograph by Carin Wilson

Festival Field and Sandlot Ballfield

Outside the village walls provide wide open space for public events, like the circus coming to town or the annual music festival. Avoid the expense of a professional stadium, instead providing a flexible, open space that can be used one day for children putting together a ball game, and the next day for a big-tent event. Set aside spaces for visiting cars, paying attention to drainage to make it useful year-round. If the site plan allows, placing the field next to the motor pool and freight depot makes some sense as this will provide overflow parking during times of high activity.

Be mindful of your noise map, choose a site where music or dancing 'till dawn doesn't affect the quiet zone, and take great care with lighting to avoid light pollution.

If water is a part of your site plan, especially navigable water, give consideration to visiting boats or ships – it's an added bonus if your audience can include them. Newport Rhode Island in the USA is famous for its music festivals, now held by the harbor. Boats and even cruise ships come from afar for this annual event. This evens out the accommodations pressure, allowing additional patrons for the event over the capacity of the hotels, B&B's and other visitor facilities.

Avoid the temptation to institutionalize the site. There is a magic to a huge tent that no auditorium or hall can match. Provide some toilet blocks, but little more. For the most part, keep it as open space.

This raises a long-term planning issue that applies to many parts of the VillageTown, but especially to open-space. A fine balance needs to be established between the benefits of the original site plan and the tendency of people over time to erode it for convenience or pecuniary interest. Once the site of amenities like the festival field are established, place restrictions on their being converted to some other use – not prohibitive restrictions, but a requirement that such a major quality-of-life decision involves the community as a whole. In making such a decision apply the same tests of social, cultural, economic and environmental well-being tests that were applied during the design brief work at the founding of the VillageTown.

> "I have heard countless people across the country use the same phrase to describe the inability of their city's leadership to adapt to the demands of the Creative Age: "They just don't get it." It is not that these cities do not want to grow or encourage high-tech industries. In most cases, their leaders are doing everything they can to spur innovation and high-tech growth. But most of the time, they either can't or won't do the things required to create an environment or habitat that is attractive to the Creative Class. They pay lip service to the need to attract talent, but continue to pour resources into underwriting big-box retailers, subsidizing downtown malls, recruiting call centers and squandering precious taxpayer dollars on extravagant stadium complexes. Or they try to create facsimiles of neighborhoods or retail districts, replacing the old and authentic with the new and generic – and in doing so drive the resident Creative Class away.
>
> At a time when genuine political will seems difficult to muster for virtually anything, city after city across the country can generate the political capital to underwrite hundreds of millions of dollars of investment in professional sports stadiums. The ostensible economic goal of these facilities is one to which they are sublimely irrelevant. The most recent studies show that stadiums do not generate economic wealth and actually reduce local incomes… Not once during any of my focus groups and interviews did any member of the Creative Class mention professional sports as playing a role of any sort in their choice of where to live and work. Why are most civic leaders unable even to imagine devoting those kinds of resources or political will to pursue the things that really matter to their economic future or to people?"
>
> *The Rise of the Creative Class p302-3 Richard Florida ISBN 0-465-02477-7 first published 2002 by Basic Books. © 2002 by Richard Florida*

We then define the Plazas – The Plaza defines the village, the streets lead to the plazas

In our research, we found one of the most important elements of the VillageTown is the paved, central square known as the plaza – not a village green or park, but a pedestrian-only cobble-stone or paver-covered open space, surrounded by shops and work places, with cafes, fountains where people can gather for a drink, light meal or evening promenade. Further, we found they work best when there are many such plazas, not just one in the center: one plaza per village, one village for, on average, every 500 people, with a larger plaza in the Town Center capable of holding the full population of the community, standing up in a crowd.

The plazas provide the stage for public connection. Children play on them; parents push babies in carriages, workers walk out to sit, have a cup of coffee, a meal or an evening drink with friends. Teens hang out on them. Old people sit on benches and talk or just watch. For actors and musicians the plaza is perfect as an impromptu stage. With workplaces and homes around them, the plaza becomes the heart of the village; it defines its living character.

Plazas serve two social functions. In a direct way, they provide a place for people to intentionally meet. Additionally, it enables people to be connected to the community without an intention to connect with anyone in particular; it creates a sense of place. Build them so one may walk from one to another for at least an hour without backtracking.

Multiple plazas provide different destinations and if each has a different character, the plazas make the VillageTown continually interesting, especially if some of that character comes from people, and is therefore continually changing.

Character

Each village will have its own character, defined by its Founders. Character is a broad concept. In defining the plazas, little attempt should be made to restrict it.

Character can be ethnic. In a multicultural, new-immigrant society like New Zealand, which places a strong value on ancestry (especially due to the fact of its founding document, the Treaty of Waitangi, which was written between the indigenous peoples and the Crown to manage the effects of large scale immigration), ethnic groups may choose to cluster around a particular plaza, and give it a flavor of their own. Maori, Pacifika, Celtic, Chinese, Indian, Arabic, African, Japanese, German, Italian, South African are just a few of the ethnic groups with strong presence in New Zealand. In more established countries like the USA, it may have different nationality themes as most Founders will have American or Hispanic accents.

Character can be architectural. Some plazas may be vernacular, hand-made, with natural tints made of whitewash or clay slurries. Others might be modern, hard edges, Bauhaus, trendy and some may choose a historic reference, to a colonial past.

Character can be creative. Imagine what would happen if the team who created the sets for Lord of the Rings were to create a plaza. Have a look at the extended DVD version of the films, in which the creative team describes how they designed and built. Extraordinary talent – so sad when at the end of filming, all was torn down. Imagine what might happen if a plaza became a collaboration between a director like Peter Jackson and the Founders, in which creative assistance was offered, to not only make a plaza, but also create a living set that could be used for future films. If some of the inhabitants of the plaza were in the creative industry, they even might find they had created a magnet for employment.

Character can be about food, slow food in particular. In this, Italians, Spaniards and Greeks especially seem to have mastered the fine art of spending wonderful hours in good company over food. Such a plaza would have more than the regular café. It might have an open fire, bread ovens, coffee roasters, olive presses and aromas wafting on the breeze. Someone may open a chocolate factory or a boutique brewery: think glorious smells.

Character can be about weather. At least one of the plazas might have a large, glass-enclosed arboretum filled with tropical plants. When the temperature dropped and the cold rains fell, residents would visit the arboretum, with its dining areas, benches amid the plants, and a visible, non-invasive children's play room (strong glass walls, soundproofed so adults can see but not hear) next to the parent's café. Build for winter, summer usually takes care of itself.

Character can be about visitors. A particular plaza can have a strong visitor component, with locals operating guest houses and B&B's and a traveler's inn with the traditional tavern on the plaza. When residents wanted a cultural exchange, they would walk to the visitors' plaza, knowing they would be sure to find someone new and interesting to meet.

Character can be about noise. Some plazas, especially ones with young-adult housing, may be loud, active, lots of fun. Others may be tranquil, with places of worship or meditation. Note: it is most important to build public, VillageTown-owned sacred buildings, regardless of which religions are popular at the time. People need places of sanctuary. If religious communities wish to use them, this is good, and their rent should be free as long as their sanctity is respected.

Noise management is a crucial element in any density-housing environment, and strict rules are recommended to control restaurant fans, heat exchangers and other generators of ambient noise so there is no such background noise. Intentional noise is a different matter. Some people love it, others don't care and others hate it. Design for quiet zones and noisier zones.

Placement

The land determines the number and location of the villages. Effectively, each village is made up of a neighborhood of about 200 homes, with workplaces and shops around a plaza. Some plazas can be very small, not more than 20 yards/meters on a side. In determining the size, we recommend viewing Pattern 123 *Pedestrian Density*, which analyses what makes a living plaza, what makes one dead. Christopher Alexander found that one needs about 150 ft² /15 m² per person to create

Scale – In Lucca Italy the Piazza del Mercado has buildings formed on the perimeter of the original Roman amphitheater. While a fascinating historic curiosity, the scale of the piazza is too big, hence the cafes tend to hug the edges and the center often feels dead, vacant.

Hands and Lips. Character is also about characters. Whether it is old men debating important matters or young lovers on the bench, the plaza becomes the theater of life.

a lively plaza, but by the time it gets to 500 ft² / 50 m² per person, it begins to die. In setting out the plaza, you need to estimate how many people will be using it. The higher the activity level, the greater the life. A big plaza where people are not moving may feel dead, but if the same number of people get up to watch street theater, it will come alive.

When you have estimated the number of people, begin by placing the buildings that form the edge of the plaza. It may be six buildings on a side (about 24 buildings surrounding a square plaza), or one may build a round plaza in which lot sections radiate outward, narrower on the plaza, getting wider as they go out (which makes some sense, if the larger homes are set further back and need more space).

Make models of café tables to show how far they spread into the plaza. Overlay with measured cut fabric or chalk to designate where children play. Think about all types of child play – kids with balls, older kids with noisy skateboards and design appropriately. Remember the school classrooms will be placed around the plaza as well.

Pay careful attention to sunlight and seasons. You want seating in the warming sunlight, but shelter from the burning sun accomplished by walls, shade-cloth or summer trees.

When you have established the size of the plaza, go outside with a tape measure and find a place, preferably a paved area surrounded by buildings (a parking lot will do). Stand people holding vertical poles at the proposed edges, to reality-check the proposed size. Too often, people, even professionals in the industry, find they build the plazas too big. Visit plazas that work and measure them as well. Use Google Earth to zoom in on famous plazas known to work and measure them.

Having said this, also keep in mind that if you have something large in the middle – say a fountain or band stand, make sure to mark that out as well, it can consume a lot of space. If you do try placing a band-stand or stage, think about making your architectural code for the buildings on that plaza include six-foot balconies wide enough for people to sit out on them and listen to the entertainment (see p 140 of *Life Liberty Happiness*).

Not all plazas need to have center piece, but they do serve multiple functions. Statues with bench seating tend to attract characters who hold court for hours on end. Ones that have niches tend to attract young lovers, especially in the evening… sweet, not sordid, because the niche is too public. Fountains can be formal things to watch, or if well designed, a place where children charge through on bicycles, clothing soaked, laughing for hours, pure joy. Budget for the center piece, just as you would for streets and sewage treatment. Engage artists and children to come up with ideas. Connect them to the life of the community.

About the Plaza in History

When we began research in 1984 on Village Towns, we soon discovered the importance of the plaza in the public life of the community. The same pattern was found in remote islands in Fiji, towns and cities in the Mediterranean, in prehistoric and classical ruins and in both large and small communities in almost every continent. As we searched back for the original archetype, we found it may have first been used by nomadic peoples, before villages and towns became a human form of fixed community.

When a campsite was selected, a place was set for the open fire, and this central fire became the gathering point. Typically, the cleared area would be large enough for everyone to gather. The people would gather in the evenings to keep warm, sit around the fire and talk, sing, eat and drink, and generally enjoy themselves. If traders or travelers approached, they would be escorted to the fire where usually a formal ceremony of some sort would accompany the greeting. In some cultures, their feet would be washed, in others they would be offered food or drink. In large nomadic tribes, one would find multiple gathering points, as clans would have their own, adding to the evening interest as one would take a walk to visit another clan – for courtship, for a different evening's experience, for different food.

When villages and towns began to emerge, these open spaces combined commerce and social contact. Socrates could be found almost every day in the Agora, the public marketplace where he engaged in dialogues – conversations of such a high level that 2,300 years later, we still read them. The plaza is a casual place, the stage for the theater of life, and its success comes from the interweaving of many different activities.

Plazas are not the village green, not the city park. Indeed, for plazas to be successful, they tend not to be places of substantial vegetation. Where they have trees and flowers, the plants are in pots or raised beds bordering cafes. The level of activity is simply too high for grass to survive, and the prospect of buzzing lawn mowers or weed trimmers is alien to the ambiance of the plaza.

In England, the climate tends to be too cold and damp to support outdoor life of the plaza. Instead one finds the larger market day open space, harking to a time when farmers and vendors would gather one day a week, Market Day, to sell goods. For the most part, these places have been taken over by parking lots, which tend to destroy the sense of place. This lack of familiar models in the mother countries of England and later the US hampers newer lands that do have the right climate.

This street in Greece is perfect for large volumes of people, yet it is relatively narrow. It can be used for truck delivery when needed, but would be too narrow for parked cars. Note also that the pavement is clean. No oil stains from leaking engines.

Pedestrian Streets

Plazas are connected by pedestrian streets of widely varying widths, but none should be wider than the adjacent buildings are high unless there is an undesirable shade effect. Watch your sunlight.

For planners in places that emerged after the automobile, such a concept may be difficult to accept. To appreciate how wonderful narrow streets can be, visit the old countries whose street networks became fixed before cars were invented. In a human scaled community, streets need to be scaled to human beings, not to motor vehicles. Those old streets demonstrate how effective and beautiful the design can be.

Set out primary streets to join the plazas. Make them logical and intuitive, but do not be a slave to straight lines – ban the grid. Zoning should allow many of the streets to have shops and workplaces, but give careful consideration to which ones. Plazas should have the most active workplaces and shops. Primary streets should have lesser activity, where fewer people enter and exit. Secondary streets should only have offices and workplaces that see a few visitors and customers in a day.

Make the primary streets the connectors between the plazas. Make minor connectors residential with front doors on the street, not set back with those sad gardens that collect trash and do nothing. If you do have front gardens, design them with great care; they are difficult to get right. In some cases, design the front of the building to be the side facing a wide street, in others, provide a wide alley for access, but keep the street frontage narrow and intimate. You only need one side to provide wide access.

We selected this photo for the book cover to illustrate that a street can be narrow but work. Indeed this street attracts millions of visitors from around the world.

Encourage small cafes along narrow pedestrian streets.

Allow and encourage potted plants and seating to intrude onto the street frontage.

"What about ambulances, fire trucks, rubbish collection?" planners might ask.

In answer, we recommend you go to Tuscany in Italy, where the town centers have special electric vehicles, small in size, made for the purpose.

Of course, if the VillageTown were built out of timber, as in new world then the streets would need to be wide enough to carry fire apparatus made for fighting major building fires. When one starts with a clean slate, one addresses this through a mandatory building specification that requires mineral based construction (stone, brick, block, poured or tilt slab, etc.) and smart fire systems in every building. This is called IBC Class IIA Masonry Noncombustible.

Narrow streets have worked for centuries, it's only with the introduction of motor vehicles in neighborhoods that the streets had to get wider.

The core of the VillageTown proposal is to make the vehicles fit the VillageTown, not make the VillageTown fit the vehicles. Large trucks are made for highways, for high-speed roads carrying large loads. The VillageTown should have a few wider streets for the occasional very large item needing to be brought in, but not most streets. Most household and office goods are made to go through a doorway.

We recommend that the VillageTown public and emergency service vehicles be included in the capital budget, if for no other reason than to assure the approving governmental officials that they are part of a comprehensive system. Simple, blanket statements similar to the following may be sufficient to allay any concerns of such officials.

- All VillageTown Buildings will be constructed of noncombustible walls and roofs and will have fire suppression or sprinkler systems as well as alarms and local fire hose, in accordance with IBC Class IIa or equivalent code.
- In-village fire fighting, ambulance, rubbish collection and delivery vehicles will be built on Low Speed Vehicle platforms, all provided as part of the VillageTown Plan.
- Each building in the VillageTown will have direct proximity to at least one street, lane or path wide enough to allow free passage and parking of these low speed emergency and service vehicles.

About The Pattern Language

In 1977 world-renown architect Christopher Alexander headed a team to write a three volume series to present a new theory of architecture, in which amateurs are given tools, or as he calls it, a language, to create master plans, buildings, living spaces. The second volume *A Pattern Language* became required reading for many first year architecture and design students. Amusingly (or sadly) some commented they slept through that class, while others, especially architects, now describe the book as passé as they promote instead the latest trend in the biz. Why? Wrong audience. Professional training often focused on developing what sociologists call tribalism in which the students bond with the profession, creating their own jargon and building a wall between their profession and the uninformed masses (also known as their customers). Christopher Alexander proposed a different approach, one which enabled the people and communities to not only participate in the process but to lead it – which makes sense when one considers they are the ones who must live with the results.

However, while we found this now quarter-century old book remains relevant, we did find that at 1171 pages, it proved – both literally and figuratively – too thick. To ask amateurs to crack open such a tome and become fluent was too much to ask. Using the book in that way fell into the "too hard" basket.

So instead, we took each pattern and reduced it to the size of a business card, and then printed each pattern on a fridge magnet, a kind of paper backed with a thin magnet that adheres to a normal steel whiteboard. We tried all sorts of other methods, yellow-sticky Post-It's®, card stock on adhesive Velcro® on cloth boards, push pins through index cards on corkboard, but in the end we found the ink-jet printed magnetic cards produced a clean, clear, easy to manage format, and if a photo-quality printer was used on a gloss finish, the ink did not fade so rapidly in the sunlight. We also found this facilitated the production of other patterns – ones taken from other books and local patterns developed by the Founders and Mentors as they articulated their own patterns.

Each card has a heading. If it comes from A Pattern Language we include the number provided in the book's index for easy cross referencing. We then extract from the two to five pages of text the pattern's core summary – often enough to enable people to master the point, but if not, then to reference to the more detailed description found in the book. We use color text to suggest additional considerations (the facilitator's notes), and at the bottom place a line where the Founder can place their name and contact details as the "Guardian" of that pattern. In this way, the group knows who to seek out to assure the pattern is not forgotten. This also satisfies the obsessive guardian that they can relax and allow the group process to proceed, knowing their particular interest stands and will not be overlooked.

> **88 Street Cafe**
> The street café provides a unique setting, special to cities: a place where people can sit lazily, legitimately, be on view, and watch the world go by. Encourage local cafes to spring up in each neighbourhood. Make them intimate places, with several rooms, open to a busy path, where people can sit with coffee or a drink and watch the world go by. Build the front of the cafe so that a set of tables stretch out of the cafe, right into the street or plaza. Note that cafes on the sunny side tend to be busier.
> *Guardian*   @   372-_____

We recommend you purchase at least one or more copies of *A Pattern Language* from www.patternlanguage.com. For fridge magnets we used Celcast® IJ37 that is owned by Avery Dennison who also provided free text software.

Pattern Cards

Having first set out a "what if" design of plazas and streets without the complete toolset, we now move to the next level of creating the design brief. A facilitator sets up whiteboards and tables with the Pattern Cards, usually organized numerically or randomly, with sufficient spacing that many people can access them at the same time. The people work in groups, select the cards and carry them over to another very large white board where they organize them into groupings. The facilitators encourage the Founders to debate how to organize the Patterns. They are encouraged to discuss what they mean and why they are important. Gradually, the board fills up and people write proposed headings (such as "make a positive contribution to the local economy"). Then the group takes a break while the facilitators clean up the board, ready for the next stage of work. The facilitators enter the headings into the card-making software to produce permanent headings (words written with white board markers are easily erased, creating confusion). The boards should stand there for the rest of the process.

After the break, members passionate about a particular pattern volunteer to become its guardian – the person who will make sure the pattern is not forgotten. Their name, phone number and email are written on the card. The group discusses the headings and rearranges cards under the headings. We strongly recommend allowing enough time to do this part right – the dialogue is paramount. For some, the process will be new, and they need to acclimate to it. Best to allow two sessions, with a day or week break in between.

The Pattern Cards will be used throughout the design brief process; indeed, it provides the most useful tool in enabling people. We encourage the professionals, the Mentors, to become fluent in the use both of the cards, and the process of creating new cards. The cards provide an external benchmark to which people and the several participating groups can reference in support of ideas they have for what should go into the design brief.

The Model Maker

It may have seemed to take a long time to actually get to the model, but if we are serious about enablement, mastering its tools form an essential foundation. Now we are ready to assign a team of model makers – people good with tools and rulers, able to measure and cut scale models of buildings. The models can be made of foams, using a hot knife (outdoors, the

melting polystyrene should not be inhaled). The key is that they be flexible, fast and of a reasonable accuracy for people to see the effects. If you are lucky (or have the budget to hire), you may find a talented model maker who finishes the buildings and details to the standard of a model train set, but this is not essential for the exercise. Most people have the capacity to visualize from simple block representations, provided the roof lines are accurately depicted. [3rd edition update: with technology we may find this process can be done using the internet, or the models can be 3-D printed]

The big picture (or jigsaw puzzle)

Before you begin to work on the detail of your village on its own jigsaw piece that is later joined with the others, the ViTo will have laid out the whole VillageTown in general form. It will have identified the best location for the Industrial Park, the placement of the Motorpool and Freight Depot. It will have set out the infrastructure and utilities within the urban core and the parts placed in the Greenbelt (for example, a greenhouse sewage treatment plant). They will have laid out the Town Center and the significant, visible public buildings that will anchor the VillageTown. They will determine the size of each village and the location of the connector streets.

Create a Noise Map

Noise is unwanted sound. Like the Londoners who for decades endured the killer fogs caused by burning coal, we get used to sound pollution. Only when we are free of it, do we notice how invasive it can be. In the VillageTowns, some places will be louder. Industrial zones typically produce more noise, as do artists using grinders on stone or steel. Young adults enjoy amplified music and parties in the street. The sculptors Guildhall should be near the industrial zone, but not the writers.

As you lay out the scale model, identify the noise zones with markers to indicate the level of background noise. Pay attention to the bounce factor in buildings and to prevailing winds that can carry noise. Do not tolerate unnecessary background noise. Noisy heat exchangers and restaurant ventilation reflects sloppy design – demand better.

Banning cars in the VillageTown will drop the ambient noise level. Designing homes so amplified noise stays inside will go far to avoid neighbor tension. Create peaceful, tranquil areas in the VillageTown – it makes a big difference.

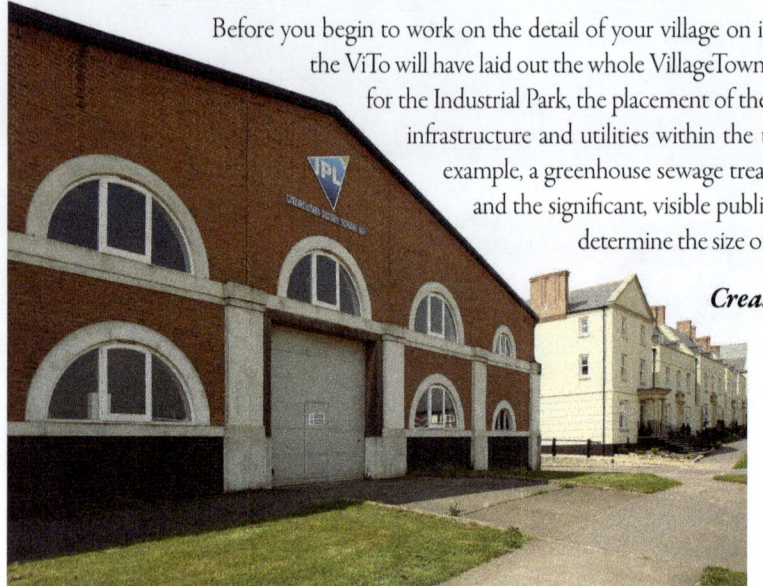

In Poundbury light industry fits within residential neighborhoods. Thick wall design blends in with the other buildings, careful attention to window and door detail provides harmony, and soundproofing becomes part of the design specifications.

Create a Smell and Odor Map

The most powerful memories are of the sense of smell. The smells wafting from village bakery next door or the fresh roasted coffee that wakes us up. For many years, the smell of the downtown waterfront in Baltimore, Maryland alternated between cinnamon and nutmeg, depending on which spice McCormick's & Co. was grinding. Tropical paradises are described not just by the beauty of the flowers, but the intoxicating smell. In contrast, the odor of too many fast food restaurants belching grease smoke on a hot, humid summer day in the city offends, and those Pacific Northwest towns in American with the sweetish fermenting odor from the town's paper mill evoke a perpetual sense of poverty.

Identify smells that are desirable, and map out where they should be. Use straws with silk threads attached and a fan to mark the wind. The baker should be on the plaza, and the flower gardens should be in the quieter parts of the VillageTown. Of all the aspects of VillageTown planning, this is usually the one ignored, yet it makes a big difference.

Create a Pedestrian Flow Diagram

Some places are easy to navigate; others so hard you can live there for years and not know how to get around. The signals people use to collect and maintain their bearings are subtle. Design street and path layout following topography. In providing cues, think of the old British line "if you follow water, you will get to the sea." Be aware of the visual landscape – providing openings to spot spires or high buildings to maintain people's orientation. Use width, curves, plants and other cues to enable people to keep their bearings. Remember, that successful VillageTowns need visitors, just as water needs motion to keep it fresh. Design it so visitors don't feel lost.

Use dotted ribbons pinned on the scale model to mark the foot flow with different colors for different routes. When you come to the delivery routes using the VillageTown vehicles mark them with solid ribbons, and be careful about conflicts.

In this Italian village, rising footpaths, outdoor stairs and an overhead bridge add considerable interest to the texture of the pedestrian flow.

The texture of movement works best when it includes variety. On main routes, you may want raised walkways along the sides, to indicate to the cyclists and VillageTown vehicles their space. All buildings should have one access route for wheelchairs and people using canes and walkers, but do not feel all routes to the building should fit this mold. Especially if the site is hilly, alternative routes should include stairs, steep paths, overhead pedestrian bridges and all sorts of accessways that give people exercise, make the whole village a great place for children to play, and add a visual tapestry of directions and verticality.

Shun straight lines unless you intend to use them for a design purpose. Surveyors love straight lines because it makes their job easy, but humans don't have a straight line in them. Nature curves. We get enough straight lines in buildings where they are needed to make construction easier and to fit normal furniture and appliances. Use straight lines when aligning with the equinox or solstice to remind the young that we live in a world governed by the sun, but avoid such lines if they create a wind tunnel. Pedestrian flow works best when the streets and footpaths gently curve.

Create a Delivery Flow Diagram

At several points in this book, we discuss the importance of adding a food box next to the mail box at each home. Instead of having hundreds of residents driving to stores to collect food, modern technology makes it possible to order on-line and have goods, especially food, delivered to the home. The delivery vehicles need not be highway-sized trucks, but custom made smaller electric vehicles that go from the freight depot to the homes. The ban on cars and trucks in the village does not include these local vehicles. Of course, not all food will be sold this way. Shops on the plazas will sell food... the butcher, baker and goats cheese maker as well as hand-selected fruits and vegetables where shopping provides both selection and social interaction.

Each building must have one access point for such vehicles. It may be a broader street in the front, or an alley in the back. A moving vehicle must be able to pass a parked one.

In setting out the street design, give thought to the delivery flow. Do not run all streets through the plazas. If you do, people in the plazas will suffer their presence, which is undesirable, especially with children playing. If a street is particularly long, consider if it is possible to put the kind of loop that gets the delivery vehicle back to the freight depot for another load. It makes more sense to keep the vehicles smaller, than a vehicle that carries a full day's load of goods. While highway-sized trucks do carry such loads, they do so because they may be far from their depot – in a VillageTown, with everything at a 10 minute walk, the proximity supports smaller load capacity.

Fresh pasta delivered daily in the Mercato Centrale in a chilled box mounted on an Italian Elektrocar.

Create a Sun, Shade, Moisture and Wind Flow Diagram

Know your seasons. Know your micro-climates. Buildings can channel wind. Trees tend to break it. Cold winter winds are no fun, yet a summer breeze makes the difference between a delightful day and a sweltering one. Dampness settles in lower areas, and can make a spot miserable. Draw these local conditions out on a side wall with a smaller scale photograph of the site, and check it regularly. Know your flood directions. Hundred year storms now seem to hit every few years. Use engineers, but also use your eyes and common sense. When you have identified the wind flow on the site, stick toothpicks with bright red silk threads into the scale model and then place a large fan to get the air moving. Observe what happens when the wind flow is broken by winding streets, angled roofs and strategically placed vegetation. The scale model will not give a completely accurate rendition, but it will get you thinking.

Moisture has two factors - movement and still. Building shadows produce damp and mold in the winter. Breezes will dry out damp places, as will the sun. In the summer, the sun can be too hot. Install a strong steel pipe bent in an arc which models the sun's daily and seasonal track. Mount one bright stage light on it that can be used to replicate the sunrise to sunset arc of the summer and winter sun. If your workroom can face the sun with a large picture window, orient the model so it is accurate with the real land. In this way, the sun shining through will show real solar conditions for that day. Design accordingly.

Then you design your village

When you have your model-made home and workplace in your hand, as a group you lay down the secondary streets and then fill in the remaining buildings in your village. What makes this interesting for the people who participate in person (as opposed to over the internet, or who ask the mentors to place their home) is that they meet their future next door neighbors.

On your building write an estimate of the expected number of people who would live or work there. This is how we will calculate how many people and how many buildings make up the VillageTown. Do not glue the buildings, streets or plazas down. Allow them to be moved as the dialogue unfolds, especially as the overlay zones (described below) are identified. In this way you get to test the ideas. Make extensive use of the Pattern Cards. Take plenty of overhead digital photographs.

While staying in a B&B in Cornwall, over breakfast I met a National Trust conservation expert who advised me that the Village of Leycock was a perfectly preserved historic village worth visiting as part of the research for this book. As it happened, on the way I stopped into a second hand bookstore where I came across an old photograph of the village of Leycock.

I went to the village to see if I could match it up with present day reality. The reader may imagine the sense of shock to find it vitally distorted in feeling by the utter domination of parked cars and trucks. While by law the buildings may not be altered – and indeed a close inspection will note a telegraph pole is all that was removed between then and now – the automobile defaces Leycock's character entirely.

I waited to capture the couple in the same place as the old horse cart – in fact they were crossing the street – but it was clear their presence was secondary to the automobile. By its size and speed, the car is dominant. Where once the village was a whole – connected by its walking pace street – the sense now is of two parts for people, alienated by its center subjugated by the car.

It would take more than banishing cars to bring back the old flavor of Leycock, however. Once the people reclaim their open space they must also regain a thriving local economy so the village sees all day activity. For a village to be alive, it needs people going about their daily activities – all sorts of people, not just the elderly or a few shopkeepers catering to tourists. It would need integration with the surrounding countryside, with a close relationship between the urban village residents and their food-supplying farmers. Indeed, at one time the wide street served a purpose, for it was the market square where farmers and artisans brought their carts and set up their stalls on market day.

In this photograph the market town of Marlborough, not far from Avebury, had a wide main street that provided space for market stalls. Now an upscale shopping town the town is wholly taken over by automobiles, the market square is now turned over to both parallel parking on both sides and angled parking in the middle. This assures the local businesses will generate a strong customer flow, but at a cost. People hug the edges and only enter the main open space to cross from one side to another. The parking is essential, as in the new economy, most of the buyers come from somewhere else: tourists visiting the stone circles of Avebury, or parents visiting their children at the nearby college.

In this photograph we find proof that not all Italian piazza design works. This modern design in a newer part of an anonymous town passed en route to Florence fails to work for several reasons. The plaza is bound on all four sides by cars, it has no connections to the buildings. The planted trees don't work. Most trees need parkland to work. There are some species that work in plazas, but not wide spreading pine trees. The plaza lacks an attraction. There is little in the way of a destination. It feels barren, lifeless, uninviting; no reason to go there except to get to ones car or take the dog out to relieve itself. Sad.

Why so many people on this street? The sign tells the story Area Perdonale Pedestrians only. With such simple design rules the whole character of the street changes. Imagine what this street would look like if cars were allowed. No people, no vendors, no street theater.

Chapter 12 – The Design Code

Up to this point we have been focused on the process of enabling people to participate in the design of their village, however a village is more than a start-up. It evolves over many decades, even centuries, and to be coherent a set of design codes need to be put into place. A design code requires a more formal approach as it implies specific language that guides the architectural framework for individual homes in that village. It must accompany the Design Brief process.

When tailored and completed for your VillageTown, such codes and plans becomes part of each village's specifications. While the design brief becomes the Master Plan, these codes become the standing rules, and in addition to being adopted by the approving agency as part of the conditions for approval, they may be placed as a condition of title. In most cases, we would expect local government planners, who must recommend approval for a VillageTown Plan, would welcome such design codes.

The codes can be explicit, to achieve social outcomes. For example, in Seaview, Florida, the code requires homes have front porches and they be close to the street. Why? Florida is warm, people sit on porches while others walk by and proximity encourages human contact. Do not be afraid to write such requirements, they are what make great places so wonderful.

Remember that the outcome is a historic district. What you see is what you get. Do it right the first time.

In this chapter, we provide suggested language to serve as the first draft for the village codes. The text in this chapter is released into the public domain by the author. If you wish to get a copy in computer readable form, please send an e-mail to contact@villagetowns.com. Please appreciate that different regions use very different language in setting out their planning or zoning rules. If you find that your local government or territorial authority uses different, but clear and relevant language, we invite you to secure copyright permission to post it at villagetowns.com so other local governments and village organizing companies may borrow from it. If possible, release it into the public domain, so it may be used without copyright concerns.

In this chapter, we also reference *A Pattern Language* by Christopher Alexander (ISBN 0-19-501919-9), and have placed excerpts from various patterns in text boxes to provide support for the recommended code language. We recommend you buy a copy of Alexander's book (try - www.patternlanguage.com) as a reference manual when writing your Design Codes.

Roads and Landscape Architecture

Streets and Lanes

A street includes mixed use and commercial activity, a lane has only residential frontage.

> Pattern 11 Local Transport Areas: "Cars are not very good for short trips inside a town, and it is on these trips that they do their greatest damage. But they are good for fairly long trips, where they cause less damage. The problem will be solved if towns are divided up into areas about one mile across, with the idea that cars may be used for trips which leave these areas, but that other, slower forms of transportation will be used for all trips inside these areas – foot [and]... a variety of low-speed, low-cost vehicles (bicycles, tricycles, scooters, golf carts...)" p. 64 *A Pattern Language*

Principle – Cars and trucks are too big for human scaled, streets of the villages in the VillageTown. The primary virtue of high-speed transport is inappropriate within the limited distance of the VillageTown. Therefore, they shall be banned from within the urban zone, where instead people will walk, or use small, slow electric or compressed air vehicles the size of golf carts.

This is a fundamental principle for VillageTown streets and lanes. It is non-negotiable.

Rule – The VillageTown shall be enclosed by walls with gates, and no automobiles or trucks shall be permitted within the village walls except by special permit, for a specific purpose, specific time, specific route, specific speed and optionally, with a guard walking ahead.

Within the VillageTown, lanes and streets shall be deemed privately owned and subject to rules and regulations made by VillageTown authority. The VillageTown shall establish a maximum width of service vehicles and design lanes and streets accordingly.

Outside the walls, a motorpool and parking lot shall provide covered parking for motor vehicles, including visitors' vehicles. A freight depot shall provide a place for goods to be off-loaded from delivery trucks and carried within the village by small Low Speed Vehicles permitted to deliver goods within the VillageTown.

Regional roads shall not pass through the VillageTown, urban core and if a right of way is required, it shall either be placed below grade (or in a tunnel), or be walled in so it shall not interfere with VillageTown life.

Road types

Pedestrian streets/roads may be as narrow as several meters/yards in width. Actual width will be determined based on projected peak foot traffic.

Connector footpaths join pedestrian lanes/streets and may include steps and gates.

Access streets/roads/alleys – Each building must have direct access to a roadway of sufficient width to deliver goods and services. Each must have at least one handicap access in accordance with law. The access may either be street frontage or alleyways – and the width must provide for (a) safe parking of a standard low speed vehicle (b) safe, slow passing room for a second and (c) pedestrians walking on the access street.

Greenstreets – The alley behind homes that has a paved footpath for walking, and then is planted on both sides. ViTo owned, the homeowner may plant a garden or the neighbors may elect to have it fenced at the ends so the village shepherd can graze the ViTo sheep.

Pedestrian boulevards connecting the main plazas may be substantially wider, but shall not be wider than the average adjacent building height.

The Village Parade is a single street wide enough to host a festival parade with all residents in attendance. It connects the VillageTown Gate to the Central Plaza.

As soon as cars and trucks are banned from the town streets, people fill them – walking, on bicycles, and using small electric carts for delivery. People stand in doorways watching the town go by. The sounds are of talking, of birds and perhaps of a street musician, not trucks. The air smells of coffee, bread and spices, not exhaust fumes.

Surprisingly, hand made street and footpath surfaces using real stone is no longer a premium priced product. While asphalt and slab cement were introduced as a low-cost solution, the overhead of the large companies and the gradual decline in competition, finds that paying a skilled laborer to set a solid base and install cobble stones may cost less, yet provide a more beautiful, durable result.

Italian pedestrian street with pavers above, Greek paved pedestrian street below.

> Pattern 247 "Asphalt and concrete surfaces outdoors are easy to wash down, but they do nothing for us, nothing for the paths and nothing for the rainwater and plants." p. 1138
> *A Pattern Language*

Road Surfaces, standards and details

Principle – Asphalt is suitable for high speed roads but unattractive and not appropriate for a human-scaled VillageTown. Better alternatives exist, which are lower cost, and when they must be dug up and reset, the result looks far better – no temporary patches.

Rules – VillageTown streets/roads shall be designed to a lighter standard than roads made to bear heavy trucks. During construction, access streets/roads shall be left unpaved so as to not be damaged by the heavier vehicles required during construction.

Street/road surfaces shall not use asphalt and slab cement as the exposed surface. Both have an adverse effect on the physical environment. Cobblestone or slab stone pavers shall be used for streets, and some lanes may use permeable grass-block in the centers (green streets).

Curbs shall be provided on busier access streets, pedestrian boulevards and the Village Parade to separate bicycles and low speed vehicles from pedestrians. Curbs generally shall be made of natural stone, not poured concrete.

Semi permeable surfaces for some sidewalks are recommended, including decorative crushed rock or seashells and pavers with openings for topsoil. This enables rainfall to penetrate the earth and slow stormwater flow. Test and select easy-to-walk on materials

Low speed vehicle access

Principle – Low speed vehicles require access and places for parking, and they must not interfere with footpaths. Pedestrians hold primacy, wheeled vehicles are secondary – the faster the vehicle can go, the lower its priority (in other words a bicycle is lower priority than a slower mobility scooter).

Rules – Off street parking and garage access for low speed vehicles shall not be paved with asphalt or slab cement. Where smooth surfaces are required, narrow strips of concrete may be used, but pavers are preferred.

In higher traffic streets and roads in the VillageTown, wheeled traffic shall be separated from pedestrian by a curb and elevation.

No wheeled vehicles, prams, carriages or trolleys are permitted on connector footpaths that exist solely for foot traffic (this is because of narrowness and presence of stairs).

In Poundbury (above) designers tried a form of stone chip to domesticate the car. Residents complained that it was messy and uncomfortable – and it was, so they reverted to asphalt. The proven system, used for thousands of years, is cobblestone, or its modern equivalent, the paver stone. Relatively smooth, comfortable for walking, they stay in place and last for centuries. If new materials are considered, test them first with elders and toddlers

Public utilities including cables, wires and pipes

Avoid wireless systems using radio frequencies (RF). The cumulative effects of RF are unknown. Use underground cables. Overhead wires or cables not permitted in the VillageTown. All services shall be installed in trenches (or walls) covered with removable panels to provide access without requiring the breaking of any surface (no jack-hammers). Pipes shall be placed in the same trenches except where engineering or safety requires separation. The trenches shall be owned by the VillageTown, which shall license any private services who require use of them.

Utility provision shall include sufficient room and access for changes in technology, so installation of new cables or pipes is a simple matter of removing lockable or heavy (if stone/concrete) panels and installing the new cables or pipes.

UTILITY ACCESS GRIDS, GRILLS, COVERS AND OTHER ACCESS;

Grills, grids, inspection covers and all visible components of service providers shall comply with a prescribed VillageTown standard, which it may from time to time update. The exposed components shall comply with an artistic standard set by the VillageTown. For example, iron grates shall be made with decorative surfaces, not just a utilitarian finish.

Earthworks including reshaping of land, natural landscape and plantings

Principle: Work with nature, do not dominate it. Let buildings and access follow the contour of the land

NATURAL LANDSCAPE INCLUDING TREES, GROVES AND OTHER FEATURES

Land contouring and earthworks shall be part of the original design brief. Any future contouring shall be subject to permission by the VillageTown and any appropriate approving agencies, in accordance with law. Design buildings that cascade down hills. Except in infirm zones, build exterior stairs – give people exercise.

In the original design brief, the VillageTown shall identify all landscape features with clear and precise language governing their preservation or removal. Any future changes to landscape features shall be subject to permission by the VillageTown and any appropriate approving agencies, in accordance with law.

Within the village walls, plants in the ground shall be subject to a comprehensive pre-planting regulatory plan to prevent them from growing into nuisances due to size, shadow, maintenance, pollen or debris. The plan shall encourage easy-to-manage plants in moveable pots and also encourage household gardens not on street frontage.

Consistency in landscape features

The VillageTown seeks to have a particular character that makes it distinctive from everywhere else. This is attained by a clear statement identifying the distinctive character and landscape features consistent with that statement. Consistency does not mean sameness. VillageTown character can include diversity, village by village, but within in each village, harmony.

This hillside town in Santorini was built with the contours of the land. The result is a place visited by millions of people.

In this Greek pedestrian street, the setback is not cluttered with walls or things placed on the ground. Instead it forms a platform for people to stand

VillageTown Layout:

- The fundamental principle of the VillageTown layout is multiple villages. Accessed by many pedestrian streets, the public life is defined by each village's mixed use plaza.

> Pattern 61 Small Public Squares: A town needs public squares; the are the largest, most public rooms the town has. But when they are too large, they look and feel deserted.
> p 311 *A Pattern Language*

- Where geography permits, primary destinations (homes, workplaces, shops, services, etc.) to be within a 10-minute walk, roughly 900 m. diameter with 15-30 units per acre.

> Pattern 9 Scattered Work: "Re-establish the connection between love and work, central to a sane society... redistribute all workplaces throughout the areas where people live, in such a way that children are near both men and women during the day... The only pattern of work which does justice is a pattern of scattered work: a pattern in which work is strongly decentralized."
> p 53 *A Pattern Language*

- Land defines the VillageTown. Work with the natural lay of the land and avoid major reshaping of the earth. Build homes and even shops on slopes, and provide for steep walks except in infirmity overlay zones.

- Within the village walls, allow 25-50% of the land for plazas, streets, footpaths, gardens, courtyards, etc. Figure 10 acres per village including streets and plaza.

- The VillageTown will benefit by a 2-3 m/yd high perimeter wall enclosing the whole of the VillageTown, punctuated with doors, gates, gateways and one main village gate. Make gates hard to open by toddlers and senile elders. Place large parks, sports and equestrian fields, major food and flower gardens, festival fields and cemetery outside village walls.

- The heart of each village is its plaza, surrounded with cafes, taverns, restaurants, shops, services and workplaces. Residences are set behind or over the workplaces. Plazas can be round, square, rectangular or of a geometry that is more complex. Figure 500 people (about 200 buildings).

- Each plaza should have at least one cafe, tavern and restaurant for gathering – perhaps funded by villagers mortgages (a cafe space adds about $5/month per mortgage). For a proprietor to keep the rent-free space, patrons must regularly rank the quality of food, drink and service as high.

- Multiple pedestrian streets and at least one access street shall connect each plaza. Plazas should be set out so a person can walk from one plaza to another for 1-2 hours as if in a labyrinth without having to retrace steps. This is to enable multiple VillageTown walks for residents that can be done frequently without becoming boring. Mark some walks with subtle signs, distinctive patterns or marker stones, so visitors can also follow the walks.

- Circular plazas will result in radial streets with tighter density closer to the plazas. Buildings along the plazas and on the pedestrian streets should share common walls (row houses). Buildings behind can stand alone, including small cottages and grand homes that would be located away from the plazas and recessed from pedestrian streets.

- In determining the level of public prominence of particular villages (the extent to which they are visited by people not resident in that neighborhood), the surrounding buildings shall be higher and the plaza larger. Identify as *primary, secondary* and *other*:

  Primary Cosmopolitan Town Center: three and four story buildings. *Secondary villages*: two and three story buildings with larger public buildings (e.g. guild halls).

- The VillageTown shall have one Cosmopolitan Town Center Plaza located in the center of the VillageTown, with the Village Parade leading to it from the main gate. The Town Hall shall be prominently located on this plaza.

- The Town Plaza shall contain an equally prominent ecumenical or institutional cathedral (use of the word implies size, not sect) for rites of passage and religious services. Management of this use shall be separate from VillageTown governance but capital and adequate maintenance costs paid for by the VillageTown.

- This plaza should be large enough to hold the full population of the VillageTown and both the Hall and Cathedral should have a balcony visible and audible by all.

- The VillageTown libraries, its school rooms, artist guilds and other prominent public buildings should be carefully distributed among the primary and secondary plazas to create a tapestry of interest VillageTown-wide.

- Provide for sensorial overlays (zone maps), including:

  Noise overlay identifying quiet and loud VillageTown areas

  Nice smells overlay: bakeries, spice grinders, roses

  Micro-climate overlay: warmer and colder places

  Visual interest overlay: framing natural and built places pleasant to view and for visitors/media to photograph

  Infirmity overlay: identify parts of the VillageTown easier or harder to access by a person needing a cane to walk

- Streets should avoid straight lines, except where sunlight is to be captured. Careful attention should be given to wind patterns to avoid creating cold wind tunnels but at the same time, supporting cooling breezes in summer.

- When setting out VillageTown blocks that are longer than wide, place their short side along pedestrian streets to provide more intersections to make walks interesting.

- All access and most pedestrian streets should connect. The exception would be small closes (enclosures) surrounded by attached homes and hotels – intimate public courtyards.

- Flowered alleyways and intimate footpaths should provide many shortcuts between pedestrian streets and accessways. Design these not to annoy residents inhabiting homes (e.g. people walking home at 2 a.m. from a nearby pub)

- Public service buildings, such as medical centers, that may be used by citizens of the region, shall be placed near the motorpool/parking lot outside the village walls.

- Most buildings should open directly onto the street. Setbacks should be used infrequently if at all, never at street corners. Avoid or design with great care, front gardens. Encourage plants and vines in pots or in window boxes.

- Food delivery boxes required at the front, or in the alley behind every residence.

In this Italian village, above (pity about the cars) with a detail shown below, a different approach was taken to setbacks – setfronts, if we may coin a word. In what appears to be the public right of way, the homes were permitted to build a covered upper floor porch so that pedestrians would be protected from inclement weather on the ground floor. This offers a different and most interesting approach to plaza design as it creates a two level plaza.

Two other patterns that works are the arches and the profusion of potted plants. The upper level plants appear to be permanent, the cafe plants probably are stored during winter.

The wide open plaza was originally designed for the market and municipal gatherings, but now has been taken over by cars. As an archetype for a plaza, it probably is too big, but with cars present, it becomes barren and lifeless. People no longer use the open space except to cross from one side to the other.

Front setbacks rarely work in urban settings and are not recommended for the VillageTown. Supposedly for gardens, most end up shabby. Better to have buildings open directly on the street with space for potted plants and climbing vines and flowering plants. Provision for front gardens may work if they are very narrow, closely hugging the wall and not more than arms length in depth. In contrast, most homes (except perhaps youth housing) should provide for gardens behind the homes (depending on solar exposure) or on upper decks and flat roofs.

Pattern 38 Row Houses

"At densities of 15 to 30 houses per acre row houses are essential. But typical row houses are dark inside, and stamped from an identical mold. Above 15 houses per acre, it is almost impossible to make houses freestanding without destroying the open space around them...

Apartments do not solve the problem of higher densities: they keep people off the ground and they have no private gardens. Row houses solve these problems. But row houses, in their conventional form, have problems of their own... The houses have a short frontage and a long depth, and share the party wall along their long side... [To solve this] give each house a long frontage and a shallow depth.

p205 *A Pattern Language*

163

Architectural Harmony and Integration Rules

The design brief created at the VillageTown founding, responding to the nature and character of the locality, shall set the architectural style and set out the distinctive character of the VillageTown and of each of its villages within.

Reference: As a general reference manual, this Design Code incorporates *A Pattern Language* by Christopher Alexander 1977 ISBN 0-19-501919-9 – buy from www.patternlanguage.com. The patterns found therein provide guidance in determining what will work, and add to the quality of life of the VillageTown.

BUILDING MATERIALS, SHAPE OF BUILDINGS AND OF ROOFS.

Principle – A general theme shall be established for the VillageTown, but within that theme, individual villages shall establish a distinctive architectural style in accordance with the character planned for the particular village. The VillageTown plan sets out the level of prescriptive rules, village by village.

Unless a village's character is set otherwise, a vernacular appearance is encouraged as the overall character of the VillageTown: Examples may include natural stone or building blocks irregular without precision edges, rusticated or recycled fired brick, earth brick or adobe. A classical appearance shall be used for prominent and public buildings.

The VillageTown design seeks to remain standing and useful for at least seven generations (150 years) and perhaps much longer. Thus, it must be of a timeless beauty, durable and functional.

Rules – All walls shall be predominantly made of fireproof, natural mineral materials. Under almost all circumstances, cavity wall construction using timber or metal studs shall be prohibited.

Construction shall adhere to IBC Class IIa noncombustible standard. Timber shall be permitted for exterior and interior ornamentation, for doors and windows, floor and wall surfaces and solid lintels if left exposed, but in all cases it shall be used in a way that does not require the VillageTown provide a Fire Department or Brigade on the same scale as communities that use flammable building materials. If for good reason such a building must be constructed, it shall have a fully automatic sprinkler system installed that even in a power outage shall fully extinguish any fires and prevent the release of toxic smoke. If metal stud walls must be constructed, they shall be insulated to limit the transmission of unwanted noise through the walls.

Comment: Architects and owners are asked to consider the overall feeling, harmony and integrity of the design of each village, and not propose to build a design intending to fly in the face of the overall design and integrity of the village or the VillageTown.

Thick walls shall be encouraged, for aesthetic purposes and for

Note: as used herein, classical refers not to a particular form of historic Greek or Roman architecture, but to timeless design requiring the skills of a highly trained team of professionals to get it right.

It is used in contrast to vernacular that uses simpler timeless design, often using well proportioned rectangular boxes with attention to their ornament and detail.

Such simpler design does not require the high art of the architectural profession, only a professional critique to assure the details and proportions are harmonious and attractive.

Classical arches, such as in this new home being built in a small town in southern Italy retain that beautiful sense that harks back to a canopy in the forest, with the columns resembling tree trucks and the arches referencing the upper branches.

thermal and noise insulation. No site coverage penalty shall be incurred by the use of thick walls less than 600 mm (24") thick.

Principle: Human-scaled buildings appear timeless when their surfaces are not completely regular, and when they have a softer feeling to them. This is best achieved by hand finishing using natural materials.

Rules:

Synthetic materials (such as vinyl cladding) prohibited

Building shapes to be variable but in harmony. Trendy styles that may soon become obsolete shall not be permitted unless a whole village is done in such a style. Simple styles are variations on angular basic forms, with set back for walls, courtyards and attached buildings. Encourage ornament and detail to break up flat surfaces. Most buildings not to exceed three stories except in the cosmopolitan town center.

Angled roofs shall be made of natural, long lasting materials that hold in highest winds. No iron or color steel (but copper can work), no asphalt shingles or synthetic roofing. Clay or concrete tile and slate are permitted. A color standard shall be set for villages. Shed and non-livable low angled roofs (3 to 19 degree pitch) shall require a VillageTown architectural review, as they tend not to work in medium density areas.

Flat roofs with roof gardens and outdoor living shall be encouraged. Such designs require careful installation to avoid leaks over time.

In locations with limited or seasonal rainfall, consider building rooftop greenhouses to collect water and extend the growing season. See below for detail.

Pattern 118 "Make parts of almost every roof system usable as roof gardens" p 577 *A Pattern Language*

Food, Water, Energy and Lifestyle Roofs

Principle – As Earth struggles to support a growing population, clean water will become scarce. As the best agriculture land is paved over for habitation, good food will become scarce. Yet we waste our roof space.

Rules – A VillageTown may establish a town-wide design designing all buildings with flat waterproof rooftop gardens and then capping them with greenhouses that combine rainwater harvesting, food growing and solar panels to collect both electric power and thermal energy to heat water and rooms. The water collection systems shall be separated from human activity. The greenhouse shall have scientific calculations to ensure sufficient sunlight for growing, as well as for solar panels.

Chimneys

Rule – Masonry clad chimneys shall be encouraged. If metal chimneys are required for earthquake safety or to control capital building costs, they shall be clad in a rectangular metal frame and mineral sheeting, plastered with a render that matches the rest of the building.

Comment: Chimneys used for wood-burning fires may encounter challenges due to the potential for local air pollution. Depending on local circumstances it may be necessary to restrict such open fires to public gathering places, or to require that the chimneys incorporate scrubber systems to eliminate particulate matter from the air. However, take care not to entirely ban open fireplaces. People need such connections, and the smell in the air can be lovely.

Pattern 197 Thick Walls: "Houses with smooth hard walls made of prefabricated panels, concrete, gypsum, steel, aluminum, or glass always stay impersonal and dead" p 909 *A Pattern Language*

(photo by Carin Wilson)

Angled rooftops made sense in traditional architecture where protecting the home from rain leakage posed a major challenge. However, as this family's adaptation shows, now that flat roof sealing is the norm, providing rooftop living space greatly enhances the utility of the home. One of the most interesting 21st century patterns is building the waterproof member as a flat roof (much easier to build structurally) and then cap it with a plant-growing greenhouse.

Pattern 239. Small Panes: "When plate glass windows became possible, people thought they would put us more directly in touch with nature. In fact they do the opposite. They alienate us from the view. The smaller the windows are and the smaller the panes are, the more intensely windows help connect us with what is on the other side. Divide each window into small panes. These panes can be very small indeed, and should hardly ever be more than a foot square."
p. 1108 *A Pattern Language*

This classic but simple Italian building derives its beauty from simple balcony doors their functioning shutters and wrought iron rails, and from the Roman arch over the door. It enhances streetscape, in this case, set back from the street.

How you select your doors and windows will do more to define the character of the plaza and village than any other feature.

Exterior Visible Doors and Windows

Comment – Fenestration: windows and doors form the faces of the community – its eyes and mouths. When they are beautiful, the VillageTown is more beautiful; when they are not – the VillageTown looks less loved. Beautiful fenestration often comes from local artisans, and for this reason, the action plan for this part of the code may include fostering such local crafts. If beautiful doors and windows are easy to purchase, and come with little overhead since the maker is the vendor, one can expect these to be the solution selected by owners, designers and builders. Beyond this economic action plan, however, the Code should set out rules for fenestration.

The art of fenestration is both demanding and too often neglected, yet it has the greatest impact on the presentation of the community – its public face. Considerable care is needed in defining the terms for fenestration, especially as recent history showed us maverick architects who rose to the challenge of producing a very controversial design that technically met the design code but upset people who had to live next to it.

Public face on the plazas and market streets

The plazas shall be surrounded with work places – offices, shops and cafes, workshops. These workplaces shall have large windows so children get to observe role models, and the workers get to keep an eye on the children.

Large windows shall be required on all ground floor buildings facing the plazas. Decorative windows with small panes shall be encouraged. Wood frame windows, especially with multiple panes provide a desirable detail and are encouraged. Each plaza shall establish a code for the windows and doors to be used on buildings facing the plaza.

Plate glass window shall be discouraged, especially at corners, unless the village intent is for a trendy look that will eventually become a historic period piece. Windows should frame rather than spread too wide or high.

Recommendation: Establish joinery (window & door making) shops on site during construction to minimize deliveries and provide high quality products for local conditions.

Doors and surrounds – Public entry doors are a major definer of the community. Encourage entry doors to be of carved or joined wood. Antique, recycled doors of distinctive character recommended where weatherproofing can be addressed. Secondary screen/storm doors to be of equal quality or installed so they are invisible from the street or plaza.

If 2% for art is used (p. 170) consider allowances for carved fenestration.

Doors and windows in private homes

Principle – The front doors of a private home, when in public view, make a significant contribution to the character of the village. The VillageTown should encourage owners to make them beautiful and substantial.

Rules – Front doors shall be hinged and open inward. They shall be made of solid core wood, and carved or paneled wood is recommended. Except in store fronts, glass is not recommended in the bottom half of the door. If storm doors are required, they must be of the same thickness, beauty and build standard as the front door. Surrounds and lintels shall be encouraged, especially carved and/or ornamental.

Windows shall be harmonious both with the building design and with the streetscape. Large plate glass slabs shall be discouraged and where used, need to be handled with great care so as to not be overwhelming in appearance and create environmental problems in terms of overheating in summer, and heat loss in winter. Placed with care, larger glass windows and doors facing the sun can be most effective in collecting solar heat in winter on heat sink floors and walls (thick stone or aggregate) and being blocked out by carefully calculated overhangs.

Window flower boxes may be encouraged on certain streets facing the public, and if they are so designated, the construction specifications shall include permanent gray-watering tubes direct to the window base, to enable automatic watering of the flower boxes so they remain alive and attractive.

Window shutters are recommended, both for their practical application in shading and cooling, and for the manner in which they dress the building.

Security Bars

If required, make security bars decorative as well as functional. Fine wrought iron sends not the message of fear and crime, but rather one of elegance.

Recommendation: Encourage the art of the blacksmith to produce works of art, not merely the utility of passive protection. Support a local blacksmith industry early in the construction phase to provide an economic opportunity for artisans in metalwork to move in and get established at the time of highest demand for services.

Consider exterior visible doors as qualifying for the 2% for art standard (see page 170)

Factories and Industrial Zone Buildings

Principle – While a walk-to Industrial Park is valuable, larger work places, factories and industrial buildings need not be banished to remote industrial parks where aesthetics matter not. Some can be within the VillageTown, to provide employment within walking distance. As larger buildings, the necessity to blend them into the overall VillageTown sets an expectation for design, especially door and window design that fits the neighborhood. Code language might be general, as below, or prescriptive:

Rule – Factories and industrial buildings that are visible by the public shall follow a building design consistent with the VillageTown master plan, and shall use doors and windows that fit harmoniously with the neighboring non-industrial buildings. This may include attractively designed false windows and doors in cases where the utility needs of the industry conflict with the aesthetic needs of the VillageTown.

Pattern 165: Opening to the Street "We passed the workshop every day on our way home from school. It was a furniture shop, and we would stand at the opening and watch men building chairs and tables, sawdust flying, forming legs on the lathe. There was a low wall, and the foreman told us to stay outside it; but he let us sit there, and we did, sometimes for hours." p. 775 *A Pattern Language*

This Italian building provides a delightful example of three false windows. Note especially the right hand window being painted as open.

Woodworking shop off a pedestrian-only street in Italy

In Poundbury this new industrial building presents a classic face, hiding the conventional shed design behind

Pattern 225 "Do not consider door and window frames as separate rigid structures which are inserted into holes in walls. Thick of them instead as thickenings of the very fabric of the wall itself, made to protect the wall against the concentrations of stress which develop around openings.

In line with this conception, build the frames and thickenings of the wall material, continuous with the wall itself, made of the same materials, and poured, or built up, in a manner which is continuous with the structure of the wall.

p. 1062 *A Pattern Language*

The Art of the Architrave (Surround)

As a picture frame can make the work of art, the architrave can make all the difference in a building. The narrow, store-bought finger-jointed timber architrave says nothing, looks cheap and degrades the quality of the building.

Architraves tell stories. New Zealand is renown for intricate Maori carvings that serve a genealogical and sacred function. In Italy, (below) and Greece (left) limestone and marble is frequently used and carvings form a high art. In Somerton, England, (right) the local Ham Stone (limestone) is carved to great effect – indeed it resembles fresh hand-hewn timber, except that we are told it was carved in the 15th century.

The photo is about the ornate surrounds – no idea why the pedestrian in front was carrying a cross-bow. Only in Italy.

169

2% for art in all public buildings and plazas.

Principle – Art is the mark of a community that values more than just the practical, the functional and the efficient.

Comment: Art often speaks to the state of humanity. If that state is confused, angry, detached from love of land, place and community, such art may undermine the sense of a village.

Thus, the Founders are advised to enter into a deep discussion about what art, before selecting it – and in doing so yield not to the experts, pundits or tastemakers – remember it's your village not theirs, and it will stand for generations.

Recommend language to accompany every title for public and commercial buildings:

2% of the construction budget for all public buildings and plazas shall be set aside for works of artistic merit. Mandatory funds for art shall be deposited in an escrow account at the beginning of the initiative to assure it remains available for art. Art may include ornament, but shall be subject to architectural harmony standards.

It is recommended that the artist guilds be invited to participate (but not dominate) the dialogue on public art. The guild members should be encouraged to bid on contracts to provide public art, understanding that as with any vendor the VillageTown decision makers must hold the artist at arms length prior to awarding the contract.

It is recommended that specifications for public art include either a durability clause, assuring the work will last, or be a time-limited lease, at the end of which the artist understand their obligation to remove the artwork at their expense. Without such clauses, the VillageTown can find they are saddled with a deteriorating work that involves unanticipated expense for the public.

The VillageTown may want to classify public art as timeless or time limited. Prior to purchase or lease, set a specific length of time when the art will be reviewed to determine if it should remain in place or be removed.

In addition to public art placed in plazas and public buildings, the VillageTown may consider sponsoring or seeking sponsorship for sculpture gardens, halls for performance art, experiential labyrinths and other creative physical environments intended to enhance the experience of contemporary art.

Note: the VillageTown may elect to permit some of the 2% to go for ornament and carving on the buildings.

Sculpture by Lorenzo Frechilla Del Rey (1927-1990) "Maternidad" Bronze, 1966, Bilbao, Spain

Example of outdoor art. My host for the Italian photoshoot was Gidon Graetz, of Castello di Vincigliata, Firenza, Italy. He is a sculptor on international renown. This is one of his stunning works.

As discussed on page 163 on setbacks, low-walled front yards in row housing is difficult to get right. Too often it becomes a shabby area. The challenge in working with low walls is sometimes best dealt with by avoidance if they embrace what in effect becomes a dead space. Of course in the VillageTown, front yards are not needed for car parking, and rubbish is handled entirely differently. Rear yards can be used for temporary delivered materials.

Better to have the attached building hard upon the street, or require very high walls, creating outdoor rooms within, or have a low sitting wall touching the building.

Walls and fences between properties

Principle – Walls and fences are a most important part of medium density housing, as they balance the private and public spaces. In some cases walls may be a full storey or even two stories in height. In approving such height, the VillageTown must give consideration to sunlight, not depriving a neighbor of sun due to extreme height. As the VillageTown sets out the wall and fence code, consider the extent that it should be prescriptive. Walls are easy to get wrong, and can have an adverse impact.

Rules: Walls shall be built of solid wall materials of a vernacular form, not exposed cinder block, as the irregular, hand-made appearance marks the difference between a lovely garden wall and a prison. Adobe or whitewashed finishes provide a low-cost, easily maintained surface.

The VillageTown shall be surrounded in most places by a high wall, both to establish a clear boundary between it and the rural aspect beyond the VillageTown, and to keep domestic pets from becoming predators for wildlife outside the walls. Some parts of that wall may form part of a privately owned building, but VillageTown controlled.

Fences shall not be purely utilitarian. Chain link fences and fences made of roof iron or other sheet materials shall not be permitted in the village except perhaps for chain link used to enclose tennis courts. Wrought iron fences are recommended. Wooden fencing is prohibited in the VillageTown due to the risk of fire.

Exterior paint, coatings and render.

Principle: Paint can be cheap to first apply, but repainting can be expensive and produce noxious noise and dust as surfaces are prepared. Render (whitewash, clay based slurry, distemper and other mineral based traditional coverings, can be exceedingly inexpensive, forgiving, easy to clean up and easy to re-apply.

Exterior fenestration and building detail may be painted provided it covers less than 10% of the building exterior's surface, and it is able to be maintained without significant noxious noise, odor or dust when it must be removed and repainted.

All exterior wall coatings to be mineral: Stone tile or native clay slurries (with sand, cement or lime) No paint.

All wall coatings to be maintained without requiring extensive scraping, sanding, blasting (other than water) or other labor intensive preparation. Recommended coatings include natural clay tints, optional supplements with oxide tints of earth tones. In area where the visual effect of white buildings is deemed attractive, permit pure white, limewashed coatings.

One of the benefits of the vernacular methods of wall coverings comes in the curious effect that wear looks good… it is described as a patina rather than looking tired.

There is no matching the brilliance of the Greek blue door or window on a pure white wall.

Principle: A long-standing tenet of architecture says that large flat wall surfaces need to be broken up if they are to be attractive. In recent times, pressure to cut costs and standardize finishing pushed architecture into large flat painted surfaces, with the unfortunate result that the buildings add nothing to the character of the community. Too often the result is boring – practical but ugly. The problem is not paint alone, but the sheet material used underneath. It lacks texture, or if it has texture it is machine applied, and the eye can immediately spot the artificiality of it. In contrast, renders that are applied with an irregular color and texture can break up the surface especially as they weather over time.

Verticality – External Staircases, Bridges and Catwalks

Principle – In medium-density, urban settlements such as a VillageTown, careful use of verticality – exterior stairways, bridges over footpaths and narrow elevated walkways (often known as catwalks) both add texture to the character of the community, and provide more efficient, lower cost land use than enclosed stairways and hallways.

Design with external staircases to homes, with upper level bridges and walkways. See page 174 for more staircase photographs.

> Pattern 158 Open Stairs: "Internal staircases reduce the connection between upper stories and the life of the street to such an extent that they can do enormous social damage... Connect all autonomous households, public services and workgroups on upper floors of buildings directly to the ground. Do this by creating open stairs which are approached directly from the street. Keep the stair roofed or unroofed according to climate, but at all events leave the stair open at ground level, without a door" p 741-4 *A Pattern Language*

Connect buildings above the street as Sir Thomas Jackson did in Oxford's Hertford College. Verticality adds great interest to a place. Cover it if you have harsh weather

Or build walking bridges open and place gathering points below.

The Greeks use of open stairs and buildings following the contour of the land to great effect. Photo taken in Santorini

Pattern 94: Sleeping in Public "In a society which nurtures people and fosters trust, the fact that people sometimes want to sleep in public is the most natural thing in the world… Keep the environment filled with ample benches, comfortable places, corners to sit on the ground, or lie in comfort in the sand. Make these places relatively sheltered, protected from circulation, perhaps up a step, with seats and grass to slump down upon, read the paper and doze off."
pages 458-9 *A Pattern Language*

A Place to Sit or Rest

The VillageTown shall provide many benches, wide public steps, low walls, buildings with places to sit as part of their structure and other comfortable places to sit and to lie down. Care shall be taken to design them for variable weather conditions, some wind protected, some shaded in hot summer, others sunny for cooler days.

In setting out both formal seating and casual seating designed for other purposes, such as steps, consider the informal communities that will gather there. Some will become places for teenagers, others for workers eating their lunch. Some will provide views, others for rest or passing the time of day. Avoid placing seating near rubbish bins. Place seating near stone or concrete walls that absorb sunlight and create a warm micro-climate in the evening.

Note that in these photos, most seating is casual. The one formal seat is serving as a bed. For more on how urban seating creates community, read Jane Jacobs *The Death and Life of Great American Cities* ISBN 067974195X

The Design of Stairs

Consider exterior staircases. They can be exceptionally beautiful, they add texture to the visual amenity of the streetscape, and they enable simpler design of buildings.

If the VillageTown has rooftop gardening with greenhouses, consider a wide spiral type exterior staircase with a small lift (elevator) running in the middle. This would allow workers to have access to the roof without disturbing the residents.

Staircases do produce empty space. If the VillageTown needs to harvest rainwater, plastic water tanks or purpose-built water bladders may be worth considering so that each house stores some of the water, even if it then fed into a central system for purifying before being piped back to the home.

Public Spaces Design and Ornament

Principle – The functionality and visual appearance of the ornament and furniture that graces the public outdoor spaces become an important part of the quality and identity of each neighborhood within the VillageTown. Decisions on their design and appearance should not be left to purchasing agents or engineers.

- Signs shall have a consistent and attractive form of design and lettering. The VillageTown shall decide if it wishes to use posts with mounted signs, or street signs permanently mounted on corner buildings, carved in stone or formed concrete. Use intuitive design to avoid dependency on signs with many rules or directions. Favor smart, design not words. Where words are essential the VillageTown shall establish a prescriptive sign ordinance requiring beautiful lettering and prohibiting signs with logos larger than one hand in size.

- Street lighting shall be selected to not spill light or waste energy. Street lights shall be ornamental, not strictly utilitarian.

- Bollards (traffic poles) and other traffic control devices shall be of a handsome appearance, not easily damaged or bent.

- Street furniture, including seats and benches shall be attractive, comfortable and placed appropriately for sun and wind.

Oxford signs (above) Italian seating (below)

> Pattern 170 Fruit Trees: "In the climates where fruit trees grow, the orchards give the land an almost magical quality... Fruit trees on common land adds much more to the neighborhood and the community than the same trees in private backyards. p 795 *A Pattern Language*

- Public gardens and plantings shall be carefully selected in location and plants to enhance the VillageTown ambiance. Low fencing should clearly delineate flower and fruit plants that should not be touched in contrast to those which may freely be picked by residents. The VillageTown should plant fruit tree varieties to encourage residents, especially children, to pick and eat. Select location carefully so leaves and peels do not become litter.

Environmental Sustainability

In 1986, the World Health Organization's Ottawa Charter for Health Promotion declared, "*Our societies are complex and interrelated. Health cannot be separated from other goals. The inextricable links between people and their environment constitutes the basis for a socioecological approach to health. The overall guiding principle for the world, nations, regions and communities alike, is the need to encourage reciprocal maintenance – to take care of each other, our communities and our natural environment. The conservation of natural resources throughout the world should be emphasized as a global responsibility.*"

PREVENT AIR, WATER & SOIL POLLUTION

Principle of Prevention – Unnecessary pollutants shall not be brought into or used in the VillageTown construction or ongoing operation.

Timber – chemically treated timbers used only where absolutely necessary. Cutting of treated wood shall be in enclosed areas where all sawdust is collected & disposed with appropriate safety handling.

Motor Vehicles – No internal combustion engines vehicles within the village walls. For motorpool cars and trucks and for farm vehicles requiring liquid fuels, the VillageTown shall seek to produce biofuel from sewage and solid waste.

Chemicals used in farming and gardens shall be limited to only that which is absolutely necessary. Organic methods shall be encouraged. Where chemicals are used, handling shall follow the strictest procedures to avoid runoff into water courses, release into the air or contaminating land. Spray drift prohibited.

Heating shall seek to use sources that do not require burning of fossil fuels – solar water heating, solar electric with heat pumps, wind, water and other technologies.

PREVENT NOISE POLLUTION

Principle of Prevention – Unwanted noise shall be avoided or suppressed in the VillageTown and its surrounding lands.

Vehicles – By designing everything within a 10-minute walk, public (and private transport) is not needed within the village. Permitted Low Speed Vehicles to use electricity or compressed air.

Motors – Stationary internal combustion motors shall not be used in the VillageTown except where essential; where they are used, stationary motors shall be housed so as to not be heard.

Construction Equipment – In construction zones a higher level of noise shall be permitted, but only if the zone's noise does not spill over into inhabited zones. If ongoing cutting or drilling is required, sound absorbing temporary buffers shall be used to minimize noise pollution. Compressors shall be muffled.

Fans, air conditioners, heat pumps – Placement of exhaust and climate control systems shall be designed so they are not heard by neighbors or on the street. Such systems shall be built into buildings so their noise is absorbed and not heard.

Amplified music and sound – Private music and sound shall not be heard outside the residence. Residential walls shall absorb sound and use windows that block sound transmission. Different residential zones shall have different sound tolerances (quiet zones, young people's party zone) with different design standards. Public music and sound shall be permitted in specified noise zones including cafe music and outdoor concerts and film showing, with appropriate standards set by the VillageTown governance.

Natural noise (loud voices and pets) – The architectural code shall provide standards in design to contain natural sound, primarily through the use of thick walls between buildings and high walls between properties, with some quiet zones in the VillageTown prohibiting pets.

ENERGY EFFICIENCY AND CARBON NEUTRAL

Principle of Prevention – VillageTown buildings shall be designed to maintain comfortable micro-climates within the structures using the minimum amount of electricity or other non-passive fuel sources. Buildings shall be constructed using advanced sustainable methods. Standby appliances (which use electricity when not operating) shall be discouraged.

Maximum use of solar gain shall be incorporated into all buildings

Very high insulation shall be used in floors, walls, ceilings and fenestration where solar gain is not a factor

Lighting shall use natural lighting where possible, and low-energy lights after dark. Electric motors shall be of a high efficiency design to consume less electricity. Integrated systems shall be used where appropriate (such as integrating HVAC with hot water/refrigeration).

SOLID WASTE REDUCTION AND MANAGEMENT

Principle of Prevention – The VillageTown local economy shall target zero-waste, reducing the need for packaging and waste products.

Waste shall be separated at the source with multiple collection systems for food, paper, glass, metals, plastics & other waste products. Advanced systems shall be adopted as they become commercially viable, including systems that convert waste into energy.

SEWAGE – TREATMENT OR USE AS AN ASSET;

Gray water and black water may be treated separately and locally. Black water shall be viewed as a valuable resource and advanced systems should be implemented as they become commercially available. This may include systems in which algae converts black water sewage into biofuel or using blackwater to grow biofuel plants.

WATER MANAGEMENT

Principle of Prevention – Water is a limited resource. The VillageTown shall be designed to use water in the most efficient manner.

Separation – Drinking water shall be purified to a higher drinking water standard than generally accepted municipal standards. Buildings shall have multiple pipe systems, one supplying drinking water, a second supplying a high quality of utility water for cleaning and bathing, and a third for toilets (black water). Where applicable, rain water shall be captured on roofs and stored in cisterns built within the VillageTown (under streets, behind buildings, under commercial establishments, in ponds and lakes).

Reuse – Where technology is available, the VillageTown will provide neighborhood launderettes that continually refilter the washing water, thus never requiring disposal of dirty water or new water. If such services are offered, private homes will not have home washers.

Street cleaning and maintenance

Principle of Prevention – VillageTown streets shall not have oil dripping cars. Trees and plants shall be carefully selected and placed with species that tend not to drop leaves that then clog up storm drains. The VillageTown governance shall have strict rules governing fouling of the streets.

Streets shall be made of materials that do not naturally look dirty or shabby. Asphalt shall not be used as a street material or patch material. Streets shall be designed so utility providers do not need to cut into the streets to access pipes or cables. Streets shall be designed so they are easy to clean with brooms or other dry systems, not requiring substantial water. Care shall be taken to not foster mold on shaded, damp streets and lanes.

Protection of flora and fauna

The VillageTown shall be designed with high perimeter walls and gates to keep domestic pets inside the VillageTown, to preserve wildlife outside. If possible, secure more land for the VillageTown, allowing 25% for the VillageTown, 10% for the Industrial Park and Motorpool, and 65% for greenspace. Outside the walls set out some land as wildlife habitat and seek professional expertise to assure appropriate plants and wildlife corridors exist to make the habitats functional.

Through neglect and monoculture farming, earth is losing its genetic stock of domesticated plants and animals. The VillageTown shall encourage community-owned gardens outside the village walls to grow heritage plants and support seed bank farming.

Environmental education and protection

Fundamental principle – All human beings require a healthy physical environment in order to maintain a sense of wellbeing. Environmental awareness comes through calling attention to the physical and natural environment, and through policies that demonstrate respect for it.

The VillageTown shall be the campus for primary, secondary and tertiary education, thus become a laboratory for environmental (and the broader standard of quality of life) education.

Healthy, low impact building design and materials.

Principle – With greenhouse gasses becoming a major global concern, the VillageTown shall design and choose building systems that overall reduce greenhouse gas emissions through a change in human lifestyle. This includes eliminating unnecessary transport and freight, require buildings that use less energy and make use of solar gain, weaning its citizens off a disposable consumer lifestyle. Healthy and low impact goes beyond greenhouse concerns.

During construction:
- Provide living space for builders so they do not commute on the public roads
- Provide silos and batch mixing plants for minerals (cement, aggregate, etc.) so deliveries are in bulk and controlled to prevent destruction of access roads, noise and congestion
- Build on-site manufacturing facilities for joinery, carvings, building materials, etc.

In design:
- Avoid chemically treated timber and other toxic materials that require special handling when being installed, when burned (including uncontrolled fires that produce hazardous toxic smoke) and when disposed either as trash during construction or at the end-of-life of the building.
- Use a single bulk building system that promotes energy efficiency. Recommended: variable density aggregate, a cement foaming system technology that produces a concrete in which heavy aggregate is replaced by closed cell air bubbles. Design thick walls, floors and ceilings to produce a high insulation factor.
- Choose bulk materials easily transformed from raw material to useful material on the job site. Choose materials with low energy components in manufacturing.
- Design winter rooms. Face thermal heat sink walls toward the winter sun. Use glass windows to allow the low sun to passively warm heat sink floors. Design internal rooms so passive heat naturally flows to areas where warmth is desired.
- Design walls that naturally "breathe" to create a lower humidity interior climate. If this is not possible in specific places, use thick gypsum (25 mm) on interior walls and apply only breathable coatings (not paints that form a vapor barrier). This is an ancient technique known to produce warmer, more comfortable rooms.
- Choose materials that do not produce toxic gasses during their useful life in the building. The oldest materials are often the safest. New materials, petroleum based or use toxic glues, may have unanticipated negative side effects not yet documented.
- Design buildings to take advantage of natural lighting and not need artificial lighting during daylight hours. Where lighting is required select low energy consumption systems, but avoid bulbs containing toxic materials that require special handling for safe disposal at end of useful life.
- Design whole building systems, so refrigeration, heat pumps and other energy exchange systems work as a single system. Use only high efficiency electric motors.
- Install food boxes at every house, so local foods may be delivered from nearby farms directly to the customer's' home. The energy component of food is related to delivery costs. Food boxes enable the shortest distance between the farm and the table, because one delivery vehicle services a whole street of customers.
- Install a high speed, high capacity telecommunications system for all buildings in the VillageTown, capable of real time video conferences so people need not travel by vehicle in order to meet and to work cooperatively. Assure the system is easily upgradable.

Checklist for the Design Code

Roads, utilities, landscape

- ☐ Road and port connections, motorpool and freight depots
- ☐ Road widths – access streets, pedestrian boulevards, quiet lanes
- ☐ Construction standards – surfaces, curbs, sidewalks
- ☐ Utility service – cables, pipe access, grills, grids, covers, other visible components
- ☐ Land contouring standards
- ☐ Tree belts, groves, landscape architecture, new structural landscape, Public spaces, streetscape, open space
- ☐ VillageTown walls define boundaries, all within a 10 minute walk
- ☐ Mix of residential, commercial, retail and industrial – 15 - 30 units per acre, multiple units allowed in a building
- ☐ Logic of human-scaled street layout and hierarchy – no grids!
- ☐ Village standards and linkages – Allow 30% of land within walls to be open space for plazas, streets, gardens, etc.
- ☐ Public gardens, landscaped edges, sitting places – smaller areas inside VillageTown Walls, larger outside
- ☐ Sports buildings, parks and playing fields outside village walls
- ☐ Dispersed public buildings and guild halls within village walls
- ☐ Building height and width hierarchy – most 2 story, some 3 and 4.
- ☐ Street frontage and streetscape standards – few setbacks, optional "set fronts".

Architecture

- ☐ Design standards and theme set by village by village
- ☐ Fireproof bulk materials (IBC Class IIa), thick walls
- ☐ Building shape standards
- ☐ Glass to wall ratios
- ☐ Chimneys, finials, fenestration, architraves
- ☐ Boundary walls and fences
- ☐ Paint, render and other coverings
- ☐ External staircases, bridges, catwalks, arched buildings over streets
- ☐ 2% for art in all public buildings and plazas

Public furniture and ornament

- ☐ Signage, lighting, bollards, outdoor seats, trash bins, etc.
- ☐ Standard on grass, plants and trees within village walls.

Environmental Sustainability

- ☐ Reduce air, water, soil pollution
- ☐ Noise control, noise zones
- ☐ Recycling, zero waste
- ☐ Energy standards in heat, lighting, cooling, etc.
- ☐ Innovations in water and wastewater management
- ☐ Wildlife habitat and native plant protection and enhancement
- ☐ Heritage husbandry and farming to protect domesticated plants and animals

---

In the sustainable society:

- Nature is not subject to systematically increasing concentrations of substances extracted from the Earth's crust
- Nature is not subject to systematically increasing concentrations of substances produced by society;
- Nature is not subject to systematically increasing degradation by physical means
- People are not subject to conditions that systematically undermine their capacity to meet their needs.

The Natural Step – Sweden (www.naturalstep.org.nz)

Chapter 13 – Building Design

The purpose of this chapter is not to dictate a particular building design that reflects personal bias. Instead it intends to set out a more general understanding of what works in a town; a compact community built for long-term habitation by all sorts of different people at all stages in their lives. In doing this some building design emerges as strong whilst other styles work poorly or not at all. The test of what works and what doesn't is set out through a series of general principles. These principles seek to be integrated, holistic. Holistic thinking is omnidirectional, understanding all the impact – not unidirectional like the hunter with tunnel vision focused only on the prey.

The intent of the VillageTown is to create a place of permanent, long-term habitation where as time unfolds, some will live for generations; and all will feel a sense of home. The VillageTown should be designed for at least seven generations (175 years), a significant challenge in this era of rapidly changing conditions, technology and perhaps climate.

A purpose of the VillageTown is to provide the option of setting down roots. In creating an environment that encourages bonding with a place, the design of the buildings comes to play a central part.

In this book, the VillageTown is a framework, not a plan. A framework is a starting point, not a prescription. As such, there are certain givens. Among these, the most apparent is that this is a town, not a suburb. Thus, almost all buildings will be attached, sharing sidewalls with the next building (but built soundproof, so you don't hear the neighbors). Also, there will be floor limits... three floors of rooms in the villages, and probably four floors in the town center. Depth of buildings is governed by streets and the need for compactness.

Santa Fe is a town in New Mexico that adopted a strong architectural code based on the historic adobe design. In part it works because the climate is desert-like; leaking buildings is not a problem in a dry climate.

Many of the new homes are not real adobe; they look like thick bricks made of sun-baked or stabilized earth, but in fact they are timber-frame structures clad in exterior wall board and then plastered. This is an outcome of globalization where materials are no longer locally sourced, but trucked in from elsewhere.

Question: How, in the short time frame of years or even months, do we create a sense of ownership and identity that naturally takes at least three generations?

Answer: With clear intent.

A new VillageTown will not have the same feeling of permanence that comes from generations of care. Unless an old tree happens already to be there, everything will look new and young. Local lore takes decades to evolve, but there are things we can do, and should do, to create a sense of ownership, identity and security that VillageTown inhabitants love about their home.

Let us examine a set of principles that may best guide the design of VillageTown buildings:

- Classical architecture for major buildings (see definition – next page)
- Vernacular architecture for the rest
- Timeless and durable – not trendy and transient
- Beauty and Color
- Ornament
- Authentic
- Harmony
- Variety
- History
- Human Ease and Unease
- Generosity
- Spirit

These are not the only principles to serve as guides. They will enable us to think about what sort of VillageTown buildings we want to design. Perhaps the most important thing to remember is that we are not seeking to create a grand architectural masterpiece in which all buildings are works of great art. A VillageTown combines ordinary modest places built by folk, with greater buildings built as civic projects or by the wealthy. Today, we have replaced modest charming homes with spec-housing and kit-set designs that look mediocre, uninspiring and sometimes awful. Yes, they keep you dry and warm, but add nothing to the visual and the unconsciously perceived amenity that is so important to creating a sense of home and place. Ordinary buildings can be simple, made of basic shapes, yet have a beauty that attracts global attention. Likewise great architectural buildings can serve as focal points and grace the VillageTown with a brilliance that enhances the overall quality of the whole VillageTown and the wider region.

This is a very simple building with plain white walls and six windows on this side. Yet it has a timeless beauty to it. What makes it so attractive?

Classical architecture for major buildings

Classical does not mean in the style of Greece and Rome. Rather it means design that requires a well educated professional architect who will design a building of significance. In times past, to become such an architect required a deep knowledge of proportion, composition, and geometry – sometimes called sacred geometry – as certain ratios produced buildings that had a striking harmony about them. Ancient geometry used the Golden Section as described by Plato.

Traditionally classical architecture was reserved for civic, religious, educational, arts and recreational buildings, the homes of very wealthy landowners and merchants, and more recently for railway stations, financial institutions as well as some larger corporations with enlightened or egotistical directors. Classical architecture is not the tawdry imitation of ornament we often hear today called classical, for such is a hodgepodge of abominations like polystyrene fluted columns plopping in front of pompous overstated front porches and oversized aluminum framed windows cut in the shape of the Parthenon's pediment. Rather classical architecture is a discipline of a highly trained professional who understands the challenge and responsibility to produce a timeless formal building that fits within the context of the site and the surrounding buildings and open space.

In identifying which buildings are candidates for classical architecture, first divide division those funded by the VillageTown and those of private enterprise. In the former, provided the VillageTown organizers have their act together, there should be little to worry about, as the organizers both control the specifications and the checkbook. However, where private enterprise wishes to erect prominent buildings, including private homes, the VillageTown needs to establish a clear protocol to assure harmony within the larger context of the master plan. This is not as easy as it seems, as rules too constraining can produce mediocrity, but too loose can create warts on the plazas and streets. If you choose to use a design code, include a plea to private architects to not see it as a challenge to design something that does not suit the VillageTown, but happens to fit within the code. It's not about creating controversy.

Vernacular architecture for the rest

Vernacular architecture is an oxymoron. Traditionally, what we call vernacular was designed not by architects but by local non-professional folk, often conservative farmers and shop keepers who needed solid, low-maintenance homes and farm buildings built out of locally sourced materials, hand shaped and showing the non-precision of the hand made. Village vernacular saw the same solid buildings sharing thick side walls, with varying height, color, texture and roof lines – but all sharing the local materials available in the region.

Now, as so much of the world has gone to the straight lines and flat planes of the machine age, these vernacular irregular shaped buildings become prized and people pay prices for them that would have the old farmer spinning in his grave. In the absence of structural engineers, mass took the place of precision. A one to two foot (300 to 600 mm) thick wall of adobe, mud-brick or rough cut stone needs not the structural calculations or careful testing of a four inch (100 mm) thick tilt-slab wall. It also provides superior climate control, especially if the roof overhang provides for winter solar gain and summer shadow. Traditional vernacular gradually figured out that while timber is easy to work, when used in walls, the buildings burn down with annoying frequency. Remember that the time frame of rural and village folk building such structures tended to be more than three generations. Thus while vernacular architecture in young western nations such as the USA and New Zealand used timber, old world countries used stone, adobe, mud-brick and similar mineral based materials.

As of late, the term vernacular has become popular, and with popularity, the word became distorted. In New Zealand, people refer to buildings made using galvanized iron sheets as vernacular when they really mean historical. Sheet iron and steel is more properly called "Cargo Architecture" because it is a product of the industrial age. To get a clay tile vernacular roof, you need a shovel, clay, a fire kiln and a hairless thigh to shape it. To get a sheet iron roof you need an iron mine, a smelting factory, a rolling factory and a huge industrial infrastructure to get the raw material from the earth to the roof. True vernacular means using local materials with as little processing and energy as possible, going from raw state to finished.

Traditional vernacular architecture therefore is unrealistic in the VillageTown. There may be a few believers who will want to erect a rammed earth or mud-brick building made the traditional way (and they should be encouraged), but for it to be effective, we need to adapt the term. Instead of adobe, in our research, we have identified lightweight concrete as the best alternative. The aggregate is local, but the cement is not. Because the material begins in a wet plastic state, it can be formed into any shape, rough or smooth, flat or irregular. This enables what perhaps we should call an evolved or hybrid vernacular.

In Prince Charles' Poundbury, vernacular architecture was attempted using architects who scoured the countryside for archetypal vernacular buildings that they then carefully set out into a village master plan. In contrast to typical English subdivisions, Poundbury results are superior, and even some critics begrudgingly conceded Charles was right. However, in my view the buildings still tend to look too architectural. They lack the individuality that comes from real vernacular. This is to be expected, as they were designed by architects and built by several builder/developer contractors. Their materials tended to be factory made where the machine is not able to replicate the fractal irregularity of the human hand. For all these reasons, to achieve a more satisfying vernacular feel to the VillageTown, we recommend the Founder-Mentor process be used in the design and many local artisans to make the components used in the building of the VillageTown.

For the purpose of the VillageTown, Vernacular Architecture should be understood to refer to all the buildings except the prominent buildings as discussed above. As such, their ornament should tend toward locally sourced materials with limited processing steps from raw material to finished, rely on mass more than precision, and not be preoccupied with uniformity, flatness or straightness. For the most part, they should tend toward the conservative end of the design scale – shunning such contemporary architectural adjectives like "quirky", minimalist or trendy.

While some may see vernacular architecture as referencing some other place (Cotswolds, Provence, Tuscany, Santa Fe, Morocco etc.), this would be getting it backwards. In those places, the vernacular architecture became famous because of its beauty, but its history shows the beauty came from working with locally sourced materials. Let the local stone, aggregate and natural earth colors define the local vernacular, not some preconceived idea taken from some other country with its own vernacular. Use other places as inspiration, but base the vernacular on local materials and local artisans and base the design on functional need and local climate conditions.

The other aspect of local design comes from the teams of vernacular builders who develop their own style. Waiheke Island in New Zealand is well known for its mud brick buildings (including ours) for the simple reason that an American, the late Vince Ogletree, arrived on the island and set about building them. He spawned an industry as his workers then went into business on their own. That industry emerged into its own Waiheke style, and ironically, builders from New Mexico have come to Waiheke to learn of the local innovations – ironic because Vince learned his trade in New Mexico.

A new building in Poundbury, it certainly is superior to most contemporary English subdivisions, but it still is a bit too precise, the stone fill too rectangular. A true vernacular would have had the lines not so precise, more akin to how nature organizes.

We decided to ride our bikes back from Dresden to Prague before flying home. Along the way, we discovered lovely towns with car-free streets. We were told that they had suffered under Communism, but when the wall fell, the buildings were repaired, and the local economies are now reviving. This image is good example of the scale of a VillageTown street.

Timeless, not Trendy – Durable not Transient

The VillageTown is too compact to suffer the perpetual tear downs and rebuilds that come with architecture that goes out of fashion. Demolition creates a mess of dust and noise, and it wastes material. We think it better to design timeless buildings that stand for centuries, because they are attractive and durable and maintain their functionality and usefulness.

Timeless is different than retro. Contemporary can be timeless, although timelessness sets a higher standard, especially in selecting materials and building methods. Looking to history shows us buildings that survived the test of time, but this should not preclude new building design.

How do we create a newly built place and assure the design will be timeless? In answer, no guarantees, but with intent and substantial dialogue, we are more likely to get there than if we hand decision making carte blanche to a professional whose training emphasizes originality as paramount. This is wrong. What is paramount is that the VillageTown feel right.

Perhaps the first assurance of timelessness is quality in materials and workmanship. There is no substitute for excellence and excellent materials need not cost more. Indeed, while a higher processed material may have less raw material cost, by the time the extensive overhead costs of manufacturing, distribution and sales are added the end price may be higher than the local.

The next assurance of timelessness is to factor in how the material ages. Patina is good, shabby is bad. Like a bespoke Savile Row suit where no label adorns, timeless design tends to draw attention to the building, not the architect. The building does not scream "look at me", but instead pleases the eye. Timeless design also tends to tap into the human subconscious.

In some of our experiments in building our own home, consideration should be given to maintenance as well. Paint can instantly change the visual appearance, but the last house we owned that was painted required almost a month of sanding the old paint off before the new could go on. On our earth-brick home, we first used a mix of clay, sand and cement, but it would not last more than a couple of years. Eventually, we found a German mix called Putztechnik, which, when mixed with oxides created a durable, lasting surface that only needs an occasional wash with a water blaster.

Choose materials that age well and require little preparation when they must be done over. Sheet copper may seem more expensive when purchased, but it lasts far longer than paint and as it ages it goes from a dull brown to a brilliant turquoise blue patina. Alternatively, you can coat it with certain salts, and the color comes in a matter of hours instead of years.

One of the unfortunate by-products of 20th century marketing economics was the view that profits are better assured selling products that wear out in a relatively short period of time and require replacement. The simple answer is not to purchase such products. Look to history to find building materials that have stood the test of time.

Beauty

If the VillageTown is to be your home, make it beautiful. Beauty has many manifestations, but usually its enemy is cheapness without imagination. Ugly places are often transient places – people who plan to be in a place a long time add beauty. In order to keep the VillageTown from becoming boring, many villages are proposed and we suggest each village develop its own character. This enables smaller groups of Founders to decide what beauty means for them. In deciding what is beautiful or what is not, avoid the tyranny of some modern professionals, who speak an esoteric language only understood by insiders and who tell you their aesthetic is superior to your taste. Keep repeating the mantra – it's your village, not theirs.

Without a doubt, beauty is subjective, but what we call "the power of the jury" comes into play here. For over a thousand years, the jury system has demonstrated that when a dozen or so randomly selected people are asked to come to a consensus on subjective matters (such as a criminal charge) with professional support they tend to get it right more often than the professionals. Each village will have about 200 families and if 10% of them participate to define the character of their village, it is likely they will come to a good agreement on what would make it beautiful.

Beautiful also has another design consideration – how it interacts with wind, rain and sun. A building can be brilliant when first built, but if it is in a dark spot that soon develops a black mold, it turns ugly. Know your local conditions; know where the winter sun shines.

Oxford copper

In Tucson Arizona this church has an iron bell that over the years has dripped brilliant rust on the whitewashed wall – an example of when the weathering works to an advantage.

Photograph by Carin Wilson

Color

The bulk material recommended for a VillageTown is mineral, which means surface treatment can be an oxide embedded, a natural whitewash or tinted wash, or it can be modern or traditional paint. It can be stone tiles embedded in the pour, or even bricks, river stones or other natural minerals.

The challenge for the village founders in setting out their architectural code includes the question of color. Walk the back streets of Venice (top photo) and you encounter a riot of bright colors, side by side, yet it works.

Travel the Elbe River by bicycle and stop into the former East German and Czech towns and you discover a revival of color, more pastel, but warm and welcoming.

Of course, the marigolds, ocher yellow and other earthen colors of Italy are renown, as are the brilliant whites of the Greek Islands.. Santa Fe, New Mexico borrowed its design code from the traditional adobe browns of the southwest.

In considering color, also consider sunlight and winter darkness. Some colors reflect the sun onto the street, making it feel warm on cold days. Whites work well in some places, but poorly selected can require everyone wear sunglasses.

The outer panels are hand-carved, took a long time to make. The inner panel looks like it was taped and blasted. With 3D technology the old look is possible.

Ornament

Buildings need to be dressed. Use texture and carvings to break up flat surfaces – employ artisans and artists, foster local artisan industries. In the 20th century, the principles of Modern Architecture declared that ornament was superfluous, that elimination of unnecessary detail and simplification of form demanded ornament be abandoned. Worshipping at the alter of the machine age, buildings became massive swaths of flat planes. Trouble is they also seemed devoid of character, as buildings became an artistic statement, and too many tended to deprive people of the joy of human scaled architecture.

Ornament is dimensional, using texture, color, shadow and light, and materials with different qualities. In the west, the Greeks were masters of ornament in stone, as were the Victorian architects in wood. In Aotearoa, the Maori are masters of ornament, not for decorative purposes but sacred and educational. The carved *wharenui* (the primary sacred community building for used for formal reception of visitors, meetings and communal sleeping) is built with large timbers carved with the ancestral story of the tribe. Between the posts, woven mats provide brilliant patterns. In many mature cultures, the ornament becomes a major defining part of the culture's identity. Chinese and Japanese ornament is well known, the ornament of African tribes less well known but equally beautiful and inspiring.

Ornament is a fine art, easily done badly. Kitsch is a disparaging term for ornament that went wrong. In the VillageTown, the way to avoid this is to encourage skilled artisans and makers of ornament to set up shop in the VillageTown at the time of its founding. If there is a skilled group, they will tend to educate the buyers sufficiently to avoid bad ornament.

Authenticity

Individual buildings must reflect the personalities and aspirations of the individuals who build and inhabit them, not the career aspirations of designers. This is a core principle of the VillageTown, as it makes the difference between a unique place and a place that looks like everywhere else. This principle is extensively discussed throughout this book, so we need not repeat it here.

How is it achieved when the individual feels they have no clue in describing what they want, and very much prefer to yield decision making to an expert?

The first answer, of course is for the individual or family to identify what they need in terms of home or workspace. In this design process, the organizers and mentors may choose to make up a set of pattern cards specifically focused on home, office and workshop. Do you need a clothes closet or a whole room? Do you want to wake up with the first sun or be on the shaded side? Sample blocks at a 1:10 scale can enable the person and the mentor to form a rough sense of the building by stacking blocks. In this way, the individual begins to put their stamp on the functional aspects of building design.

The next answer is to have a large number of small business artisans – proprietor owned and operated – offering a selection of components and ornament from which to choose. People may lack the imagination to come up with ideas, but find it considerably easier to select in the marketplace when ideas are on display. In this it is most important that materials actually be what they purport to be. A column can be made of stone, or of concrete – even lightweight concrete, but when it is made of polystyrene with a plastic casing it lacks authenticity and soul – it "thumps" wrong, and if damaged looks awful. A while back, some bright spark came up with imitation stone molds that one pressed into wet concrete and then sprinkled with a colored dye to resemble a stone patio. It fooled no one, and as it wore through, the color it looked worse than badly patched asphalt. If you are going to dye concrete, use oxides in the mix, not color on the surface, and don't try to imitate nature unless you can do it perfectly and artistically. By having many local skilled artisans working with vernacular, local materials, this aspect of authenticity is more likely to be secured.

The third answer is to rely on the group planning process where a village is formed around a plaza. We can safely bet that in any such group there will be several Founders with great imagination, and others will get caught up in the process. Just as a charismatic music teacher can prove that almost everyone can sing – it's a matter of getting over the self-censoring unconscious – all people can be involved with design of their home and community.

The final answer is based on the head-space of the mentors. These architects and designers are there to empower the Founders. If they are prepared to work in groups, their expert knowledge will stimulate the Founders and together a design will emerge that is authentic.

Left and Right – Two buildings on the same street. Different era, different character. The building to the left uses ornament to produce a more finished, dressed appearance, which adds to the character of the streetscape. The gray building is built of flat panels punctuated by unimaginative windows. One may expect that the gray one was cheaper to build but built neither to grace the streetscape nor add to the quality of the community. Instead – as its signs declare – it's solely about money, and partially vacant as well, which is a fitting allegory.

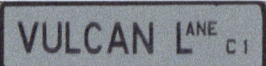

Harmony

Vulcan Lane in central Auckland is a classic Victorian era street now populated with cafes, shops and top fashion designers. A while back, the city council decided the old pavers needed replacement and proposed to replace the warm toned pebble design with the cold, dark bluestone pattern they have set as the new city standard. A howl of protest followed, during which the press secured release of an internal memo under the Official Information Act in which the project leader wrote prior to the consultation process that *"we should establish our preference and not present to stakeholders anything we don't want"*. To explain, under New Zealand law, the local government is required to consult with the people, especially those with a stake in the matter (such as being a neighbor) and to take those views into consideration before formulating a plan.

How remarkable to secure evidence of the state of mind of professionals charged with consulting on the city's landscape architecture – although I fear the wrong lesson was learned: project leaders will no longer reduce their real intent to writing.

Harmony has two parts – securing harmony of the stakeholders and then securing harmony in the results. The photo below illustrates both the failure of harmony and the different underlying values. In Vulcan Lane, the contrast is striking.

Different eras, different values. The Victorian era was a time when the businesses that commissioned buildings expressed pride in architecture. Visual amenity was as important as interior functionality. Somehow we lost those values in the 20th century, as architects took their instructions from investors who cared only about the profits. Minimalist architecture is cheap. No matter what words are used to dress it, the king has no clothes.

The bank building is about fast money, nothing more. Cheap to build, with purely functional windows, the two steel bars affixed most likely because the awning is otherwise not safe. What local government systems failed so badly to foist on to the public such a clashing building on such a charming street?

In contrast, the cafe building next door is about quality of life, taking time with friends, acknowledging that thousands of people will appreciate the careful design and ornament for many decades – long after the architect is dead and gone.

Harmony is a complex and subjective concept, best achieved with open and frank dialogue among all stakeholders – which is why we propose involving Founders at the onset.

Variety

A VillageTown where all plazas and streets look the same induces boredom. As discussed in other places in this book, the primary way to introduce variety is in the different plazas and streets – especially the plazas. Of course, this presents a challenge – achieving harmony yet maintaining variety. You achieve this best through active dialogue during the Design Brief process and through self-education. In writing this book, I travel both overseas and throughout New Zealand with a camera to capture photographs of some ideas difficult to convey in words. In the process, I had to look at a lot of different communities and buildings, and to challenge myself to see them with different eyes. When I went in search of the perfect village and perfect plaza, I found it difficult. For example, my memory of the plaza in Pietrasanta, Italy proved to not supported by the plaza's present day reality – in part because many of the stone carvers had been driven out by higher real estate prices – gentrification.

Avoid banality, where the designer and builder seem to conspire to degrade the streetscape to earn a fast buck at the public's expense. There is no better way to educate your eye to the variety of architectural choices than to take a camera and travel – with specific intent to look at building design and streetscape.

The challenge around the question of variety comes in mixing conflicting styles. In England and Europe, placing a wildly modern building exuding ego next to an icon of classical design clearly offends, sometimes I wonder if not intentionally. In the new worlds of North America and Oceania, I observe that sometimes mixing styles does work, that it adds vitality to the streetscape… not always, of course, but enough to support coming to the table with an open mind.

Why do Auckland's two Vulcan Lane buildings (left photo) fail to work but the three in High Street Oxford ones do? While the High St. design (above) and colors are different, the windows bind them. Also, the shop fronts have a harmony in appearance and in sign scale and lettering. In Vulcan Lane (left) the older building is rounded, the new one shows no respect for this, but instead asserts it property rights – let the streetscape be damned

History

Honoring ones past, ones roots is an important part of what it is to be human, especially when so many of us have lost our ancestral stories and moved from our ancestral lands. In the new world, this opens the possibility of plazas and particular streets being founded by peoples with a common history and making reference to it.

One principle of modern architecture rejected historic references. We heard aggressive and disparaging characterization to historic reference as **pastiche** architecture, which was applied as a slur. Pastiche originally referred to a musical, artistic or written work intended to imitate an earlier artists' style, or a hodgepodge of different styles. In architecture, it is used disparagingly by critics of buildings based on historic reference.

A rejection of history is one of those cerebral rule-making exercises that fails to serve humanity. The expectation that architecture must come up with something new, even if banal, shocking or ugly, subverts architecture's primary purpose – to design human habitat in accordance with human scale and sensibility. Instead some observe that it becomes an insider's contest to win accolades of ones peers. Historic reference has a place, not necessarily as replicas (although in certain circumstances even that may be appropriate), but in honoring ancient tradition in present day design.

History is about geometry, symmetry, harmony, ornament, inspiration and longevity. The column that historically referred to nature – the tapering tree trunk – remains valid today. Trees are still with us, and still important in the scheme of life. The vaulted ceiling remains inspiring, and today with inflatable molds, it's easier to build, but equally as beautiful as those examples we find in our historic buildings.

Curiously, the masters of historic architecture today are the designers and builders of film sets. In doing historic and fantasy films, they create remarkable architecture that sets the mood of the place. In designing a VillageTown, I have often thought we should strike a deal with filmmaker Peter Jackson, inviting him to design whole plazas as permanent sets which could be used for films but which would be live-in communities for the rest of the time.

Historic does not mean antiquated engineering. Unlike the Santorini buildings wrecked in its 1956 earthquake as still seen in the photograph below, New Zealand has one of the highest earthquake building codes in the world, thus the bricks we made had specifications where reinforced steel ran the full height of the building, from foundation to bond beam. Our engineers did advise us that the steel might shorten the life of the walls – perhaps creating problems in 350 to 500 years depending on when dampness or salt would penetrate the concrete sufficient to spall the rods.

In the VillageTown where Founders wish to make historical reference in building and streetscape design, we recommend that authentic materials be used with the non-uniform construction process of many small teams of builders.

Human Ease and Unease

Most humans exhibit an innate sense of comfort or discomfort in response to a local physical environment. Some of this may come from ancient cellular memory – just as Darwin found the animals of the Galapagos had never learned to fear man, humans pass down a memory of place that makes them feel unease or its opposite. Some of this may be validation of what the Chinese call Feng Shui that sets out a world of unseen energy.

Whatever the reason for the feeling response, many ignore or override these feelings, and then do not understand why their life manifests a grayish background of undefined tension and stress.

Few would call Oia on Santorini pastiche, yet most of what one sees has been built in our lifetime. Old Oia was destroyed in an earthquake in 1956. The ruins are extant on the right. Examine this photo carefully and you will see a new building being constructed.

In the photograph to the right, the living room has been extended over the driveway by pouring a steel reinforced concrete slab – very practical – but something about it feels unnatural, something inside of us nags that a room is not supposed to hang in mid-air. While our engineer, or at least our rational self convinces us that the steel will hold it up, at the subconscious level it aggravates, in induces unease. Further, this unease is not simply affecting the occupant, who probably ignores it, but it affects the streetscape in delivering a message of dissonance.

In contrast, in the photograph to the left, the overhanging floor is suspended in a way innately understood – it feels right, and of course is far more beautiful. The same holds true for placement of buildings. People look for a sense of enclosure that offers security. This can be accomplished using walls, or placing the buildings in right proximity to a hillside. Whole books have been written on this subject, but people can learn to trust their feelings – if it feels wrong, there probably is a good reason why. Listen to your senses.

Generosity

One of the most peculiar aspects human belief in the affluent 21st century western world is the belief in scarcity – that there are not enough resources to go around, and for every winner there must be a loser. No matter how much you have, it is never enough.

20th Century Modern architecture set out the principle *Form Follows Function,* often resulting in low ceilings, soldier-course windows, detail eliminated as unnecessary, bare boned materials using straight lines and flat planes – cold places, unwelcoming, ungenerous. I am uncertain if form follows function meant a lack of generosity, or if that was an unfortunate outcome, but if by their fruits ye shall know them, I'm left unfed.

Indoors, "functional" buildings sometimes seem to drive people crazy. The problem stems from how designers view functionality. People need space to gather, and also space to be alone. This is especially true in families with children, but also true in work places. If funds are short, perhaps skip on a formal dining room and instead invest in a larger country kitchen with lots of places to sit – the place people congregate. Make the bedroom a meditation place, not just a place to sleep. Be generous with water spaces; give your morning kitchen sink a view.

Yes, buildings need to be functional but make functionality generous: if funds are limited build fewer rooms but make the remaining ones bigger spaces. If the rules allow it, make the ceilings higher in some places, especially where there is light. Where it is dark and low, build rooms as cloisters – vaulted low ceilings. I am reminded an old castle cellar, dark and low, transformed into a place of meditation and retreat, cloistered with candles.

When selecting windows, place them so they frame a special view or work well with light. In window placement, avoid uniformity for its own sake.

Consider the generosity of this street corner in Florence in the photo to the left. The street sign is carved in stone, a beautiful carving that gives pleasure as well as orientation. A streetlight is needed, but instead of a utilitarian sodium vapor crime light, the fixture is more elegant, and then in addition to lighting the way, it lights a framed-in-stone icon. Less is less. More is generous. Choose to be generous.

Getting it wrong, getting it right

In the photo above, it doesn't work. The windows are at knee level, the proportion is all wrong. In contrast, in the photograph below, it looks a textbook on different forms of block work and plaster. The same basic materials and forms are used, but with a sense of harmonious design. In the photo above, one may speculate that the designer was the block layer – familiar with the elements, but lacking any understanding as to how to put them together. Below the skills of both architect and builder are apparent. Design does not necessarily require an architect skilled in geometry, but good design demands an innate sense of balance and proportion. Another detail to note is after-construction wiring. In the upper photograph wires are run on the surface. When making a solid wall building include plenty of cable channels inside the walls – even empty ones, and mark them to be easily found.

In my view, this modern design appears to be about maximizing profit and perhaps complying with setback rules. With it's In and Out signs on the ground floor to prompt me, is this why am I reminded of the file boxes stacked on my desk?

"I would say this one looks contrived, ill thought out and wacky for wacky's sake." These words were not written by me, but by an architect who kindly subjected this book to two critical passes. In my view, I don't understand why the porches are so narrow. For a porch to be used, it needs to be at least as wide as a person is tall. Not sure why, but it seems to work out that way. These look unused.

This private home (I assume) resembles nothing so much as an industrial air conditioning unit. Such architecture seems to be about being entirely inwardly focused, with the front door being the minimum required to receive people who don't enter the house through the attached garage. This design may be an appropriate response to the modern suburb with its crime problems.

This neoclassical design has a calm feeling about it, no doubt helped by the subtropical plantings. It provides for a more open, outdoor life. The wall serves as a boundary from the busy street.

Amusing story: After the publication of the first edition of this book, our next-door neighbor on Waiheke Island told me the photograph was of their town house in Auckland... good thing I wrote kindly about this one.

"Building Form around Spirit"

We built a large earth brick compound on an island in the South Pacific. We used the local clays and aggregate to make the bricks. Most of our workers were semi-skilled: Maori elders, a Czech chemist, a graphic designer, and a former mechanic turned earth-brick builder. Design details were decided as we went along. When completed, a visiting Maori elder commented "you have built form around spirit." Thought provoking comment – what did he mean?

What is spirit? The dictionary covers a wide range of meanings, from the fundamental principle of life to a general term for alcohol. When we speak of the spirit of a place, we instantly know it. We can feel it even if we cannot identify what causes the feeling. We want to live in a place with great spirit, avoid one with a low or mean spirit. Religious institutions come to mind – but mostly because of their extremes. I visited monasteries with a wonderful spirit – peace, tranquility and sacred consciousness. I visited others with a spirit of repressed anger, an air of decay and deprivation. I can only say it was a form of energy where English lacks precise words – we felt it but lack the words to name it.

Let me be clear, this discussion is not about religion or religiousness. Religion speaks of spirit, but spirit can exist independent of religion. Spirit can be perceived regardless of ones beliefs. In Greece we drove into a small mountain village where, as we passed the village boundary sign a strong sense of foreboding, of oppression and even danger came over us. We then drove around the curve in the road, and saw a huge compound that obviously was some sort cult – barricaded, with military camouflage and human squalor seen over the barriers. We perceived the spirit of the village before we saw the site.

Even those of us who only believe in what our five senses perceive, understand spirit – especially those who have experienced a loved one dying. One moment there is a living person you know, lying in the bed speaking final words to you. Next moment they "slip away" – all that remains is the deathly still corpse – all that really matters is gone. Let us define spirit as the missing part, the departed, the part that passed away.

In order for us to make sense of this as it applies to architecture, we may need to find language, but in doing so we may need to take a long walk through history and other cultures. In classical times there was a word for this sense of spirit in day-to-day life, and not surprisingly we find it clearly articulated by Plato over two thousand years ago. He called it ether (aether) and he described it simply as what God used to delineate the universe. Along with the other four elements of the universe – solid, liquid, gas and energy (earth, water, air and fire) – ether was one of the five elements instrumental in ancient architecture, and these five design principles continued to be instrumental in architecture all the way through the Middle Ages.

When we use the word elements, we must not confuse it with the modern scientific elements found in the periodic table. The ancients were referring to an understanding of states of energy, not different metals, liquids and gasses. Plato is clear when he discusses reality that he considers the image of a chair to be less real than the physical chair. He considers the "form" of the chair – that which exists in the perfection of the transcendental chair, the idea in our mind from which the physical chair is then created – to be more real than the chair we sit upon.

In Japan, we find a similar hierarchy: Earth, Water, Fire, Wind, and Kū – where Kū may be translated as Void, but also is understood as spirit, intelligent and creative energy. Kū is also a state of mind sought by practitioners of the martial arts to shift their awareness to the unseen, to what they are picking up subconsciously, to tap into a different level of reality. Likewise, in Tibet's earliest known spiritual practice of Bön, the hierarchy of these same five elements is set out, and it later influenced Buddhism and other eastern wisdom.

As we go from spiritual practice in one culture to that in another, we repeatedly find the pattern of the four visible elements and the fifth unseen,

Waiheke Island

and we find architects in all those cultures worked with all five. In fact, as we look at cultures throughout time and throughout the world – from the most primitive to the most sophisticated – we find the same hierarchy. We find this way of thinking about architecture, especially in the ethereal dimension, to be what our Maori elder referred to as building form around spirit.

We also find that many Westerners, lacking the language to put it into words, describe using feeling words to identify particular emotions or a state of mind that occurs when they walk into places in which it is believed the original architects worked the etheric.

Visit the Acropolis or Delphi and one immediately feels the power of the place. Visit thousand year old great cathedrals or modest chapels of the same era, walk within the circle of Stonehenge or the cave-monastery Mega Spileo founded in 362 A. D. and one feels something one may describe as awesome.

Of course, in these places, one may be picking up more than the architecture. It is said that the earth has lines of etheric energy that the ancients identified and upon which built their temples. The line said to run through the Acropolis and Delphi also runs in a straight line through Skellig Michael, St. Michael's Mount, St. Mont Michel, Pisa, Siena, Assisi, Delos, Rhodes, Mt. Carmel and Armageddon. It is said that these temples were built in those places because of the etheric energy that was there first. In ancient times and in other more indigenous cultures this is accepted. In modern culture it seems to be relegated to either those practitioners of the esoteric and those called new age. So we do not confuse different energies, let us consider an experience in which the spirit of the place can be said to be in the walls alone.

Three decades ago, I went to the Old Bodleian Library in Oxford England to do research on the 9th century Clarke manuscript of Plato's works. As I walked up the well worn white marble steps and then over to my desk to await the manuscript being delivered, I was overwhelmed with a sense of scholarship – that I would be perfectly happy spending the rest of my life reading and doing research in that room. Not being particularly bookish by nature, I wondered at this, and wondered if scholars emit brain waves that embed in the walls, and after many centuries the walls glow with a kind of scholarly radioactivity. I was in an atmosphere highly conducive to deep study. In contrast, in my undergraduate days, I spent many hours in a modern library designed by Edward Durrell Stone, a white box with faux Grecian columns. While it was functional – stacks of books, desks and chairs for study, it failed to engender any feeling that inspired study. What was it about the Bodleian library that induced a spirit of scholarship? I believe it was the architecture – the architect understood the ether of a library.

Visit Japan and find a completely different spirit in its traditional architecture. To begin understanding it, one must delve into the principle of *kami,* which like ether crosses the boundary into the metaphysical. Japanese belief says that trees have kami, a spiritual essence, and when they build out of wood they honor the tree's kami – thus the effect would be entirely different than the spirit of wood in modern timber-framed suburban house. Walk into a traditional Japanese home or monastery and one experiences a sense of peace – one is calmed. Some of the effect can be seen in how the materials are selected and formed. Wood is chosen for its color and grain, and then hand shaped. Shoji screens use natural washi paper to transform harsh sunlight into a soft, diffused light that furthers the sense of calm. In describing how this effect is included in the design, the Japanese will speak of Kū in the same way European architects worked with ether.

Why is it that in the modern arts and sciences of the Western World, this wisdom and understanding is relegated to the museum as archaic remnants of superstitious primitives who lack the knowledge base we have to discern what is truly real, and what is not? Just because it is old does not mean it is without validity. Modern man should be more cautious about rejecting thousands of years of collective wisdom because they believe we now have the right answers.

But modern man is not cautious. Indeed to the contrary, modern man is remarkably arrogant in the comfortable belief that we are on an upward slope in terms of our knowledge, and no man has ever been as knowledgeable as we are today. What if we are wrong and they were right? Rather than try to answer that question, it may be useful to understand how we got here – because western human beings descend from a remarkable event that I call the Great Bifurcation, an event that may explain why we have come to deny the place of the spiritual or ethereal in architectural training. To appreciate it, a history essay needs to be inserted at this point. If history is not your thing, you can skip these two pages.

Beginning in the fifteenth century western humanity began to bifurcate reality into the seen – the physical, given over to Science, and the unseen – the metaphysical, retained by the Church. Science agreed to only focus on reality that is apprehensible by the five senses – not crossing the line into that whole other realm that is deemed real by most other cultures. Initially the Church held the balance, but over time, Science gained power to the point where today reality is solely defined as that which stimulates nerves (sensorineural) or is provable. The scientist who crosses the line is anathematized by his peers.

It has its roots in earlier history – indeed one particularly hard-to-find marker occurred in 869 AD at the 8th Ecumenical Council in Constantinople where Edict 11 defined what it means to be human. For the scholars among us, permit me to quote it in full in Latin:

> XI Quod oportet anathematizare omnem qui impie ac laesis sensibus habere hominem duas animas opinatur.
>
> Veteri et Novo Testamento unam animam rationabilem et intellectualem habere hominem docente, et omnibus deiloquis Patribus et magistris Ecclesiae eamdem opinionem asseverantibus, in tantum impietatis quidam, malorum inventionibus dantes operam, devenerunt, ut duas eum habere animas impudente dogmatizare, et quibusdam irrationabilibus conatibus per sapientiam, quae stulta facta est (1 Cor. 1), propriam haeresim confirmare pertentent.
>
> Itaque sancta haec et universalis synodus, veluti quoddam pessimum zizanium, nunc germinantem nequam opinionem, evellere festinans: imo vero ventilabrum in manu veritatis portans, et igni inexstinguibili transmittere omnem paleam, et aream Christi mundam exhibere volens, talis impietatis inventores et patratores, et his similia sentientes, magna voce anathematizat, et definit, atque promulgat, neminem prorsus habere, vel servare quoquo modo statuta hujus impietatis auctorum. Si autem quis contraria gerere praesumpserit huic sanctae et magnae synodo, anathema sit, et a fide atque cultura Christianorum alienus.

In essence the Church Fathers declared that human access to spirit was not within, but was through dogma and the Church. For the next five hundred years, the Church compelled mainstream Europeans to comply. Those who resisted were anathematized, the first step toward being burned as a heretic.

The upshot was that Europeans gradually yielded spiritual sensitivity to the Church. Those with strong natural propensity were taken into the Church where they took vows of chastity and were physically separated from the normal family life that constituted the education milieu for most of the young. If spiritual sensitivity is genetic, chastity was an effective way to breed it out of Europeans. If not inherited but learned, building walls around such people, housing them in monasteries and abbeys is equally effective to assure the young are not exposed to spiritual perception. It is unlikely the church fathers intended to breed out sensitivity; it is a logical result. Some in Christendom resisted, notably the Celtic Christian Church.

After about five hundred years of such selective breeding, the Church became corrupt, and began to weaken as the spiritual portal for Europeans. The Church had formed an agreement with the landed aristocracy and as power shifted from them to the rising merchant class, the Church lost control. Selling indulgences didn't help as it damaged its moral authority and gave rise to Protestantism.

As discussed elsewhere in this book, a shift in technology shifts the definition of wealth, bringing a new class of power holders. In Biblical times, wealth was in livestock – wealth of nomadic tribes. Then technology shifted with mounted warriors wielding metal weapons, so wealth became land as castles and walls defended the food. A newly emerged landed aristocracy benefited from this shift in mobile warring technology – a land based system based on feudal armies.

Around 1400 - 1600 technology shifted again, as a new class of power holders arose, the merchant and trader class. New technology in shipping enabled merchant traders to redefine wealth as gold and jewels, spices and silk, not aristocratic controlled land. Navies became the new arm of enforcement. The merchants had little love of the Church, but they found Science of great value. Thus, somewhat parallel with the Reformation, we saw the Renaissance, the Scientific Revolution and the Enlightenment, as Science began to articulate what is real and what is not.

Initially the Church declared aspects of Science as heresy but eventually we saw the emergence of the Great Bifurcation. The Church fathers and the scientists began to stake out territory – the Church would refrain from declaring the scientists as heretics and science would pretend their universe was purely mechanical and except for human beings, not intelligent. Eventually, in architecture this gave us Le Corbusier's "A house is a machine for living in."

The problem with this detente emerged as subsequent generations of scientists withdrew from the Church, or joined a protestant church that focused on simple answers, discouraging spiritual questioning or exploration. This brings us to the present. The Great Bifurcation is complete and you get to choose sides – reality is defined either by Science or by your Religion. If you are a scientist, you must not factor in the metaphysical into your research.

This bifurcation has a profound effect on how western man conducts his affairs. Business bases its predatory linear thinking on Darwin, and seeks to transform every problem it produces into another financial opportunity – look at the Kyoto Protocol, which creates a market to trade air pollution and greenhouse gas production. If we truly understood what we were doing – asking nature to absorb our pollutants – humanity would do the sane thing and cease polluting overnight. Instead, much science has become the handmaiden of huge corporate interests, which through trusts and foundations, provide funding for studies that ask questions expected to prove outcomes favorable to the industry.

Likewise, artists express the subconscious agony of their unacknowledged bifurcated being by producing works that shock, in which harmony and beauty are eschewed. Art must be new; it should be edgy; it should cause controversy.

As people cannot find their internal spiritual foundation, they go out to find answers. To supply them, rigid religious organizations emerge which provide absolute answers. We now witness rapidly expanding organizational forces which recruit new believers, providing them with a package of answers. Each believes they are right, and the others are wrong.

With all of this serving as a cacophony of competing belief systems, it makes it very hard to engage in a meaningful dialogue to explore the possibility that the spiritual plane acknowledged by so many people throughout history might actually be real.

There is hope. Humanity is indeed intelligent, even if some of our present day leaders and decision-makers try to prove it not so. For me this awareness came in 1971 when I was an undergraduate student one summer in University of California in Berkeley. Resident in my dormitory was a conference of nuclear physicists. I made a point of sitting at the cafeteria tables across from the old fellows with the scruffy gray beards; asking them questions. I found these physicists were inquiring human beings who were pursuing the questions as to the fundamentals of reality, the meaning of the universe, and in doing so were finding answers remarkably similar to ancient wisdom, only the old ones used allegory while the new ones use mathematics.

At the risk of packaging the western world's scholarship into a nutshell – the boundary line between matter and energy is being blurred. Further, some boundary pushing scientists are allowing for the possibility that some forms of energy may be intelligent rather than random. In other words, Science may discover the universe is not just a marvelously complex mechanical device, but that it is fundamentally intelligent. If they get there, the Great Bifurcation may prove simply to have been a necessary step in human evolution.

What does the Great Bifurcation have to do with building design?

It comes down to a simple question. If you accept my thought that what the ancients called ether is worth considering, then we ask, is it possible to design ether in inanimate objects like a building or a community? Or to put it more directly, was that Maori elder talking nonsense, or is it possible to build form around spirit?

Consider the two photographs below. Both are Christian churches, one Orthodox, one Protestant. Both are white in color. Both display relatively little ornament – in the Cycladic architecture one finds a traditional form not that far from the modernist Presbyterian church built in an elegant New Zealand suburb. Yet there is a fundamental difference between the two – their measure of spirit. In the modern church, this comes across in the thin panels, the huge slabs of box-cut glass, the frontal placement of the carport and the utility shed (which seems like an afterthought). One gets the sense of the architect and the parish wanting to make a bold minimalist statement, but not of the spirit of the place. It also exudes a sense of transience, a drive-in place that won't be there in fifty years – most likely because the old parishioners will die off, and the young will see no relevance to supporting this dated monument to a passing architectural phase.

If we were to accept the possibility that one can design and build a place or a whole VillageTown with a particular spirit, how would we proceed? Let us begin with a working definition. Spirit in architecture and in landscape design may be described as the intelligent energetic fields which create resonance or dissonance that affect human beings – some consciously and others at the subconscious level. Such resonance and dissonance influences how people feel, behave and interact with others. In this definition we use resonance and dissonance in a similar context to music. Most people prefer resonance.

In this definition, the observable effect is reported as a feeling: *the old Victorian mansion felt creepy. The newly built suburban McMansion felt vacuous, devoid of any feeling. The country house in the sun felt loved*. In Christopher Alexander's *A Pattern Language*, many of the patterns are given over to archetypes "deeply rooted in human nature", which is to say that rather than look for *why* they produce good feelings, the book simply lists them. Some are obvious – damp rooms create dissonance, a warm fire creates resonance. But why do "Houses with smooth hard walls, made of prefabricated panels, concrete, gypsum, steel, aluminum, or glass always stay impersonal and dead", as Alexander writes in Pattern 197 (Thick Walls)? Why do thin walls feel dead?

> **Build a Cemetery** – Go to a modern community and look for the cemetery. It's not there. Why not? Because the developer wants to maximize profits; a place to bury the dead is not profitable. Also modern society treats dying as a disease.
>
> In a VillageTown, continuity and connection become important parts of daily life. People will die in the VillageTown, and a place should be set aside for their bones or ashes to lie in peace. Make it a beautiful place that welcomes the living, and design it to need little maintenance. If grass needs to be mowed, use sheep or goats fenced in, and let families plant real flowers.

Consider the experience of the Maori elder when he came to our earth brick compound.

In a world of highly machined, rigidly straight lines, the buildings showed the fractal irregularity of nature – in this case because they were hand made: their straight lines not perfectly straight; the flat walls not perfectly flat. The surface coating (not paint) made with lime, clay and sand are of materials near to earth, not petrochemical based – yielding an irregular color that changes with sun, driving rain and aging.

On entering through a bell tower – complete with a 150 year old bronze bell – the elder came not into a hallway, but an open courtyard with high walls and no roof. It invites one to pause – providing an immediate sense of enclosure, of protection. Like most visitors, the elder paused and looked up to the open sky. At this point the elder reported on the energy of the place: both quieting and safe as the ancient, large oak door closed behind him blocking the wind blowing off the sea.

Following protocol the visitor was then offered water, tea or light food. The elder walked into large country kitchen with a massive stone slab for both food preparation and dining. The elder's experience shifted, this time one of hospitality. The thick white-washed walls enhance the quality of the air, and their solidity engenders a sense of security.

Later, after visiting for a while, the elder walked into another courtyard and into the art studio that has what the elder described as Tapu, having a sacred feeling to it. The elder instinctively remove shoes before entering, and spoke in hushed tones. The elder was not told to do this by anyone, instead the architecture itself spoke. Photographs are on the next two pages.

The archetypes in materials, in the shape of the building, including generous use of open space courtyards, were not new. Selection of the right materials play an important part, as does layout and design. However, perhaps the most important element of designing for spirit would be *intent*. Unless you intend to achieve a particular feeling, you won't design for it. Because so much of modern design focuses on other intent – low cost, the "wow factor" or using generic materials available from catalogues and professional supply houses, the possibility of designing a place which moves one when one walks into it is unlikely.

In this discussion, I would prefer we end it not with answers, but with a question that perhaps may become a subject of discussion in the Dynamic Engagement process, or on VillageTown web site:

Can we design form around spirit?

An Experiment in Present Day Vernacular

I asked the town officials what makes their job easier – sustainable management of resources. What does that mean on Waiheke? Earth Brick. So I contacted the local earth brick builder and set out to build a home, office, studio, workshop and a place where community events could occur. It's one thing to talk about sustainable building, it's another to actually do it.

As it was to be vernacular, we did not hire an architect. We used simple, proven forms – basic boxes, variable roof pitch, various window shapes. The design changed as we went along, our plan had minimum-maximum specifications that meant such changes did not require amended plans. We hired semi-skilled laborers and paid by the hour, which allowed flexibility as we built.

The challenge of contemporary architecture

"*Architecture is the will of an epoch translated into space.*" So, we are told, said Ludwig Mies van der Rohe, the architect who gave humanity the pattern of the glass and steel skyscraper. He also said "*And just as we acquaint ourselves with materials, just as we must understand functions, so we must become familiar with the psychological and spiritual factors of our day. No cultural activity is possible otherwise; for we are dependent on the spirit of our time.*" Perhaps what he says is true. If the psychological factors of our day are neuroses and psychopathy and the spiritual factors of our day are alienation, distress and a loss of our roots, a loss of connection to all that once was human scaled, then one may agree that much of our architecture reflects the spirit of our time. Is architecture the reflection or the cause?

Why is that so much of what is acclaimed architecture of our day seems to be exercises intended to win prizes in architectural magazines not timeless places the citizens love? Or as we hear architect George E. Hartman observed "*The architectural profession gave the public 50 years of modern architecture and the public's response has been 10 years of the greatest wave of historical preservation in the history of man.*" The profession and the public are out of sync.

I have been a historian, educator and businessman not an architect, so I look to others to state the professional concerns. Let us first hear the views of architect Christopher Alexander – but this time his recent book, not his 1977 book of patterns.

"In the 20th century we have passed through a unique period, one in which architecture as a discipline has been in a state that is almost unimaginably bad. Sometimes I think of it as a mass psychosis of unprecedented dimension, in which the people of earth – in large numbers and in almost all contemporary societies – have created a form of architecture which is against life, insane, image-ridden, hollow. The ugliness which has been created in the cities of the world, and the banality and pretentiousness of many 20th century buildings, streets, and parking lots have overwhelmed the earth. Much of this construction is caused by developers, housing authorities, owners of hotels, motels, airport authorities. In this sense architects might be considered blameless, since in some degree the ugliness of what has been created is caused by new relations between time, money, labor, and materials, and by a set of conditions in which the real thing – authentic architecture that has deep feeling and true worth – is almost impossible.

But architects are not blameless. For the most part, architects have stood by, content to play their role as part of the 20th century machine. In many cases they make it worse. They guild the lily of commercial development with pretentiousness. Many architects have raised the designer-consciousness fashion of building to new levels, have invented absurd ways of thinking about architecture, have altogether poisoned the earth with an abundance of terrible and senseless designs which have few redeeming features." *

---

* The Nature of Order, An Essay on the Art of Building and The Nature of the Universe - Book One – The Phenomena of Life, Page 6 OUR CONFUSION IN ARCHITECTURE by Christopher Alexander: ISBN 0-9726529-1-4 © 2002, Center for Environmental Studies, publisher

Next, permit me to quote from a controversial speech by a critic of contemporary architecture, HRH Prince Charles and his famous speech given in 1987 at Mansion House (see www.princeofwales.gov.uk/speechesandarticles):

In the space of a mere 15 years, in the Sixties and Seventies, and in spite of all sorts of elaborate rules supposedly designed to protect that great view, your predecessors, as the planners, architects and developers of the City, wrecked the London skyline and desecrated the dome of St Paul's…

You have, ladies and gentlemen, to give this much to the Luftwaffe: when it knocked down our buildings, it didn't replace them with anything more offensive than rubble. We did that…

I believe I have been accused of setting myself up as a new, undemocratic hurdle in the planning process – a process we are supposed to leave to the professionals. But the professionals have been doing it their way, thanks to the planning legislation, for the last 40 years. We, poor mortals, are forced to live in the shadow of their achievements. Everywhere I go, it is one of the things people complain about most and, if there is one message I would like to deliver this evening, in no uncertain terms, it is that large numbers of us in this country are fed up with being talked down to and dictated to by an existing planning, architectural and development establishment.

…architects and developers have the wrong kind of freedom – the freedom to impose their caprice, which is a kind of tyranny. Competitions even encourage them to come up with the voguish innovations and fashionable novelties that appeal to nobody but other architects. One prominent architect recently confessed, airily and with no apparent sign of shame, that some of his earlier buildings have ceased to interest even him, now that the thrill of creativity has worn off.

Well, what kind of creativity is that? To put up a building which other people have to live with, and leave them to live with it while you wander off saying you're tired of it, and then to put up another one which you will presumably get tired of too, leaving yet more people to live with the all-too-durable consequences of your passing fancy. There is a terrible fecklessness to all this, when grown men can get whole towns in the family way, pay nothing towards maintenance, and call it romance.

To comfort architects who find difficulty with the process set out in this book, I caution them to consider that the VillageTown is competition to the suburb. Unlike grand city buildings, most suburban home designs are picked out of a catalogue. Inviting architects to help design VillageTowns, we venture into territory where today architects find little work.

In creating the VillageTown, the principal of authenticity precludes the option of picking homes and offices out of a catalogue. Design matters, and for the VillageTown to feel authentic, we can either let it take several hundred years to evolve, or we must develop a new process for its design. The answer, we propose, is to make the owner primary and the professional designer secondary. Remember, the owner has to live with the results as do the neighbors.

This means that professional designers are needed, but at the same time, need to keep their egos in check – the homes and work places they help make manifest cannot be trophies. This is our challenge – on the one hand we have trophy architecture where the building is often referred to by the architect's name – and on the other we have cookie-cutter mediocrity in which design is little more than what is required to secure a permit to build. In conceiving the VillageTown, we need to find a new way that avoids both extremes of contemporary architecture.

With the VillageTown process the architect has a career opportunity – but to be a useful part of the process, they need to come to the table with a very different head space. They need to come as a learner, with open ears to listen, and a heart open to perceiving at a different level. They need to be open to a sense that there is more to life than the physical and observable; that buildings can hold a spirit that can be nurturing and wonderful, inspiring and life affirming, and that when this is accomplished the physical design is often timeless. They need to have excellent people skills. For some this may be an impossible task, it is alien to much professional training. For others it will seem a dream come true, an opportunity to collaborate at a deep level.

Conclusion

Building design has two parts, outside and inside. Both are equally important. The inside is about functionality and ambience, creating a stage set in which life is lived when weather is inclement. The outdoors, especially the streetscape, is the other stage, and it should be one that never gets boring or drab – but should be one that inspires and nourishes.

One of the blessings of our time in our Western world is the unprecedented level of democratic affluence. We really have created democratic levels of wealth never seen before in history. However we don't do enough with this wealth. In the old days, erecting a building was a major event, and people recognized they and their descendents would be living with it for many generations. Therefore they built more than just the purely practical. Today, we tend not to do this. Buildings are viewed as disposable, and made of components that end up in the garbage heap within years, not centuries.

Commerce triumphs over streetscape in Oxford

We can attribute some of this to transience. Home no longer means putting down roots. It's not that people don't yearn to put down roots, it's a product of a transient society where one moves to get a better job, to find a better place to raise children, or to get a change of scenery because the scenery is no longer fulfilling.

In the VillageTown, these factors are addressed to enable people to put down roots. Self employment or contract employment using the Internet as virtual office enables people to pick where they want to live, not have to select what is on offer because of the job location.

When one puts down roots, the quality and character of the place becomes more important. Places with graffiti tend to be places of transience, the residents are not stakeholders. Places with flowering plants growing up the walls are places of permanence, the residents expect to be there to enjoy them for many years.

Perhaps one of the biggest differences comes in the thinking when deciding on a style. If a building is viewed primarily as an investment, one tends to listen to the real estate agents to hear what sells best. Decisions are based on resale, not the pleasure one may derive from living there. One approaches house building completely differently if one builds not for resale value, but for long-term living. Space is set out as it fits ones needs, ones aspirations and ones imagination.

If there were to be a primary goal of building design, it would be to make the building and the surrounding neighborhood the Center of the Universe. Of all the places to be, this would be the place one is happiest; the place where one wants to be.

Building design plays a major part in achieving that goal.

Someone once said invest well in a good bed and good shoes, you will spend most of your life in them. Likewise, and for the same reason, design for a good home and good village within a wonderful town.

This is the street front not the back alley.

Building Design Checklist

Classical architecture for major buildings
- ☐ Architect designed
- ☐ Formal statement
- ☐ Sophisticated design that fits streetscape

Vernacular architecture for the rest
- ☐ Simple, familiar shapes
- ☐ Individual exterior treatment
- ☐ Strong use of artisans for detail and ornament
- ☐ Functional, intelligent design of interior and access
- ☐ Low maintenance, low pollution during maintenance

Timeless and durable– not trendy and transient
- ☐ Agreement on what this means in an architectural code
- ☐ Beauty
- ☐ Ornament
- ☐ Create a local ornament industry

Authentic
- ☐ A formal process implemented to achieve authenticity
- ☐ Harmony
- ☐ Variety
- ☐ History
- ☐ Human Ease and Unease

Generosity
- ☐ Create incentives to encourage generosity in building design

Spirit
- ☐ A clear VillageTown agreement as to what designing with spirit means
- ☐ A clear agreement as to how it is to be achieved

On Architectural Style

While my personal taste tends toward the timeless forms of architecture, it is important to understand that this bias does not extend to what happens in VillageTown design. The framework is there to enable people, not to create a particular style (as is the case, for example, in Poundbury, England).

In *Life Liberty Happiness* (see page 148) I wrote about one village in the VillageTown where the Village Coordinator (the person who defines the features that attract the villagers) set a visual theme that was about architectural cutting edge creativity. Within the framework of a two or three story attached home, architects were invited to design the front and back face of the homes with a fixed price if a villager selected their proposal. The result was a riot of color, shape and ornament which worked because it was cutting edge.

The important thing to appreciate in such a process is that it is not mob rule, where the loudest voice dominates, but a formal process more like how a jury works, where ordinary individuals are empowered to work within a structure of support, so their collective wisdom comes out.

I probably won't live in the cutting-edge architectonic village, but I may visit it from time to time.

This window was set for the winter equinox so it would capture the sunrise everyday.

Chapter 14 – Building Materials and Process

Problem Statement

Complexity

The average wall in a new home probably contains about 40 components and for the most part these are assembled by hand using methods that have not changed much for over a hundred years. The hammer has been replaced by the hammer gun, the hand saw by the circular saw and the paint brush by a spray gun, but that is about it. This is because buildings are generally built one at a time, or at best in a series of subdivision homes that cannot get ahead of the sales curve if the developer does not want to go bust. The sales curve is driven by growth in the regional economy. For this reason, the building industry is probably one of the most out-of-date in the world.

Because homes tend to be hand-assembled, building materials tend to be ones that can be lifted by one or two men. Frame houses use wood or steel studs, plywood, building wrap, fiberglass insulation, painted gypsum plaster board and outside some sort of weatherproof cladding (siding)... wood, vinyl, brick veneer or stucco.

Each of these steps requires a different trade, which adds the complexity of scheduling. Because many are subcontractors, they promise to arrive on Tuesday morning but show up Thursday afternoon. The job of project manager seems to involve a cell phone permanently screwed to the manager's skull as he tries to track down the delivery truck stuck in traffic. Today they even make reality television shows about the endless crises that are status quo in the home construction industry.

In commercial construction, increasingly tilt-slab concrete walls are used because they are fast, inexpensive and meet international building codes on non-combustibility. However they still need to be insulated and clad if they are to be made into attractive, livable environments. As a result, commercial buildings, which at one time were the pride of community, now tend to resemble big shoe boxes covered with signs and logos. They are bland at best, and too often downright ugly.

Building one house at a time, complexity is forgivable. When building thousands at one time, simplifying is essential.

Health

Some of the newer materials used in building construction create new problems. Consider these comments from the United States Environmental Protection Agency web site. It clearly states the health related problems caused by buildings:

> The term "sick building syndrome" (SBS) is used to describe situations in which building occupants experience acute health and comfort effects that appear to be linked to time spent in a building, but no specific illness or cause can be identified. The complaints may be localized in a particular room or zone, or may be widespread throughout the building. In contrast, the term "building related illness" (BRI) is used when symptoms of diagnosable illness are identified and can be attributed directly to airborne building contaminants...
> A 1984 World Health Organization Committee report suggested that up to 30 percent of new and remodeled buildings worldwide may be the subject of excessive complaints related to indoor air quality (IAQ). Often this condition is temporary, but some buildings have long-term problems. Sometimes indoor air problems are a result of poor building design...
> Most indoor air pollution comes from sources inside the building. For example, adhesives, carpeting, upholstery, manufactured wood products, copy machines, pesticides, and cleaning agents may emit volatile organic compounds (VOCs), including formaldehyde... Research shows that some VOCs can cause chronic and acute health effects at high concentrations, and some are known carcinogens. Low to moderate levels of multiple VOCs may also produce acute reactions.*

* http://www.epa.gov/iaq/pubs/sbs.html

Fire

The first edition of this book was favorably reviewed by conservative op-ed journalist Jim Bacon, editor of the Virginia-based BaconsRebellion.com. About the same time, he wrote a piece entitled *Design by Fire Truck* in which he demonstrated the character of new community design is dictated by the demands of the Fire Marshall, requiring wide streets and wider turnabouts so his fire trucks can get to fire.

It seems fire trucks have grown larger because they now need to be a combination of apparatus delivery and bus. No longer are fire fighters allowed to ride of the back of the truck, they must be safely belted inside. The trucks get bigger. Thus, we end up with truck-sized communities where destinations are separated to accommodate the size of these infrequent-visiting trucks.

Because the developers want to get on with building, and because they use combustible materials, they do not argue. They comply to get their permits with an outcome of sprawl.

> Further to your recent discussion with our Group Manager with reference to "property fires" in the new Poundbury area of Dorchester in the last 10 years, I have checked our records and have listed the information below:-
>
> 11.07.02 fire in light fitting
> 06.09.02 fire in a window frame during re-decoration (blowlamp)
> 14.12.02 light socket overheated
> 01.04.03 unattended cooking
> 05.03.06 fire in microwave oven
>
> There have been several false alarms with various automatic detection systems in premises on this site, but the only "fires" recorded are listed above.
>
> Please also note that, due to current building regulations requiring smoke detectors to be fitted in all new premises, some owner/occupiers may have had a fire, but due to early detection by the smoke detectors were able to deal with the incident themselves and saw no reason to call the Fire Service.

Major cities of the world were originally built of timber. Rome learned the lesson in its great fire of 64 AD. It rebuilt in stone and concrete. London paid the price in its fire of 1666. New York burned in 1835. When Prince Charles built his archetypal Village, Poundbury, the buildings were of stone, brick and other mostly non-combustible materials – the Dorset Fire and Rescue Service, located in Poundbury reports no houses have burned in Poundbury since it was constructed 10 years prior. I know because I asked them to send me their records (copied above).

"A Fascinating Material" - Variable Density Aggregate (VDA)

Simplicity

In constructing a building, Christopher Alexander in *A Pattern Language – Pattern № 207 Good Materials* observed that as much as 80% of the total volume of the materials used in a building consists of "bulk materials". If the same raw material can be used for all the bulk materials, manufacturing and assembly are less complex. While this is helpful for building ones home, it becomes important when building several thousand buildings in a very short period of time.

The challenge when using a single base material is to avoid uniformity – one does not want a design that resembles 1950's Soviet architecture. Once again, it is useful for us to turn to Pattern № 207 for advice:

> "We believe that ultra-lightweight concrete is one of the most fundamental bulk materials of the future".
> "Regular concrete is too dense. It is heavy and hard to work, is ugly, cold, and hard in feeling unless covered by expensive finishes not integral to the structure.
> And yet concrete, in some form, is a fascinating material. It is fluid, strong and relatively cheap. It is available in almost every part of the world...
> Is there any way of combining all these good qualities of concrete and also having a material that is light in weight, easy to work, with a pleasant finish? There is. It is possible to use a whole range of ultra-lightweight concretes that have a density and compressive strength similar to that of wood. They are easy to work with, can be nailed with ordinary nails, cut with a saw, drilled with woodworking tools, easily repaired."

When Christopher Alexander and his team wrote this in 1977, product development in lightweight concrete or what we now call variable density aggregate (VDA) was still in its first generation. Reportedly developed in Germany about 60 years ago, the principle is simple. Concrete and mortar consists of three parts... cement, water and a filler (sometimes with additives). The filler tends to be stone of various sizes from sand or stone dust up to what is called builders mix. In VDA the much of the filler is air, held in place by a foaming agent so the air bubbles evenly disperse in such a way that they make the concrete less dense.

To avoid confusion, VDA is not Autoclaved Aerated Concrete (AAC). Known by brand names such as Hebel Block®, AAC is a different product, not in our view the right bulk material for the Village Town. AAC is sold in blocks, made off-site in a factory, using aluminum powder and lime that react when cooked in an oven to produce hydrogen bubbles – a bit like baking bread. Typically it comes in blocks that are glued together. It is more suitable for one-off house building.

Since 1977 when A Pattern Language was published, the industry has seen substantial product development and now the foaming agents are in their second generation of technological development. While one may argue that the air acts as filler, when reviewed by building inspectors, the foaming agent is generally understood as an approved additive.

The Qualities of Lightweight / Variable Density Aggregate (VDA)

- Non-combustible, low heat transfer in fires
- Does not rot, termite-proof at prescribed densities
- Non-toxic, insulating, creates a healthy micro-climate, feels warm
- Sound absorbing, neighbors cannot be heard through the walls
- Reliable and proven – timeless and familiar to inspectors
- Efficient bulk material, little residual waste
- Fast & cheap to build, low transport costs of materials
- Easy to shape, drill and cut
- Low-on going maintenance
- Opportunity to produce beautiful buildings by molding
- Same base materials for most structural parts of building

Foam Generating Machines 2014 © litebuilt.com

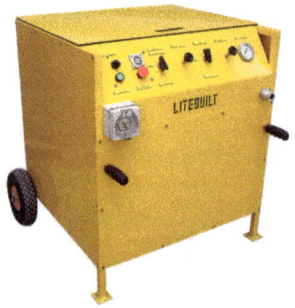

Insulation

The simplicity of VDA comes from its structural and insulating qualities. Built as a foot-thick wall, VDA needs no other internal components other than reinforcing steel. It provides a high level of insulation that is inherent in the bulk material rather than being applied on the inside afterwards.

Standard concrete is a poor thermal and acoustical insulator. In other words, by itself, it makes cold, clammy buildings where you can hear the neighbors, especially the thump of their stereo. The foaming agent overcomes the limitation of traditional concrete, which is simply that normal concrete is too dense. By adding the air bubbles, the density is reduced, making it a delightful, highly flexible building material with almost infinite possible variations on what can be designed and built.

VDA is made in a machine that adds air to a foaming agent to produce an additive that looks like shaving cream. The mix is added to concrete in a precise variable measure to get the right density.

To understand the density issue (*if you don't like numbers – and metric numbers at that – skip this section, written in brown*), a conventional cubic meter of concrete weights 2,400 kg. Adding the foaming agent reduces the weight as space becomes occupied by air. The weight can drop to three quarters (1,600 kg), half (1,200 kg), one quarter (600 kg) or even as low as 95% air (100 kg which is about 200 pounds per cubic yard), although this latter is a limited-use product with the strength of meringue.

Using different ratios of foam to aggregate, the foundation can be poured with a strong (heavy) mix, and then lighter mixes used for walls. The roof is thicker still, as thick as needed to get the right insulation numbers. Just dial in more air, so it does not add weight, but only greater thickness.

The controls are relatively simple, and the testing is by weight, as the air makes the mix lighter. In a settlement the size of a VillageTown, production would be computer controlled with constant batch measurement to assure precise quality control.

The trade off comes in strength. The lower the density, the lower the compressive strength (mPa or psi) of the wall. Structurally, this is not a problem because the engineer calculates the right combination of reinforcement in the slab.

To understand the insulation qualities, you need to understand the mythology of r-factors. A 13" (305mm) thick VDA wall at 500 kg/m^3 (31 lbs/ft^3) will have an r-factor of R19 (US) / R-3 (metric). However, this number does not compare to an R19 conventional wall made of timber or steel studs packed with fiberglass insulation. This is because a conventional wall has leaks, gaps and conductive components that result in a colder room in winter or a hotter one in summer. The VDA wall is solid. It has no gaps. Its insulation qualities are therefore consistent, meaning it will keep the house warmer with the same R-factor.

Molded finish

When mixed and poured, VDA has the consistency of porridge. In other words, it molds to the form that holds it until a chemical reaction turns it into a form of aggregate stone. The potential of this characteristic is almost unlimited. At its worst, we get Soviet style cheap housing made of flat forms that is functional but ugly. At its best we can get a building that is high art.

The secret is in the mold. And, while concrete is one of the oldest building materials in the world, and VDA a product that has been around since the 1920's, the potential of mold-making is something new. The new tool is called a CNC router. CNC stands for Computer Numerical Controlled and it is a computer controlled machine for cutting wood, plastic, or metal. In essence, it is a three dimensional printer. If you can design it on a computer, the CNC router can cut it. And CNC routers can be huge, meaning the panels they carve can be wall height.

The VillageTown stewards include a team of specialists who have developed a computer program that converts 2 dimensional images into 3-D carving instructions. The potential of this is broad. A classical building that took decades for the exterior ornament to be carved can now be completed in formwork in a matter of hours. The limitation is imagination and good taste. In addition to the ornament panels, these same forms can include precise locations of doors and windows, as well as inserts for stone tile. Instead of a tiler spending weeks precisely applying marble or granite wall times, a semiskilled laborer drops them in face down with no ability to set them in wrong. In this image below, an intricate Maori fractal pattern is designed using a computer. It then is scaled up (zoomed) with no loss of resolution, carved, molded and cast.

These panels are inserted in the forms and then fitted with doors, windows, rebar and conduit for wires, cables and pipes, all affixed in air. When the panels, forms and inserts are installed, the wall is then poured with VDA. If it is steam cured, the panels can be removed two hours later. Otherwise they are left for 24 hours. They are then set in final place. Roofs and interior floors are then installed using cranes from the top. Having a rooftop garden makes a big difference, because the roof is nothing more than a waterproof top floor.

Afterwards detail and ornament is applied and the exterior lock-up shell is complete. In a high-production operation running 24/7 using mobile tents and cranes that span the building and have their own lights and roof, finished walls can be erected in less than a day, at a substantially lower labor and material cost. Such a mechanized system can build a village of 200 homes in a matter of months, in lock-up stage, ready for interior finishing.

The potential of these molding systems is almost unlimited. A talented designer can design the wall surface on a computer and it will be instantly cut to scale, ready to insert.

The standing walls with their molded shapes can be plastered, or they can be left as is – especially if tints or oxides are added to the VDA so it does not have that off-white concrete look. One proposed approach involves spraying a very strong (95 mPa / 14,000 psi) thin layer of special cement mixed with color first and then pour the VDA immediately afterwards. This gives a hardshell render with a wide range of natural, long-lasting colors that do not require future painting.

The walls can be whitewashed on the inside, or for the Greek look, on both sides. Whitewash is another one of those ancient materials that costs next to nothing, is easy to maintain, and does not require expensive preparation when it needs to be re-coated. Using the lightweight slab method, the whitewash is sprayed on the slab as soon as it is poured. Whitewash slows down the curing process by keeping the slab moist, which is a desirable quality on cold-cure pours. Any damage done when the slab is being put up is easily touched up because whitewash is a very forgiving medium.

Whitewash

The oldest materials are still sometimes the best. Whitewash is lime with a bit of binder – glue. Distemper is chalk. These coatings can be applied with brushes and left brilliant, soft white or tinted to produce those spectacular colors featured in photography and travel books about the Mediterranean. They are easy to mix (dry powder, about $10 a bag, add water and a dollop of glue). They are easy to clean up (use a sponge, even a week later). They are easy to recoat. Ready-to-use costs about a dollar a gallon. Why are these coatings not used more often? The simple answer is it's too cheap. Who can support a sales department promoting a product that costs $20 to do the whole interior of a home?

The Freedom of Hand Made

Except for water on a windless day, very little in nature is straight and flat. Yes, the construction process works easier when building with straight lines – or to be more correct, building using materials that require straight manufacturing, work best when they are plumb and level. Why is it that we must accept this? In timber buildings, boards are made straight because saw mills use rotating blades, and it is most efficient to ship straight timber. Same holds true for steel girders and for plywood, gypsum wallboard, rolled steel roofing, and other familiar building materials. When building materials are pre-manufactured, and the construction industry becomes one of assembly, then we are stuck with flat planes.

In contrast, by using VDA we are not bound by the tyranny of manufacturing and delivery costs. As soon as one shifts to mineral based materials – and we recommend ones based on light weight concrete because of its inherent flexibility – the raw materials arrive in bags or tankers, and they can be formed in any shape, any curve. What we then need to do is to free our thinking so we don't set out pouring straight, flat tilt slabs or make flat, straight walls.

Material Handling and Efficiency of Scale

Elimination of components speed up construction. Bulk materials are delivered to the Industrial Park in bulk. Cement comes by ship, rail or hopper truck and is stored in silos, not bags.

By using a few bulk materials for 85% of the buildings, the ViTo realizes substantial savings in wholesale purchasing. It goes direct to the bulk market, to the producers, bypassing the middlemen who serve the smaller volume markets.

In some cases, it may prove more efficient to mix the aggregate at the Industrial Park and transport it to the mobile factories not in mixing trucks but through pumping pipes, where the foam additive is dialed in at the mobile factory.

In addition to these bulk structural components, VDA opens up a whole new world for secondary uses, especially in ornament. Examples of intricate Greek columns – made with VDA using fine-grained sand – suggest the possibility of a carving industry that creates both molds and one-off blanks to be directly carved. One could make a simple mold for a round column or square door surround of a density far easier to form than traditional marble.

Health

Noting the EPA concerns about *sick building syndrome* and *building related illness,* the best way to avoid the risk is to select non-toxic materials. Human beings and life evolved in the presence of calcium sand, water and air. When it comes to interior finishes, we recommend following the same timeless approach, rather than go with recently invented products and materials, most of which derive from petrochemicals. The choice on materials is up to the home buyer, but the ViTo can play an important role in bulk material selection.

We built this building using local adobe called earth brick – a crushed aggregate from the local quarry is used in a 13:1 mix with cement. Blocks are hand-made on site. It took over three months to get to this point. It is a wonderful place to live and work. It has a special quality to it that visitors comment upon. Guests consistently note how well they slept "best rest in years". This comes from the solidity. However, as the photograph shows, the job site is a mess, and it remained that way for over a year. Had we used VDA and preset molds, it would have gone much faster but it would have cost to much to only do one house. The lessons leaned played a big part in the search for the right system to be used for Village Towns.

Fire

VDA is non-combustible. More importantly, its vendors state that it has a 5 hour burn rating, which means it is especially slow to transmit heat through the wall where it would heat the next room hot enough to spontaneously combust. All rooms will have smoke alarms and sprinkler systems. Each block would have hose storage so trucks need not bring hoses with them. All of this is done to get away from the requirement that streets be wide enough to support the conventional large trucks used by fire departments. This becomes a compelling argument for the materials we recommend. Design by Fire Truck simply is not acceptable. Assuring safety is paramount, but there are better ways.

Greenhouse Gasses

In the past decade, climate hysteria seems to have hijacked environmental consciousness to the point where *green* means an obsession with greenhouse gasses, and scientific analysis appears to have declined into a tribal contest between histrionic alarmists and abrasive skeptics. We seek to stay outside that brawl, taking the precautionary approach, but for better reasons. Thus, on page 101 for example, the 20 reasons to not use cars in the VillageTown intentionally do not include global warming or peak oil. However, because it is such a passionate issue, we do need to address it, noting this is not a complete analysis.

VDA uses cement or MgO. Cement manufacture generates CO_2. For the average VillageTown home, CO_2 impact is 17± tons – about the same as making a new car. For 4,000 homes this works out to about 68,000 tons – one time, not ongoing.

The offset comes in eliminating ongoing pollution, most notably in eliminating driving, but also with buildings that require less heat or cooling. Of these, driving is easier to document. A gallon of gasoline generates 19 pounds of CO_2. The average US car travels 20 miles on one gallon. The average American drives 35 miles a day, of which only 15% is commuting. Multiply this by 8,000 VillageTown adults who no longer need to drive, and *every day* it eliminates over a quarter million miles of driving. This saves about 50,000 tons of CO_2 per year. Thus in about 16 months, by itself, no-driving offset the VDA cement CO_2.

Note that this gasoline calculation only used CO_2 from the tailpipe, whereas the cement calculation included its manufacture. It is exceedingly difficult to find the total impact of gasoline, but any calculation of its CO_2 content should include:

- Manufacturing and running petroleum drilling rigs and the support vehicles (trucks, helicopters, ships).
- Transporting crude oil including loss and damage due to ship crashes, explosions, spillage and oil well blow-outs.
- The cost of refining oil including the energy and pollution involved in building and operating oil refineries.
- The cost of transporting wholesale gasoline and diesel, and the cost to build and operate the retail fuel stations.
- The cost of fighting wars over oil. For example, the US Department of Defense is America's largest consumer of fuel.

Add up the CO_2 component of all of those necessary steps to make that gallon, and the gasoline offset is probably under a year. Remove the manufacturing footprint of 2 cars in the garage, and the offset comes faster.

2 November 2003
The day before a strong storm blew through, dumping snow on Sausalito and clearing the air of Los Angeles. Landing at LAX one could actually see the mountains in the distance, and real blue skies.

18 May 2006 Landing at the same airport and on the same flight path, the sky this day was much more typical for Los Angeles. On landing, the day felt oppressive, although the locals seemed not to notice it.

It's not that LA generates more pollution, it's only its location in an air trap means people see it more often.

Chapter 15 – Building the VillageTown

Taking an average of 2½ people per home, a 10,000 population VillageTown will have 4,000 homes. We can allow ten years to do a settlement in the conventional staged process in which a master plan is then contracted out to several high quality developers who do their particular part. However, this makes it impossible to establish a local economy for the businesses that need a critical mass of 5,000 to reach break-even. Additionally, because the best way to fund a billion dollar settlement fund is by consolidating individual construction loans, the carrying time (when the buyer is paying for their existing home while accruing interest on the new one) must be as short as possible. For these reasons we examined industry best practices, brought on board experts, and asked what is the shortest reasonable time we could go from Stage 1 funding (start-up) to completion.

The reasonable answer was three years. To put this in perspective, consider that Prince Charles' Poundbury set a schedule of 25 years. The difference is how the local economy is structured. A VillageTown draws upon a national or (if immigration policies support it) a world-wide market. On the back of an envelope we estimated worldwide 100 million people may move to a VillageTown if it was on offer. A VillageTown only needs to attract 10,000. So how do the experts propose we accomplish this?

They suggested three stages, about a year for each stage, meaning three years after getting seed funding it should be done.

Stage 1 - Begin the Initiative

Stage 1 begins when the initial funding is secured. Hire the best top executives to run the initiative, retain the best engineering and logistics companies. Look to the level of companies that handle projects on the scale of the Olympic games – the better ones that deliver ahead of schedule, below budget and above standard in quality. In this stage, there are multiple streams that will occur, but the most important is to identify the Village Coordinators who put forth their vision for their village (its theme). Driven by passion not pecuniary interest, the Village Coordinator will be the person who will recruit the 500 people who will live in the 200 or so homes that are in that village. A VillageTown of 10,000 people will have about 20 villages plus the Town Center where taller and larger buildings are built. That means 20 or 21 coordinators who set the themes and attract the people.

By the end of Stage 1 critical mass will have been reached. Critical mass means enough buyers to support construction. In order to prevent people from having to suffer living in a construction site, a village cannot proceed until almost all of its homes are presold. It is hoped the vision will be sufficiently attractive

Photograph of Poundbury, where work began in the mid 1990's with the aim of completing development in 2025. Not only do the homes resemble ones built hundreds of years ago, as the stacks of materials suggest, the building methods also resemble methods of yore. Poundbury was an example I studied with care, seeing both good patterns, and finding things that could be done better, such as more focus on the local economy.

to generate a waiting list.

One of the more important elements to note in Stage 1 is to avoid the temptation to identify and commit to a particular piece of land. If it happens, so be it, but be aware that the critical relationship between the local government that must grant rezoning and settlement permits shifts as soon as the developer, the ViTo has established where they want to build. Do an internet search on competitions by various state and local governments to woo corporations that are looking for a new site to move their business. The concessions offered for what may be dozens or hundreds of jobs can run into the hundreds of millions of dollars, sometimes in cash, other times in tax concessions.

Now consider how they would compete (presuming of course the jurisdictions in question are not verging on bankruptcy) if they were invited to compete for a corporation that would bring in, let's say, 6,000 new jobs worth a quarter billion dollars a year or more, that would have no adverse environmental impact... no burden on the roads, public utilities or school system. It is safe to say they would compete vigorously, with attention paid at the policy level... by the elected officials and the top administrators.

This leverage goes away as soon as the ViTo locks in land. The competition for the best concession package is over, and the job is then handed to officials in the planning and zoning departments. Because some of the core elements of the VillageTown do not fit neatly in zoning and building regulations designed to serve car-based development (suburban sprawl), the approval process promises to be a long, hard slog. Thus, it is far better to hold off on finding the land until the policy has been adopted that sets out the process whereby the VillageTown plan will be developed and approved.

At the end of Stage 1, which is estimated to take one year, the buyers are known and enrolled in the process. They have demonstrated their ability to pay, and their ability to bring their work, or their income with them. Some buyers will be investors, looking for rental tenants, but even in this, we suggest the process be turned on its head. Seek out the tenants first, the people who want to live in the VillageTown but not buy a house. Then, when they are qualified, seek out investors looking for good solid rentals that originally can be managed by the VillageTown corporation... perhaps even setting up real estate investment funds to spread the rental risk.

Stage 2 - Planning, Preparation and Permits

Stage 2, which also is estimated to take a year, is when all the preparatory work kicks into gear. With the buyers known, it should be easier to secure Stage 2 investment funding. Stage 1 funding will require less than 1% of the total initiative budget. Stage 2 will require about 4% of the total budget, with the big variable being the price of the land, and when it must be paid. With the buyers known, and the rezoning policy approved, the land is identified and secured. The Dynamic Engagement process begins, so the complete plan can be approved and be ready for Stage 3. Construction begins on the infrastructure including the roads and on some of the industrial park buildings that will be in operation during Stage 3 to supply the materials needed to construct the villages. In most cases where dormitory living will be required for the workers, the motorpool will be constructed with dormitory bathrooms and kitchens. In some cases, where companies will start in the industrial park making products for the VillageTown construction (such as 100,000 doors and windows) and then continue in operation selling local to global, the industrial park workers village may need to be constructed in Stage 2, so the workers have permanent housing. The VillageTown bank, or its mortgage banking equivalent) will be established and buyers will begin the process of applying for construction loans that will be consolidated into mortgage backed securities. Design of the mobile factory begins. They must be on site, ready to build, at the start of Stage 3.

Stage 3 - Construction

Stage 3 marks the beginning of construction of the villages. Experienced builders in the construction industry may question the ability to construct 4,000 homes in 12 months. It is easier to think about constructing 200 homes in that time frame, and then run 20 jobs in parallel, sharing the industrial park resource that provide the building materials. The engineering firm retained in Stage 1 will have determined the level of tooling required to build in the time frame. It may turn out that one mobile factory can build 400 homes in a year, which means one for two villages, or the engineers may recommend one for each village.

Stage 3 funding comes from the buyers. Each home is built in a very similar way to an individual buyer purchasing a building lot and securing construction financing to build. Each buyer has a separate contract with the ViTo to build their home. They have a site they have selected in the Dynamic Engagement process. They will have determined the size and shape of their home and in the Dynamic Engagement process generally agreed on what it will look like. Most buyers who finance will arrange that through the VillageTown bank to combine their purchasing power to get better rates; however this would be a choice, not a requirement. The bank will manage construction loans with appropriate probity, with funds paid to the ViTo only on performance standards as agreed at the beginning... as with other parts of the VillageTown, checks and balances are important to securing a good result. The engineering and logistical team will schedule which villages to build first based on access. The intent is to enable the citizens of a VillageTown to move in as soon as their village is complete and certificates of occupancy issued. This will be of benefit to people who run local-to-global businesses. The end of Stage 3 is when the construction is complete and everyone else moves in. Construction loans are converted to mortgages, and the final payment to the ViTo provides for its profits. The investors are paid, and then relinquish their stock. The ViTo then is recast as the VillageTown operating corporation and new stock is issued, one share per title, one vote per citizen, meaning a home with five citizens gets five votes, and a home owned by a landlord has tenant votes only unless the landlord also lives in the building.

The Importance of the Artisan Sector

In the industrial sector establish the artisans' workshops where the doors, windows, decorative lintels and other details of buildings are made. Consider having the ViTo invest in expensive tooling that might not be affordable by artisans. Make the tooling available to keep building details cost-competitive so the buyers buy local. The ViTo will establish technical standard for things like doors and windows (so they work with the VDA pouring process for example), but will encourage home owners to dress their own home in a way that reflects their personality, provided it fits within the design code their village established.

Encourage multiple artisans in each trade and encourage competition not simply on price, but on quality and artistry to enhance the visual amenity of the VillageTown. We sometimes presume that beautiful places got that way by the brilliance of the designers when in fact history reveals that often it was due to particularly talented local artisans offering products that designers then incorporated.

Hamstone

One of the cross-over industries will be in employing artisans to work with the VDA. The material can be mixed to the consistency of sandstone or limestone that makes it easier to carve. This architrave (door surround) is carved of local Ham Stone quarried near the market town of Somerton, England. A Jurassic Limestone easy to shape, it gives the town a distinctive and warm feeling that adds to the character of the town.

Presuming such natural stone is not found locally, VDA, using a sand, cement and oxide mix can serve as a starting point for such carving. In addition to carving, VDA permits artisans to make molds and pour architectural details either in finished form, or as a raw material for further hand carving.

Conclusion

The residential construction industry has not changed much since the industrial revolution. The VillageTown promises to be what Silicon Valley calls *market disruptive*. It proposes to use some of the oldest materials in the industry, yet to apply tooling and technology in ways that speed up the process, lower the costs and make it possible to be more beautiful than much of what is built today. This promises to be very difficult for some lifers in the industry to digest. The implications of an instant market of 4,000 buyers who can combine their purchasing power and spark the local economy is outside the scope of professionals whose career has been based on regional market expansion. It becomes a challenge to digest the compelling reasons that will attract buyers... a secure and diverse local economy, excellent education for children, a place for elders, and a culturally and socially enriched community whose purpose for continuing are the five elements of a good life. Some people will get it. Others will remain skeptical. But remember, you don't have to convince everyone. Just get on with it, and it will happen.

Chapter 16 – Getting There… Funding and Organizing

Each Initiative will be different

The purpose of a book is to set out a framework to go from a good idea worth doing to a settlement that people live in. A framework is not a plan. It is a starting point that removes enough variables so that people can get their head around the concept and see a way forward. A plan emerges out of a specific place, with specific needs, characteristics and challenges. The land will have its own climate, its own shape and its own geography. The host population will have their own needs and expectations. But to get from here to there, the VillageTown initiative will need some structure and some seed funding.

The VillageTown Stewards and Company

We begin with the VillageTown Stewards, a group of volunteers from around the world who are committed to creating a better way for people to live. As the concept emerged, the stewards saw it as important to create a company to hold the intellectual property of the VillageTown™ (the word is trademarked in order to prevent someone else from claiming it). As the people with the most expertise, the VillageTown Stewards and Company serve as the trustees to "name" and then incorporate a "civitas corporation", the ViTo that will build a specific VillageTown and then transform into its operating company.

The stewards hold the stock of the ViTo in trust until the settlement is built, whereupon the stock is transferred to the citizenry, with the preferred ownership being one share per house, and one vote for each VillageTown citizen. The ViTo will collect a 10% reinvestment premium on its revenue that the stewards will manage to fund future VillageTown settlements. The stewards will also retain ownership of the tooling, that will be moved to the next VillageTown to be built. Other than this, all the net profits of the ViTo will remain in the ViTo, so that the home buyers will get an operating company with a lot of cash.

First Step, The VillageTown Ad Hoc Committee

As a settlement, the VillageTown process begins when the local people (the hosts) invite in the stewards to explore the potential of a VillageTown in their jurisdiction. The first questions relate to feasibility. Is there land? Is there a decision-making process that will support an initiative that does not have a deep-pocket investor/developer? Is there sufficient local support? Does it make sense? Are there any "drop-dead" issues that would render the initiative unlikely to succeed?

When it seems the answer to these questions are favorable, the stewards then recommend that a committee of local host citizens come together to serve in the host role. The duties of this committee will depend on how the decision-making process works. What needs to happen? Who decides what?

The Purpose of a Host Ad Hoc VillageTown Committee

Unlike the ViTo that will build the VillageTown, a local committee is made up of supporters of the idea – hosts who want to see the VillageTown happen for the common good. This kind of group is exceptionally powerful, because they are by definition the interested public. They hold the high ground in terms of motivation and public perception. If they attract a wide range of people, especially key influencers in the many communities that make up a region, they can make the VillageTown happen in what developers would consider record time. The Committee is not the Founders Group of villagers that engages in the actually planning process of their future village, as described in Chapter 3. Some of the same people may belong to both, but the Committee role is to help at a higher level.

The first job of the committee members is to make sure they understand what a VillageTown is. For some, this can be exceptionally challenging, especially if its members are already involved in the real estate industry in one form or another. For example, typically the committee members will want to focus on "where" – a search for land. As discussed in the previous chapter, this is not necessarily the best idea unless the local government elected officials have already stepped forward and committed to adapt their policies to enable the VillageTown to proceed without distortion or delay. Another tendency of committee members is to want to take on the job of pulling together a 1-2 billion dollar initiative. We gently suggest this is a role for the best professionals the ViTo can hire. Having seen intentional communities struggle to self-form, I say, hire the best.

In essence, at this point, the most powerful thing a committee can do is to enroll people in the passion. Avoid the nay-sayers and keep an arms length relationship with conflict-of-interest people who have a private agenda. The committee will not be hiring, nor will it be buying the land. Those are jobs for the ViTo.

Building Momentum

There will be many practical details needing attention. At the same time that the local focus is on finding the land and going through the many steps required to succeed, the host community will want to begin the process of attracting jobs and industries. In some cases, this will involve a "bring our kids home" campaign, if the host community finds its best and brightest have moved away to take good jobs in the cities. Prepare a brochure that states the case for moving a business, or opening a branch office in the VillageTown and encourage the young to approach their bosses, boards and decision-makers with the proposal to move to the VillageTown. Help the idea go viral and see what happens. If it is meant to be, it may spread like wildfire.

Attracting Funding

The business plan for the VillageTown calls for a three stage process:

1. $5 million: Employ the senior management team, establish the ViTo. Critical path, attract Head-of-Household jobs for at least 50% of the projected total. Qualify buyers in preparation for mortgage applications. Initiate Dynamic Engagement
2. $50 million: Convert applications into construction loan/mortgages to be sold as securitized bonds or PMBS. Repay principle of Stage 1 loan. Prepare the land and the construction process ready to begin in Stage 3.
3. $1-2 billion: Funded by the wholesale placement of the loans/mortgages. All investment funding paid; risk eliminated. Build each village as a separate job site. Target completion within 12 months using high-tech manufacturing systems.

The greatest challenge will be to secure the first stage of funding for the first VillageTown. The key question" Will it sell" can only be answered by the market. Thus, the first stage of funding is required to answer that question. We believe it will sell; we can see the market is crying out for an alternative to the status quo, but believing is not the same as knowing. The market has the answer.

Professional Management

The business plan calls for the most experienced, competent senior management team that can be found. We expect these people to have recently retired from top management jobs only to find they are too young and have too much energy to chase a golf ball around a groomed course or putter around the house. However, life has a way of surprising, so we really have no idea who will show up when they are the right person at the right time. What is important is that the stewards acknowledge that first-in is not a sufficient qualification. For example, I have written the books, have woven together a lot of good ideas, but I'm not qualified to run a $1-2 billion job site. Those people are out there. We need to find them.

Chapter 17 – Recap

The purpose of this book is to set out practical, do-able ways to build and live in thriving communities that enable people to meet their needs and pursue their aspirations while protecting the planet and its life-giving capacity. It is about enjoying life, taking care and growth.

It focuses on common locality, because everyone has to be some place, and the quality and character of that place has a great deal on influence on the quality of people's lives. It is a sad fact that far too many people have seen their quality of life decline as we monetised place. When the average person has to spend one quarter of their income on transport and then spend additional time moving from one place to the next, it becomes a burden rather than a joy. When that transport demands immense amounts of energy, land and materials, the cost to the planet and the burden laid on future generations increases.

Transport

Car and mass transport was necessary in the 20th century because large factories and offices required many people converge on the same buildings to work. But those conditions have changed, and they are changing even more rapidly now. Most white collar work is now being conducted via the Internet. With 3D printing, blue collar work will make the transformation as well. It's happening very fast.

It is this change, this shift in technology that is creating ripe conditions to decentralise and demonetise common locality. As long as the locality has an economic and social critical mass (enough jobs and enough people), the need to travel from one place to the next is eliminated.

The effects of this are profound. But let's start with the simple effects:

- The average person gets a 25% tax-free raise, by not having to pay for transport
- The average person gets about 90 minutes a day back in time by not having to drive or ride
- The businesses no longer need to provide off-street parking. Cost of business is lower.
- The town does not need to provide on-street parking. Less land is needed, costs less
- The streets are quieter, outdoor dining is more pleasant, sleep with windows open is not disrupted with vehicle noise
- The surrounding region gets growth without congestion
- The nation reduces its carbon emissions without pain

Affordable Housing

When one builds a settlement instead of a development, the cost of housing is less . the economies of scale kick in but the profits that a developer extracts are left in the community. This is then augmented with the parallel housing markets that acknowledges certain classes of work cannot compete in a single market. In order to have a complete community, about 25% of the housing should be limited to parallel markets.

Rapid, durable housing

The building industry has tended to build bespoke, one at a time, each hand made. Unlike tailor-made suits however, bespoke housing is not a status symbol, it's merely slow, inefficient and overly expensive. It is the logical outcome of building one at a time. It is absurd when one needs 4,000 units at about the same time. At that point, one needs to look to other industries to see what is possible. While factory-build housing is not a new idea, for the most part, these designs occupy the bottom of the market – boring budget homes that look bland and cookie-cutter. This is not a necessary condition.

Buildings can be generous, beautiful, functional, safe, durable and flexible; and this can be done for less money than inferior bespoke housing. It takes a reset of the mind.

Beautiful Housing

Change the basis of decision-making. It's that simple.

When developers make decisions, almost all are monetised: design and ornament is based on what will sell. When settlers make the decisions, it's a bit like fashion. People make atheistic decisions that reflect their tastes. Some will buy a front door that will never see a return on investment, but will give them pleasure every time they walk in.

When one examines beautiful historic places, one finds that the beauty was often personal, meaning that town had artisans who made beautiful things. Beautiful places are a collaborative relationship between the professional, the expert, the master who knows how to make beauty, and the decision-maker who will live with the result and is willing to pay for it.

Wealth

Wealth creation is different than wealth conversion, although both operate concurrently and interchangeably in today's local and global economies. In the beginning of this book (pages iv-v), I wrote an essay that discusses it. Presuming the reader has read from front to back, it is time to revisit the concept.

The VillageTown is about creating wealth. It is about creating broad-based wealth, using the market economy rather than a collective model. Collective models appeal to idealists, but in practice they rarely work because they require a higher level of consciousness on the part of every member of the collective, and an agreed common purpose. Usually, such systems end up being dominated by overbearing egos and ruined by corruption.

In a market economy, individuals specialise, form companies ("group shares bread" is the original meaning of that word) and they produce goods or services that provide for the basics or make life better. They cooperate, and they compete; competition can make them more effective. They use money as a medium of exchange, and they measure their success by how much money they control. However, success does not mean a good life. When people pursue money for its own sake, they lose the plot. When they pursue money to gain power for the sake of power, they become toxic to civilization – as can be seen today with many of the global problems that we are told may threaten the way of life we have come to enjoy. The hierarchy of conviviality, citizenship, and artistic, intellectual and spiritual growth is the framework for a good life. That becomes the purpose statement from which very specific infrastructure investments are made.

Sustainability

Harvest rain water, store it, create a hierarchy of uses, beginning with pure water that goes into or touches the body, then clean and reuse it for lesser purposes, such as cleaning, and finally for effluent. Don't build a sewage treatment plant, build a surplus resource processing plant. Do the same with solid waste – don't dump it, reprocess it

Grow food for local consumption. Cut out the transport component of food not based on price, but quality. Eat a wide variety of foods that don't travel well, but taste wonderful and are more nutritious. Take time with food, enjoy it.

Stop driving. Don't give up driving, just eliminate the need to drive every day. Move destinations not people.

Build for seven generations. Design durable, efficient homes and workplaces that can respond to changing conditions.

Put the word out that a 10,000 population community is looking to implement the most sustainable designs that are proven and affordable. Expect to be overwhelmed with brilliant designs.

Live your dream

In the end, most of us want to live a good life. Human beings are, by nature, social beings. The natural form of society is defined by common locality.

While at present humanity is making great strides in technology, human nature changes much more slowly. When people lose themselves in glass screens, be it televisions, computer displays, tablets or smart phones, life becomes curiously thin. This is because people need real communities; they need face-to-face contact to form and support friendships. When they are strong, they support the weak. When they become weak, the strong support them. All of these qualities are core to what it means to be human, but for such qualities to thrive, they need fertile ground in which to grow.

At its essence, that is what this book is about. How to create that fertile ground so that what people naturally do, will naturally happen. How to create that fertile ground; how to build a VillageTown.

Index

A
Active Listening and Active Dialogue 130
Aging population 28
Alexander, Christopher 3, 5, 21, 33, 34, 49, 96, 110, 117, 119, 123, 131, 148, 152, 199, 202, 207, 208
A Pattern Language 3, 5, 33, 34, 117, 119, 173, 199, 207
A Place to Sit 173
Architecture Code 164, 177
Art 51, 61, 122, 169, 170, 202
Artist 37, 126

B
Baby Boomer iii, 8, 10
Banks 89
Biochar ix
Biofuel 105
Bremer, John 23, 116, 123
Broadband 13
Building and Building Ornament Industries 81
Build the Workshop 140

C
Carving 228
Character 146, 148
Classical architecture 179, 180, 205
CO_2 31, 104
Collaborationz 2007 16
Construction Waste 110
Creative Class 17, 78, 120
Critical mass 14, 20
Curriculum 124

D
Delivery Flow Diagram 155
Deming, Edward 122
Design brief 137
Design Code 158
Destinations 66
Diversity 78
Dorchester 207
Dynamic engagement 33

E
Education 116
Elder housing 11, 28
Electricity 108
Energy 105
Environmental Action Plan 175, 177
Executive Department 131

F
Fireproof 62, 164
Florida, Dr. Richard 120, 145
Food Waste 111
For Profit Operations 134
Four Hour Chair 82
Fuller, Buckminster 178
Furnishings Industries 83

G
Gateways 69
Governance 128
Graetz, Gidon 170
Great Bifurcation 195
Gregorc, Dr. Anthony F. 117
Greenhouses viii-ix
Guild Hall 15-16, 119, 126, 154

H
Hartman, George E. 202
HBDI 117, 140
History 101 14, 29
Hock, Dee 47
Human Ease and Unease 190

I
Industrial Zone 80, 168
Integrated thinking 102, 117

J
Jackson, Peter 17, 146, 190
Judicial 132

K
Kū 194

L
Law Enforcement 134
LAX 29, 212
Leycock 157
Lipton, Bruce 94
Local Food Economy 79
Local Transport Area 96
Low Speed Vehicles 96, 159, 175
Luftwaffe 203

M
Maslow, Abraham 18
Massachusetts 31
Millspaugh, Marty 2
Motorpool 115, 134, 142, 154, 159
Musical Instruments 225

N
Noise Map 154
Non Profit Operations 134

Nursing care facilities 20

O
Ogletree, Vince 182
Ornament 81, 179, 186, 205

P
Parallel market 27, 39, 44, 134
Pastiche 190
Pattern cards 186
Pattern Cards 33, 117, 153
Pedestrian Streets 150
Plantings 70
Plaza Design 21
Poundbury 36, 44, 98, 182, 207
Prince Charles 36, 44, 98, 182, 203, 207
Proximity 14
Public Spaces Code 177
Public Works 133

R
Real-time resolution 139
Recycling 112
Reducing Crime 30
Regional economic industries 86
Regulators 138
Resource Management Act 49
Retirement Income 84
Rouse, Jim 2, 44

S
Schaefer, William Donald 2, 45
Services and Shops 87
Settled Work 21
Sewage treatment 106
Side Effects 75
Slow Food 92

Smell and Odour Map 154
Solid Waste 110
Storm Water 110
Students 86

T
Terra Preta ix
Travelers Inn 85

U
Urban Form Code 177
Urbis 142

V
Ludwig Mies van der Rohe 202
Vernacular architecture 179, 181, 205
Verticality 172
Village Institute 85
Village Prosecutor and Conflict
    Resolution 132
Visitors 45, 65, 85, 142, 147, 154
Voting 130
Vulcan Lane 188

W
Walls 44, 70, 135, 159, 196
Water viii, 31, 67, 102, 109, 110, 115,
    175, 194,
Weston 31
Wind/Moisture Flow Diagram 156
World Health Organisation 94

Y
Youth housing 26

Z
Zero Waste 110

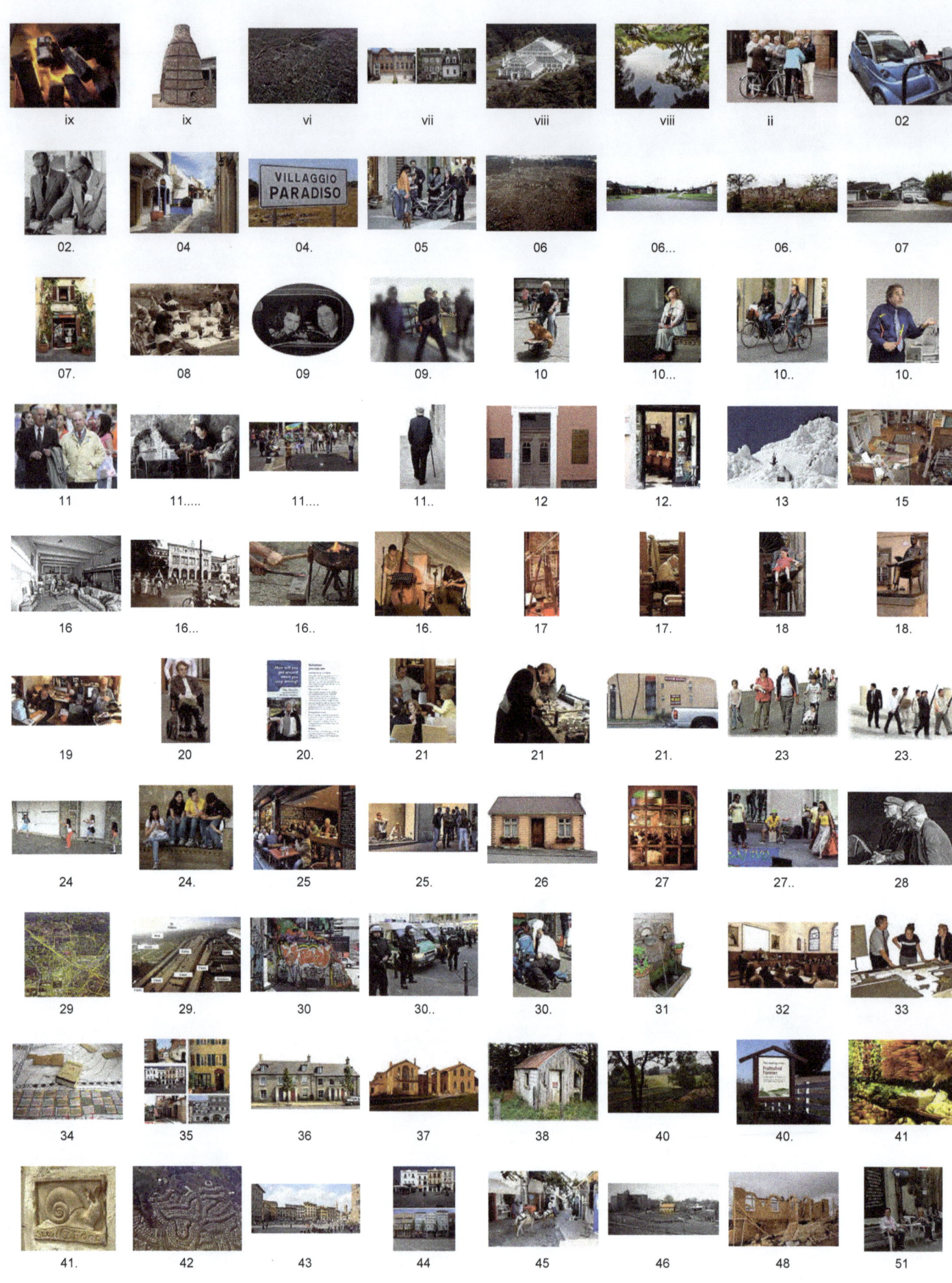

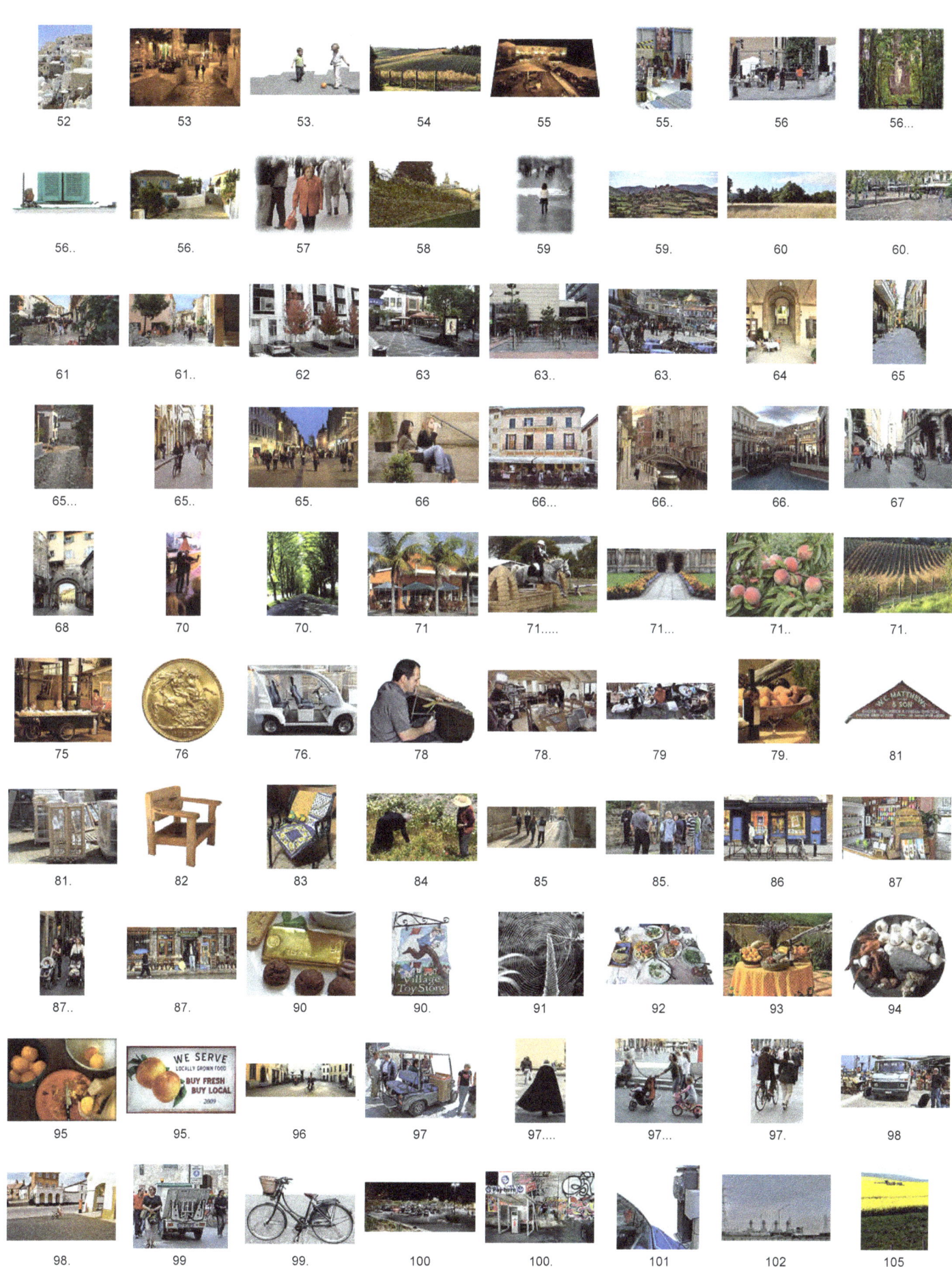

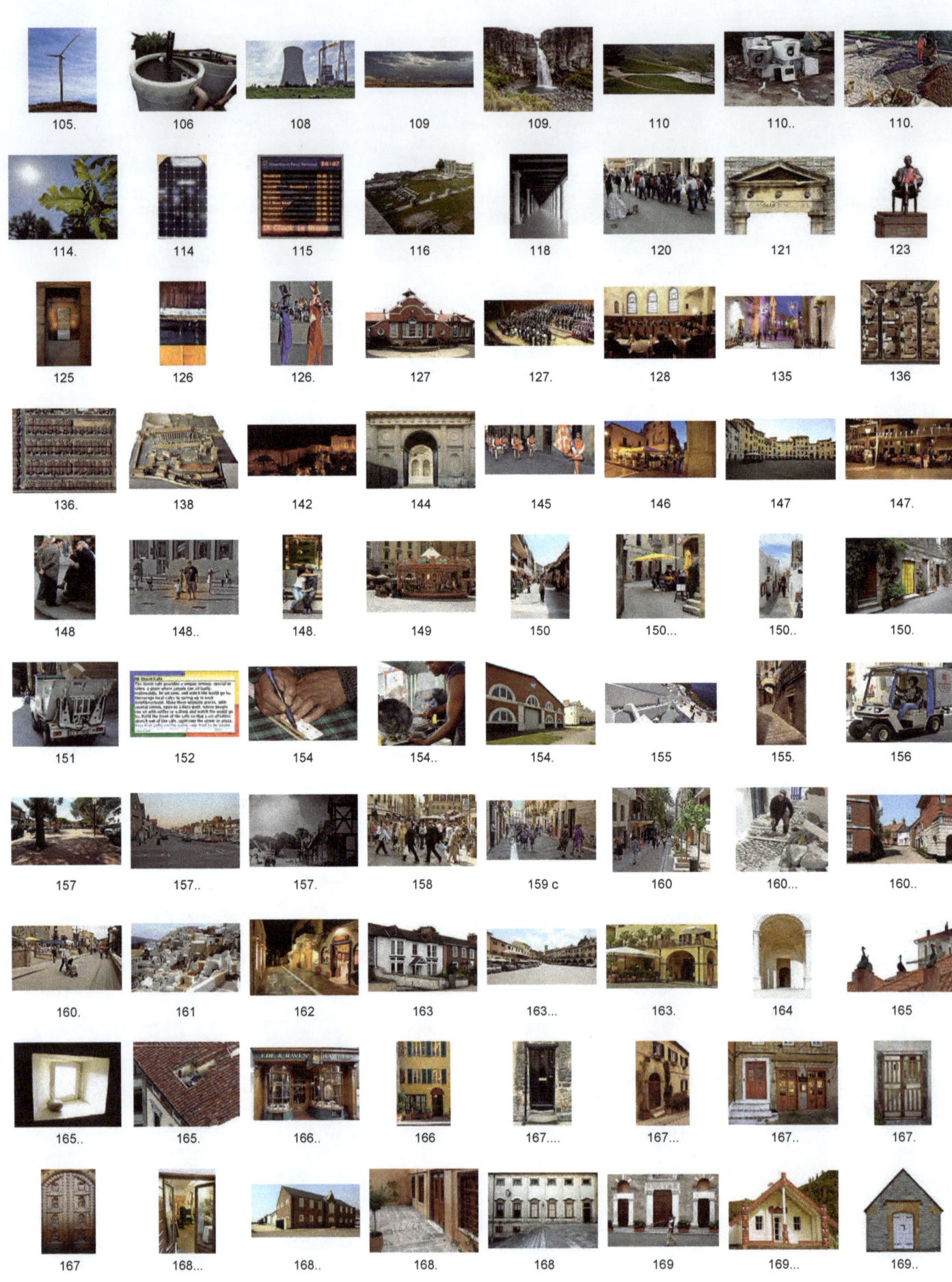

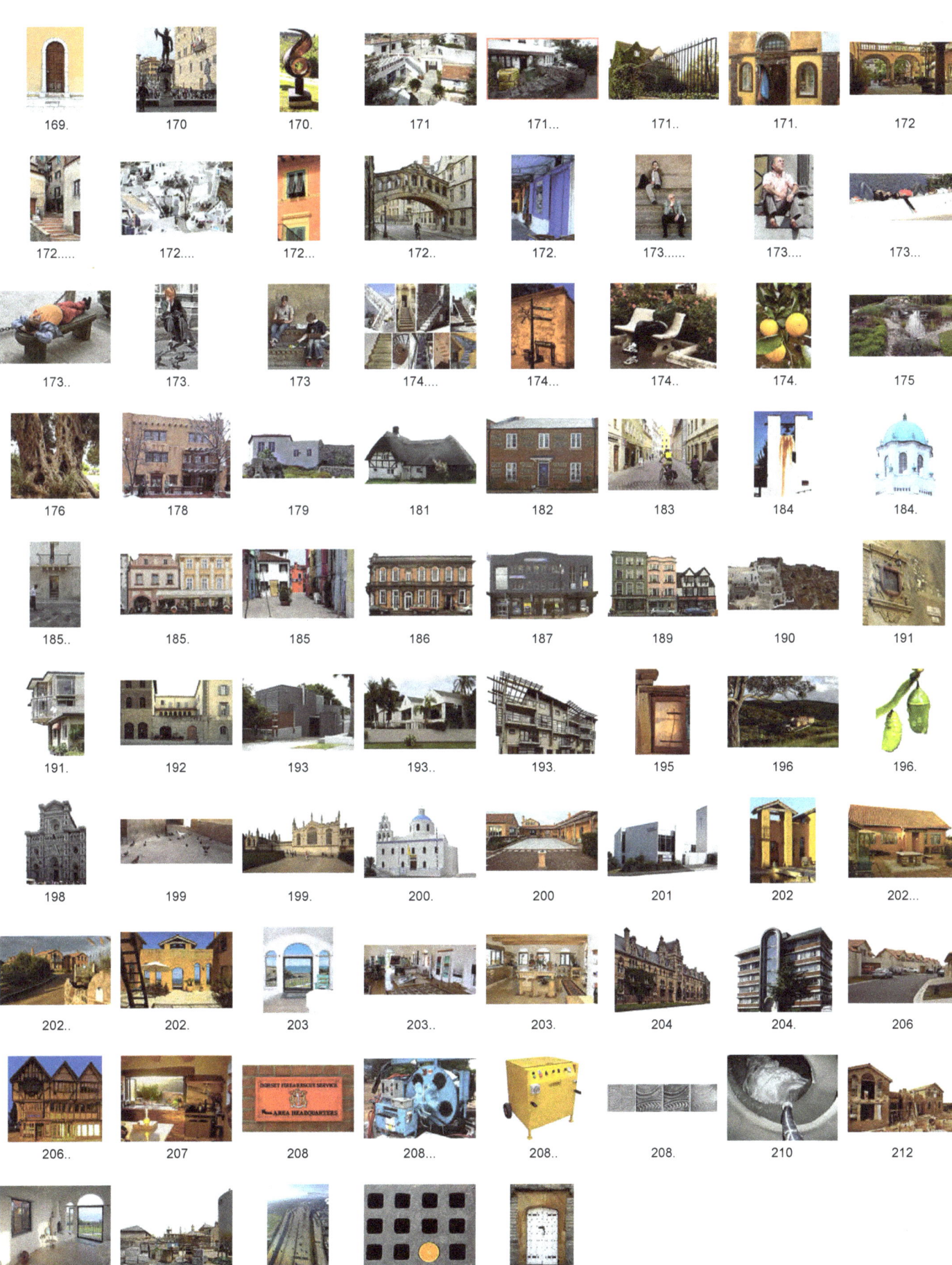

www.ingramcontent.com/pod-product-compliance
Lightning Source LLC
Chambersburg PA
CBHW061211230426
43665CB00032B/2978